hotel bars and cutting edge contemporary venues.

Our drink offer is also pretty unique. Beers range from traditional real ales, stouts and cider to the best imported brews from Europe, America and beyond, while the average wine list in the capital includes bins from all of Europe's classic regions, alongside Africa and the Americas. London remains gin's spiritual home, and the range of spirits and liqueurs available in the best bars is truly extraordinary.

This is a vast city and in this guide we have concentrated on the seventeen areas with the most important pub and bar scenes. Of these, I'd advise a visitor to start with:

Soho & Mayfair – W1, London's core bar zone, contains colourful, edgy Soho and posh, exclusive Mayfair.

Shoreditch –Once a rundown industrial area, today Shoreditch offers London's most vibrant bar scene.

Notting Hill – Still home to good looking, young trustafarians, along with some great bars and gastro pubs.

Knightsbridge & Belgravia – These well-to-do locales offer plenty of places with a long and distinguished pedigree, from classic hotel bars to ancient pubs.

Every single one of the 252 places in this guide has its own individual character. I visited all of them, and many more, often several times, before deciding which were special enough to include. (As always, please let me know if you agree with my selection and assessments.)

This is a guide to London's best pubs and bars. So who better than London's very own gin, Beefeater, to help us publish it? We don't accept – let alone ask for - payments from the venues we feature, and Beefeater's support has helped us stay dispassionate.

Beefeater is one of the last true London Dry Gins, as Desmond Payne, Beefeater's Master Distiller, and his team still make it in central London – in Kennington, to be exact. So please think of them when you order your next G&T, whichever pub or bar you choose.

Cheers

Simon Difford

simon@diffordsguide.com

ISBN: 0-9546174-9-5 (10 Digit) 978-0-9546174-9-3 (13 Digit)

THE BEEFEATER DISTILLERY - LONDON

DISTILLED IN LONDON

Beefeater has been distilled in London since 1820. Since the late 1950s its home has been among the Victorian terraced houses behind the Oval cricket ground in Kennington.

THE NAME

Beefeater has its roots in London, inspired by the yeoman warders – also known as 'Beefeaters' – who stand watch at the Tower of London.

THE RECIPE

As well as carefully selected Italian, Serbian and Macedonian juniper berries, Beefeater is flavoured with coriander seeds from Eastern Europe, angelica from Flanders and Seville orange and lemon peel. Liquorice, almond and orris root are also used.

24 HOUR STEEPING

Unlike other gins, the natural botanicals that flavour Beefeater are steeped in grain spirit for 24 hours. This allows the full flavour to be extracted before the 8 hour pot still distillation begins.

DESMOND PAYNE

Beefeater is a premium gin crafted by a small, dedicated team. At the head is Master Distiller Desmond Payne.

THE FLAVOUR

Beefeater has a clean, fresh juniper flavour and is noted for its fresh citrus character. To bring out the freshness, a Beefeater Dry Martini is best served with a lemon twist.

A KEY TO THIS GUIDE

The pubs and bars in this guide are in our view the very best in London. Some have a great atmosphere, some enjoy an idyllic location, others benefit from bar staff who are not only friendly but can also serve a decent drink: a rare few offer all the above and more. Those that I have judged worthy of a high grade not only offer great drinks (be they wine, beer or cocktails), but good service and, ideally, good food too: these are the kinds of place you'd want to return to time and time again.

We DO NOT accept payment from featured establishments or run advertising of any form for them.

GRADES – I have awarded each pub and bar a grade out of five according to its range of drinks, service, décor, food and ambience. These grades reflect my own tastes and yours may be very different – please let me know. (simon@diffordsguide.com)

They range from:

● ○ ○ ○ ○ - Dismal

to

● ● ● ● ● - Outstanding

HOURS – London's licensing laws have supposedly been liberalised, amid great furore, but it is still common for traditional pubs to close at 11pm (10:30pm on Sundays). On the other extreme, a rare few venues now open 24 hours. The opening hours of various establishments were still settling down after the change in the law as we went to press, but we have endeavoured to list the opening hours of every venue in this guide.

TYPE – This should be a good first indication as to whether a venue is the kind of place you're looking for. Categories include: lounge bar, café bar, cabaret bar, hotel bar, members' club, traditional pub, gastro pub, contemporary pub, nightclub and wine bar. We are a bar guide, not a club guide, and prefer relaxing with a great drink to getting hot and sweaty on a dancefloor.

ALFRESCO – This indicates whether or not a venue offers drinking under the sun/stars/clouds.

ENTRY – Here I've attempted to show how easy it is to access a venue. 'Open door' means just that while 'subject to management & capacity' means you may encounter a rope, a clipboard and a guest list policy. 'Members & guests only' means exactly that, so entry may be difficult or even impossible.

HIGHLIGHTS – These are simply what we liked best about each bar.

ATMOSPHERE – Obviously, atmosphere varies in each pub and bars according to day and time but we've tried to give you an idea of what to expect.

CLIENTELE – An indication of the kind of people we saw when we visited.

DRESS CODE – Unless a code is stipulated – for example, 'jackets requested for gents' - this is an indicator of roughly how people we encountered were dressed.

PRICE GUIDE – This is a very rough guide to how expensive the drinks are in each bar. £ means cheap and £££££ means megabucks.

FOOD – It's better to eat while you drink than hit the kebab shop on the way home. Where venues serve food we have tried to indicate the style of cuisine available.

REVIEWS – While I (Simon Difford) may agree with the views expressed in diffordsguide - and, let's face it, they are mine anyway - they are not necessarily the view of Sauce Guides Limited, so please don't try and sue the company! I have personally visited and reviewed all of the pubs and bars in this guide, many of them on several occasions. Please feel free to email me with any comments - or even your own reviews: simon@diffordsguide.com.

RECOMMENDATIONS
The following symbols appear at the foot of bar reviews where we consider the establishment is reliably good at offering the following. A food icon indicates that the food offer is well above the average for a bar: we are a bar guide, not a restaurant guide.

🍸	COCKTAILS
🍴	FOOD
🍷	WINE
🍺	BEER
	SPIRITS
	MUSIC
H	HISTORIC INTEREST

ACCURACY OF INFORMATION
- While every effort is made to ensure the accuracy of information contained within this guide at the time of going to press, no responsibility can be accepted for errors or omissions. If you are making a special journey to visit somewhere we have reviewed, please use the telephone or internet to check before leaving.

diffordsguide **are:**

CEO Ricky Agnew, **Publisher & Editor** Simon Difford, **Art Director** Dan Malpass, **Photography** Rob Lawson & Dan Malpass

Cover Venue: The Light, Shoreditch

Published by Sauce Guides Limited, Milngavie Business Centre, 17 Station Road, Milngavie, G62 8PG. www.diffordsguide.com

ISBN: 0-9546174-9-5 (10 Digit) 978-0-9546174-9-3 (13 Digit)

THE DISTRICTS

THE BARS IN THIS GUIDE ARE GROUPED INTO SEVENTEEN AREAS, INCORPORATING THE FOLLOWING DISTRICTS. TO FIND BARS IN YOUR AREA PLEASE SEE THE LIST BELOW AND THE MAP OPPOSITE.

BLOOMSBURY & HOLBORN
PAGES 20-27
BLOOMSBURY (WC1)
GRAY'S INN (WC1)
HOLBORN (WC1)

CAMDEN & MARYLEBONE
PAGES 28-35
CAMDEN TOWN (NW1)
MARYLEBONE (NW1)
KING'S CROSS (NW1)
REGENT'S PARK (NW1)

CITY
PAGES 36-45
ALDGATE (EC3)
BANK (EC2)
BISHOPSGATE (EC2)
BLACKFRIARS (EC4)
FLEET STREET (EC4)
LIVERPOOL STREET (EC2)
MONUMENT (EC3)
MOORGATE (EC2)
ST. PAUL'S (EC4)
TEMPLE (EC4)
TOWER HILL (EC3)

CLAPHAM
PAGES 46-55
CLAPHAM (SW4)
NINE ELMS (SW8)
SOUTH LAMBETH (SW8)

CLERKENWELL & SHOREDITCH
PAGES 56-71
BARBICAN (EC1)
BETHNAL GREEN (E2)
CLERKENWELL (EC1)
FINSBURY (EC1)
FARRINGDON (EC1)
HACKNEY (E2)
HOXTON (N1)
SHOREDITCH (E2, EC2)
SMITHFIELD (EC1)

COVENT GARDEN
PAGES 72-81
ALDWYCH (WC2)
COVENT GARDEN (WC2)
KINGSWAY (WC2)
STRAND (WC2)

EAST END & DOCKLANDS
PAGES 82-89
BOW (E3)
BRICK LANE (E1)
BROMLEY-BY-BOW (E3)
DOCKLANDS (E14)
ISLE OF DOGS (E14)
MILE END (E1)
MILLWALL (E14)
POPLAR (E14)
SPITALFIELDS (E1)
STEPNEY (E1)
WHITECHAPEL (E1)

FULHAM & CHELSEA
PAGES 90-99
BROMPTON (SW3)
CHELSEA (SW3)
EARL'S COURT (SW5)
FULHAM (SW6)
PARSONS GREEN (SW6)
WEST BROMPTON (SW10)
WORLD'S END (SW10)

GREENWICH & BLACKHEATH
PAGES 100-105
BLACKHEATH (SE3)
DEPTFORD (SE8)
GREENWICH (SE10)
WESTCOMBE PARK (SE3)

HAMPSTEAD & KENTISH TOWN
PAGES 106-115
BELSIZE PARK (NW3)
HAMPSTEAD (NW3)
KENTISH TOWN (NW5)
KILBURN (NW6)
QUEENS PARK (NW6)
ST JOHN'S WOOD (NW8)
SWISS COTTAGE (NW3)
WEST HAMPSTEAD (NW6)

HIGHGATE & ISLINGTON
PAGES 116-125
ARCHWAY (N19)
BARNSBURY (N1)
CANONBURY (N1)
HIGHBURY (N5)
HIGHGATE (N6)
HOLLOWAY (N7)
ISLINGTON (N1)
TUFNELL PARK (N19)

KENSINGTON & SHEPHERDS BUSH
PAGES 126-133
HAMMERSMITH (W6)
KENSINGTON (W8)
SHEPHERDS BUSH (W12)
WEST KENSINGTON (W14)

KNIGHTSBRIDGE & BELGRAVIA
PAGES 134-147
BELGRAVIA (SW1)
KNIGHTSBRIDGE (SW1)
PIMLICO (SW1)
ST. JAMES'S (SW1)
SOUTH KENSINGTON (SW7)
WESTMINSTER (SW1)

NOTTING HILL & PADDINGTON
PAGES 148-163
BAYSWATER (W2)
HOLLAND PARK (W11)
LADBROKE GROVE (W10)
MAIDA VALE (W9)
NORTH KENSINGTON (W10)
NOTTING HILL (W11)
PADDINGTON (W2)
WARWICK AVENUE (W9)

SOHO & MAYFAIR
PAGES 164-197
FITZROVIA (W1)
MARYLEBONE (W1)
MAYFAIR (W1)
OXFORD CIRCUS (W1)
PICCADILLY (W1)
SOHO (W1)

SOUTH BANK
PAGES 198-207
BERMONDSEY (SE1)
BOROUGH (SE1)
LAMBETH (SE11)
LONDON BRIDGE (SE1)
ROTHERHITHE (SE16)
SOUTH BERMONDSEY (SE16)
SOUTHWARK (SE1)
SURREY DOCKS (SE16)
WATERLOO (SE1)

WANDSWORTH & BATTERSEA
PAGES 208-215
BATTERSEA (SW11)
CLAPHAM JUNCTION (SW11)
EARLSFIELD (SW18)
WANDSWORTH (SW18)

All Star Lanes

Let' em R

BLOOMSBURY & HOLBORN
(WC1)

CENTRAL THEY MAY BE, BUT BLOOMSBURY AND HOLBORN RETAIN A QUIRKY, CHARACTERFUL CHARM THAT'S MATCHED IN THEIR SCATTERED, ECLECTIC BARS. LOOKING FOR A BACK STREET POLISH VODKA JOINT OR A HIGH STYLE 50S BOWLING ALLEY? YOU'LL FIND IT HERE.

AKA

● ● ● ● ○

West Central Street (off New Oxford St),
Bloomsbury, London, WC1A 1JJ, England

Tel: +44 (0)20 7836 0110,
www.akalondon.com
Hours: Tue-Thu 7pm-3am, Fri 7pm-4am,
Sat 10pm-4am, Sun 10pm-4am

Type:	Lounge/nightclub
Alfresco:	No
Entry:	Subject to management & capacity
Highlights:	Atmosphere
Atmosphere:	Clubby
Clientele:	Party animals
Dress code:	Cool casual
Price guide:	£££
Food:	Pizzas from Pizza Express

This excellent pre-club venue is attached
to the renowned End nightclub and since
opening in 1998 has built up something of
a reputation in its own right.

The 19th century building was once the
Royal Mail's Holborn district sorting office and
the names of local postal districts are still
visible on the wall opposite the bar. The
warehouse-like industrial feel derives not only
from its scale, but also from the exposed
steel beams, service pipes and wires.
There's a mezzanine overlooking the action
and the 15 metre long bar is illuminated by
fibre optics and covered in zinc.

Various DJ residencies attract a
young, funky, energetic crowd. Be warned,
this is not a destination for courting or
business. Unlike most music-led venues,
AKA prides itself in its drinks offering and
300 different spirits, including 59 individual
rums, line its impressive back bar. Thanks
to a nearby Pizza Express, the food served
here is also well above the standard typical
of similar establishments.

All Star Lanes

All Star Lanes

All Star Lanes

ALL STAR LANES

● ● ● ● ●

Victoria House, Bloomsbury Place (off Southampton Row), Holborn, London, WC1 4DA

Tel: +44 (0)20 7025 2676,
www.allstarlanes.co.uk **Hours:** Sun noon-10:30pm, Mon noon-11pm, Tue-Wed noon-midnight, Thu noon-1am, Fri-Sat noon-2am

Type:	Lounge bar & bowling alley
Alfresco:	No
Entry:	Subject to management & capacity
Highlights:	Cocktails, atmosphere & bowling
Atmosphere:	Fun, friendly & relaxed
Clientele:	Local office workers & style set
Dress code:	Designer casual & bowling shoes
Price guide:	££££
Food:	Salads, burgers and steaks

All Star Lanes is a decidedly boutique bowling alley with an equally slick lounge bar. It is tucked away on a side street and an illuminated sign is the only indication that the break in the iron railings has significance and the steps lead down to its basement entrance.

Formerly bank vaults, this sizable space is now a celebration of Americana. The bowling hall houses four lanes and is serviced by the attached vault bar, so named because bolts from the place's original incarnation adorn its pillars. The concealed VIP room houses a second bar and two further lanes. Its wood-clad walls make it feel a little like a huge sauna.

Fashionable 20- and 30-somethings pack the place to eye each other up and rattle the pins while sipping on beautifully balanced cocktails. A range of iced teas, shakes and malts suit the theme, while salads, burgers and steaks are washed down with an all American wine list (11 by the glass). Beer drinkers are well served with Anchor Steam and Liberty, plus the excellent Goose Island IPA.

BAR POLSKI

● ● ● ● ○

11 Little Turnstile (behind Prêt a Manger High Holborn), Holborn, London, WC1V 7DX

Tel: +44 (0)20 7831 9679
Hours: Mon-Fri noon-11pm, Sat 6pm-11pm

Type:	Polish vodka bar
Alfresco:	Tables in pedestrian lane
Entry:	Subject to capacity
Highlights:	Range of vodka
Atmosphere:	Fun, friendly & relaxed
Clientele:	Local office workers & Poles
Dress code:	None - suits to jeans
Price guide:	££
Food:	Traditional Polish fare

Formerly Na Zdrowie, this very Polish place is tucked away down an alleyway round the back of Holborn tube. The name hints at its raison d'être – a vast range of Polish vodka, beer and food at affordable, almost zloty prices.

Fifty or more Polish plain and flavoured vodkas are on offer, all served in functional shot glasses on small plastic trays. I recommend ordering a round of Polish beers and a selection of the aforementioned spirits, then finding a corner to peruse the food menu, most of which is impossible to pronounce. Persevere, however, and you'll find it tastes great.

If you've not visited for a while, you'll find that the old utilitarian design has gone. In line with the new Poland a clean, slick, modern look prevails and traditional wycinanki art graces the walls, but the familiar fun and friendly mood endures.

Bar Polski

Bar Polski

THE BOUNTIFUL COW
● ● ● ● ○

51 Eagle Street (corner Dane St.), Holborn, London, WC1R 4AP, England

Tel: +44 (0)20 7404 0200
Hours: Mon-Sat 11:30am-11pm

Type:	Gastro pub
Alfresco:	No
Entry:	Open door
Highlights:	Steaks & burgers
Atmosphere:	Laid back
Clientele:	Local office workers
Dress code:	Office attire/casual
Price guide:	£££
Food:	Great burgers and steaks

This gastro pub's location - the corner of a sixties carbuncle of an office building - is neither beautiful nor bountiful. However, the tiny interior is quirkily fascinating: a cross between an American diner, a pub and a vintage poster shop, decorated in a mish mash of colours and textures with patches of insulating material and splashes of colour pasted about like sample swatches. The movie posters that adorn the walls all have meat references, e.g. Travolta in 'Urban Cowboy', for the emphasis here is on all things bovine: thick steaks and succulent burgers are tantalisingly displayed in the refrigerator.

The Bountiful Cow is owned by the Australian personality, Roxy Beaujolais, former front-of-house manager at Ronnie Scott's, now cookery-book writer, TV cook and proprietor of the excellent Seven Stars (also in this guide).

While this place is not for vegetarians, real ale drinkers are well served with four brews on draught, including Adnam's Broadside.

THE LAMB
● ● ● ○ ○

92-94 Lamb's Conduit Street, Bloomsbury, London, WC1N 3LZ, England

Tel: +44 (0)20 7405 0713,
www.youngs.co.uk
Hours: Mon-Sat 11am-11pm, Sun noon-4pm & 7pm-10:30pm

Type:	Traditional pub
Alfresco:	Small beer garden & pavement tables
Entry:	Open door
Highlights:	Ambience
Atmosphere:	Traditional local
Clientele:	Locals, office staff
Dress code:	Suits to jeans
Price guide:	£££
Food:	Sandwiches & traditional pub grub

This unspoilt Victorian pub, like the street that houses it, is named after the Kentish clothmaker who was responsible for bringing the first fresh water supply to Holborn in 1577. Its flowing window boxes and green tile and mahogany frontage grace the north end of the street.

The central mahogany bar still features original cut-glass, swivelling snob screens. Either side of this are built-in green leather banquettes below walls lined with sepia photographs of 1890s music hall actresses. 'The Pit' is a cosy sunken seating area at the back of the pub with a door that leads out to a small patio garden.

This is a small, very traditional pub which serves its very traditional clientele Young's cask ales and old-fashioned pub grub.

PEARL RESTAURANT & BAR
● ● ● ● ○

Renaissance Hotel (left side), 252 High Holborn, London, WC1V 7EN, England

Tel: +44 (0)20 7829 7000,
www.pearl-restaurant.com
Hours: Mon-Fri noon-3pm & 6pm-10pm, Sat 6pm-10pm

Type:	Lounge/restaurant bar
Alfresco:	No
Entry:	Subject to management & capacity
Highlights:	Service & wines by the glass
Atmosphere:	Stuffy but informally so
Clientele:	Hotel guests, business types
Dress code:	Smart (not strictly)
Price guide:	££££
Food:	Full restaurant menu

Pearl takes its name and design cues from its home in what was once the banking hall of the Pearl Assurance Company. In the Grade II listed room original marble columns rise to a high corniced ceiling from which hang oversized lampshades surrounded by strings of pearls. Illuminated strung pearls also serve to divide the sofas which line the room. More privacy is provided in secluded walnut booths with velvet banquette seating.

More than forty wines, including many of the world's most celebrated, are available by the glass. A Cruvinet system ensures that these are preserved and served at their peak. Cocktail lovers are also well served by the attentive staff who skilfully prepare both classics and contemporary creations.

Perhaps it's the wine, perhaps it's the serenading pianist, but on my visits I've noticed that Pearl predominantly attracts young, female business types. Chaps, you're missing out.

The Lamb

The Perseverance

The Perseverance

THE PERSEVERANCE

● ● ● ○ ○

63 Lamb's Conduit Street, Holborn, London, WC1N 3NB, England

Tel: +44 (0)20 7405 8278
Hours: Mon-Sat noon-11pm, Sun noon-4pm

Type:	Gastro pub
Alfresco:	Bench tables on street
Entry:	Open door
Highlights:	Food
Atmosphere:	Can be very smoky
Clientele:	Hospital staff & locals
Dress code:	Casual
Price guide:	£££
Food:	Modern British gastro grub

Flock wallpaper of the curry house variety and a generally burgundy colour scheme make a refreshing change from the usual gastro pub clichés. You'd think the décor would be oppressive in this smallish room, but with its comfy brown banquettes and mismatched old chandeliers the place feels homely and cosy.

By day The Perseverance is very much a restaurant but come evening the atmosphere of a traditional boozer prevails as the excellent food moves upstairs to the candle-lit dining room. Those left waiting for a table downstairs can console themselves with one of the two traditional ales on offer. Lamb's Conduit Street is practically pedestrian so the outside bench tables feel almost villagey in summer.

The Perseverance is popular with staff from the nearby Great Ormond Street hospital and other local workplaces as well as the hip and wealthy who live nearby.

The Perseverance

VATS WINE BAR

● ● ● ○

51 Lamb's Conduit Street, Holborn,
London, WC1N 3NB, England

Tel: +44 (0)20 7242 8963
Hours: Mon-Fri noon-11pm

Type:	Wine bar
Alfresco:	Pavement tables
Entry:	Usually a spare table
Highlights:	Wine, food & conviviality
Atmosphere:	Very relaxed
Clientele:	Businessmen & locals
Dress code:	Suits to jeans
Price guide:	£££
Food:	Charcuterie to mains

Vats opened in 1972 and its far from plush décor has changed little since. It is a privately owned traditional wine bar and those seeking beer or spirits will be disappointed. An electrified oil lamp hangs in each front window and a heavy green curtain waits on its circular track to be pulled in front of the door. This quiet, relaxing place with its friendly staff attracts a broad cross-section of drinkers ranging from businessmen to groups of girls in everything from jeans to posh frocks.

A dusty bike hangs above the bar, crying out for a string of onions to accessorise the French foods and cellar of classic Bordeaux and Burgundies. The bar also boasts a line of cut glass decanters filled with vintage ports, which makes ending the evening with the cheese board almost a necessity. Vats is far from being fashionable, trendy or star-studded – perhaps that's its attraction… That and, of course, the homemade fishcakes.

Vats Wine Bar

Vats Wine Bar

Vats Wine Bar

CAMDEN & MARYLEBONE

(NW1)

FROM THE GRUNGY HUBBUB OF CAMDEN'S MARKETS AND LIVE MUSIC JOINTS TO THE ELITE STREETS OF NEARBY MARYLEBONE (THE 'Y' IS SILENT) IS A SHORT WALK BUT A LARGE LEAP. YOU'LL FIND THE ODD DECENT BAR ALONG THE WAY.

Cottons

COTTONS

●●●●○

55 Chalk Farm Road (opp Roundhouse),
Camden, London, NW1 8AN, England

Tel: +44 (0)20 7485 8388,
www.cottons-restaurant.co.uk
Hours: Mon-Thu 5pm-midnight, Fri 5pm-
1am, Sat noon-1am, Sun noon-11pm

Type:	Caribbean restaurant & bar
Alfresco:	Couple of pavement tables
Entry:	Open door
Highlights:	Food, cocktails & rum range
Atmosphere:	Buzzy, often DJ led
Clientele:	Homesick Caribbeans & locals
Dress code:	Casual
Price guide:	£££
Food:	Authentic/modern Caribbean

When this little place opened back in 1985
it was the UK's first Caribbean restaurant
and bar. Today it stays true to its roots,
serving a wide range of dishes drawn from
the various islands of the Caribbean. The
front, AKA The Rum Shack, operates as a
rummery-cum-cocktail bar, with DJs playing
R'n'B, reggae and 80s classics on Friday
and Saturday evenings. Behind lie three
atmospheric dining rooms, named for the
islands of Margarita, St. Lucia and Barbados.

Since 2003 Cottons has also been the
lair of Ian Burrell, London's self-styled rum
ambassador. His influence is evident on the
shelves which groan with around 200
different rums, many rare and some unique
in the UK. Unsurprisingly, the cocktail list is
dominated by rum-based drinks, including
a variety of Daiquiris, Reggae and Sorrel rum
punches and the infamous Strong Back.

This good time venue always has a
warm buzz. This, coupled with the food and
rums, attracts the likes of Sol Campbell and
Samuel L. Jackson.

Cottons

THE ENGINEER

● ● ● ● ○

65 Gloucester Avenue (corner Princess Rd),
Primrose Hill, London, NW1 8JH, England

Tel: +44 (0)20 7722 0950,
www.the-engineer.com
Hours: Mon-Sat 11am-11pm, Sun noon-
10:30pm

Type:	Traditional pub/gastro pub
Alfresco:	Large rear garden
Entry:	Open door
Highlights:	Food & garden
Atmosphere:	Public school canteen
Clientele:	Pretty Primrose Hill types & celebs
Dress code:	Yachting casual
Price guide:	££££
Food:	Modern British with Pacific Rim touches

The Engineer in question – and the man in
the tall hat on the sign outside - is the
celebrated Victorian bridge-builder
Isambard Kingdom Brunel. He is an
appropriate symbol, since this corner pub
was built in 1841.

Once a boozer, this is now a very
upmarket gastro pub. The lounge bar is now
an informal dining room decked out in
wallpaper with a purple and mauve cow
parsley print. In the public bar, similarly
psychedelic wallpaper is toned down by
original features and stripped pine. During
summer the secluded garden is the place
to be for both drinkers and diners.

Although this pub has served locals for
over a century and a half, its stratospheric
rise to fame came when the excellent
restaurant opened in the summer of 1994.
Now posh Primrose Hill types and local
celebs flock here to enjoy a modern British
menu (with a hint of Pacific Rim), washed
down with a couple of good ales and some
very serious wines from the well-priced list,
which includes 15 bins by the glass.

The Engineer

The Engineer

Gilgamesh

GILGAMESH

● ● ● ◐ ○

The Stables, Camden Market, Chalk Farm Road, Camden, London, NW1 8AH, England

Tel: +44 (0)20 7482 5757,
www.gilgameshbar.com
Hours: Mon-Sun 11am-late
(closing times vary)

Type:	Pan-Asian restaurant & lounge
Alfresco:	Retractable roof
Entry:	Subject to management & capacity
Highlights:	Food & decor
Atmosphere:	Only when full
Clientele:	Jet set & wannabes
Dress code:	Go for it – style togs
Price guide:	£££££
Food:	Pan-Asian & sushi

This sumptuously decorated Pan-Asian restaurant and lounge bar-cum-club perches above Camden's Stables Market in what I can best describe as a cross between an aircraft hangar and an Indiana Jones set. It is named for and inspired by the palace of an ancient Babylonian king, Gilgamesh of Uruk.

Beyond the clipboards and the escalator, the vast interior is divided into four distinct areas: restaurant, tea house terrace, lounge bar and the VIP Babylon Lounge. The ceiling, the walls and even the throne-like chairs are covered in intricate Indian hand-carvings, while friezes and hieroglyphics abound. The roof, which curves to a height of forty feet, is retractable, turning the dining room into a virtual roof terrace.

Celebrity chef Ian Pengelley and a team of sushi maestros ensure the food is as ostentatious and spectacular as the décor. Cocktail standards vary according to your server so you might want to opt for one of the 26 sakes. Gilgamesh is the kind of O.T.T. themed place you'd expect in Las Vegas. How it will fare over the market stalls of Camden remains to be seen.

Gilgamesh

Gilgamesh

THE LANSDOWNE

● ● ● ● ○

90 Gloucester Avenue (corner Dumpton Place),
Primrose Hill, London, NW1 8HX, England

Tel: +44 (0)20 7483 0409
Hours: Mon 6pm-11pm, Tue-Sat noon-
11pm, Sun noon-10:30pm

Type:	Traditional / gastro pub
Alfresco:	Tables on pavement
Entry:	Open door
Highlights:	Food & atmosphere
Atmosphere:	Very casual/relaxed
Clientele:	Upscale locals
Dress code:	Casual
Price guide:	££££
Food:	Modern British/Mediterranean menu

The second upmarket gastro pub on
Gloucester Avenue is more relaxed and
pub-like than The Engineer along the road.
The open plan ground floor with its black
anaglypta ceiling, creamy walls, bare board
floor and old wooden tables is homely
rather than designer.

The dining room is concealed upstairs
so this remains a pub first and a restaurant
second. A good beer selection, including
a couple of quality ales (Bombardier &
Deuchars) is on offer, along with well
chosen wines (13 by the glass) and various
champagnes. This is Primrose Hill so it's
not uncommon to see a young couple
enjoying a bottle of vintage fizz with their
evening meal.

The food here is remarkably good and
the menu ranges from snacks and stone-
baked pizza through to Mediterranean
influenced modern British mains. Pretty
young Primrose Hill types crowd here and
evenings late in the week can be chaotic
but this just seems to add to The
Lansdowne's character and appeal.

The Lansdowne

The Lansdowne

The Lansdowne

THE LOCK TAVERN

● ● ● ○ ○

35 Chalk Farm Road, Camden, London,
NW1 8AJ, England

Tel: +44 (0)20 7482 7163,
www.lock-tavern.co.uk
Hours: Mon-Thu noon-midnight, Fri-Sat
11am-1am, Sun 11am-11pm

Type:	Music venue/gastro pub
Alfresco:	Roof terrace & back yard
Entry:	Subject to management & capacity
Highlights:	Music
Atmosphere:	Music led, relaxed
Clientele:	Young trendies
Dress code:	Trendily casual
Price guide:	£££
Food:	Soup, sandwiches, pies & gastro grub

The Lock describes itself as a "tarted up
boozer on Chalk Farm Road" but it's hardly
your average boozer and the decor is
rustic pub meets New York loft rather than
tarty. It's music-led, slightly scuzzy,
ultra-trendy but strangely appealing – and
an "old boozer", if you must.

Downstairs feels like a scruffy gastro
pub and bench tables line the partially
covered and heated back yard. A narrow
staircase winds up to a second, loft styled
bar with bare brick walls where cutting
edge light shows are projected onto a big
screen. The adjoining roof terrace
overlooks the bustle of Camden Market.

One of the partners behind this place
is the DJ Jon Carter, and the thing The
Lock does best is attract the ultra-trendy
through great tunes and talented DJs.
Drinks standards are generally at the lower
end of bog-standard but the food,
including great pies sourced from the
Square Pie company, is much better than
you'd expect of such a venue.

Made in Brasil

Made in Brasil

Made in Brasil

MADE IN BRASIL
●●●●○

12 Inverness Street (off Chalk Farm Rd),
Camden Town, London, NW1 7HJ, England

Tel: +44 (0)20 7482 0777
Hours: Mon-Sat noon-1am

Type:	Brazilian cachaçeria
Alfresco:	Back yard
Entry:	£5 with free caipirinha
Highlights:	Caipirinhas
Atmosphere:	Often Carnival-like
Clientele:	Brazilian expats
Dress code:	Casual
Price guide:	£££
Food:	Brazilian tapas

Preparation for a ski trip often includes a practice visit to a dry ski slope. Londoners should similarly head to Made in Brasil to acclimatise before visiting that nation because this place is more a spiritual home of Brazil in London than the Brazilian Embassy.

The food, the beer, the cocktails, the staff, the atmosphere and even the clientele are all authentic. Cachaça (a rum-like liquor) is Brazil's national spirit and there are seventy different types to choose from when ordering the national cocktail, the caipirinha, plus a wide range of tropical fruit juices with which to flavour it. Other Brazilian drinks include the Batida cocktail and Brahma beer. While this is more bar than restaurant the tapas style dishes are surprisingly good, if you can get your mouth around the names.

The somewhat dingy interior is long, narrow and usually crowded. Try heading downstairs or best of all, in summer, to the courtyard out back.

If Brazil are playing football the big screen induces a carnival atmosphere.

QUEEN'S HEAD & ARTICHOKE
●●●●○

30-32 Albany Street (corner Longford St),
Marylebone, London, NW1 4EA, England

Tel: +44 (0)20 7916 6206,
www.theartichoke.net
Hours: Mon-Sat 11am-11pm,
Sun noon-10:30pm

Type:	Gastro pub
Alfresco:	Small yard & pavement tables
Entry:	Open door
Highlights:	Food, bright interior
Atmosphere:	Relaxed
Clientele:	Medical students & 30-somethings
Dress code:	Casual
Price guide:	££££
Food:	Modern British meals, tapas & pinchos

The Artichoke dates from the 16th century and its strange name is attributed to Daniel Clarke, master cook to Elizabeth I and James I: the first landlord is said to have been the queen's head gardener. The original pub was demolished when Regent's Park was laid out and rebuilt on its current site in 1811. However, its present day incarnation was built around 1900.

Those rebuilds have resulted in a beautiful corner pub. Mottled mullion windows wrap around the street sides, throwing abundant natural light into the polished, mahogany panelled interior. Sturdy wooden tables and chairs dot the room and a few leather sofas rest by the Victorian tiled, cast iron fireplace.

This pub offers a couple of traditional ales and a fair wine list (with 12 by the glass), but food is the real draw. A daily changing modern British menu is supplemented by tapas and pinchos (snacks on a stick). In summer the best tables are in the tiny back yard but more refined surroundings are available year round in the upstairs dining room which is lined with girly portraits.

Queen's Head & Artichoke

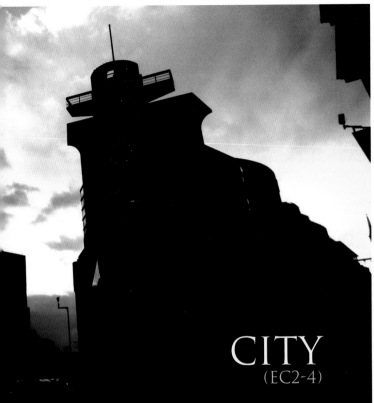

CITY
(EC2-4)

THE HISTORIC HEART OF LONDON, AND THE CENTRE OF ITS VAST
FINANCIAL INDUSTRY, THE SQUARE MILE FEATURES ANCIENT PUBS, THE
ODD FINE WINE BAR AND THE OCCASIONAL STYLISH LOUNGE, AMID
ACRES OF IMPERSONAL, CORPORATE CHAINS. THURSDAY EVENINGS
ARE WHEN THE MONEYMAKERS COME OUT TO PLAY.

AURORA BAR

● ● ● ○ ○

Great Eastern Hotel, Liverpool Street,
London, EC2M 7QN, England

Tel: +44 (0)20 7618 7000,
www.aurora-restaurant.co.uk
Hours: Mon-Fri noon-3pm & 6pm-11pm

Type: Lounge/restaurant bar
Alfresco: No
Entry: Subject to management & capacity
Highlights: Cocktails, wine & decor
Atmosphere: Restrained, calm
Clientele: City types
Dress code: Suits preferred
Price guide: ££££
Food: Caviar, smoked salmon, canapés

Long before Conran, the Great Eastern
Hotel was a style icon. Its flagship
restaurant, Aurora, first opened in 1884
and the splendid interior has been
beautifully restored to its former glory. The
most striking feature is a stained-glass
dome, which is backlit at night, while the
specially commissioned chandeliers are
made from hundreds of sheets of thin
porcelain and appear to glow from within.

The bar itself was added at the end of
2001 but its polished pewter finish works
well within this opulent room and its lines
curve elegantly like a cruise liner's bow.
Comfy armchairs invite one to sit and enjoy
a fine Armagnac, a Cognac or one of the
excellent classic cocktails produced by
Aurora's skilled bartenders.

The atmosphere is calm and relaxed
- something of an oasis amid the bustle of
Liverpool Street. Here you will find suited
City folk enjoying the peace and
discussing the business of the day over
wine or Martinis.

THE BLACK FRIAR

● ● ● ○ ○

174 Queen Victoria Street, Blackfriars,
London, EC4V 4EG, England

Tel: +44 (0)20 7236 5474
Hours: Mon-Sat 11am-11pm, Sun noon-
10:30pm

Type: Traditional pub
Alfresco: Pavement tables
Entry: Open door
Highlights: Architecture
Atmosphere: Hardly electric
Clientele: Sightseers / after office crowd
Dress code: Office wear to casual
Price guide: ££
Food: Rolls, jacket potatoes, hot pub fayre

The Blackfriars area of the City of London
is named for the Dominican monks, or
black friars, who once resided here. This
pub was built in 1875 on the site of the
brothers' medieval monastery, jammed in
between other buildings - hence its
curious, wedge-like shape.

At the beginning of the last century
the artist and architect Henry Poole, a
leading figure of the Arts & Crafts
movement, was commissioned to
redecorate. His spectacular, witty interior
includes art nouveau friezes of jolly monks
backed by Florentine marble walls and
pillars. The small back room features a
vaulted mosaic ceiling, yet more friars and
some wise advice to drinkers.

The Black Friar is popular with office
escapees and on warm evenings the
pavement is thronged with people. The
drinks are very basic but it's worth visiting
just to see the interior.

BOISDALE OF BISHOPSGATE

● ● ● ○ ○

Swedeland Court, 202 Bishopsgate, City of London,
London, EC2M 4NR, England

Tel: +44 (0)20 7283 1763,
www.boisdale.co.uk
Hours: Mon-Fri 11:30am-11pm

Type: Wine bar, lounge bar & restaurant
Alfresco: No
Entry: Subject to capacity
Highlights: Wine, whisky and jazz
Atmosphere: Gentleman's club cum pub
Clientele: City types sans jackets and ties
Dress code: City smart
Price guide: £££
Food: British with a Scottish leaning

Not content with being heir to large swathes
of Scotland, Ranald Macdonald Younger of
Clanranald, the elder son of the 24th
Captain of Clanranald, continues to expand
his interests in the capital. In 2002 he
acquired that former bastion of Englishness,
Bill Bentley's, and converted it to his second
restaurant and bar. The original Boisdale
club is over in Belgravia and even there
attracts its fair share of City types, so this
newer outlet is well positioned opposite
Liverpool Street Station. It takes its name
from Loch Boisdale in South Uist in the
Hebrides and has a suitably Scottish theme.

Just as in Belgravia, you'll find a
gentleman's club style interior with dark
green and lacquer red panelling, aged oak
floors, leather seats, marble topped tables
and an eclectic collection of framed art.
Upstairs operates as a wine bar, while the
basement restaurant mutates into a live jazz
club each evening between 6 and 9pm.

The beer selection is disappointing but
the wine list and choice of malts more than
make up for it.

COQ D'ARGENT
●●●○○

1 Poultry, City of London, London, EC2R
8EJ, England

Tel: +44 (0)20 7395 5000,
www.coqdargent.co.uk
Hours: Mon-Fri 11.30am-11pm, Sat
6.30pm-11pm, Sun noon-4pm

Type: Restaurant & rooftop bar
Alfresco: 3 terraces on rooftop garden
Entry: By express elevator
Highlights: Roof terrace
Atmosphere: Chilled
Clientele: Successful City boys & girls
Dress code: Business suits
Price guide: ££££
Food: Roasted nuts to charcuterie & lobster

Part of the Conran estate, the Coq perches
at the very heart of the City, on the roof of
the extraordinary No.1 Poultry building.
Walk off the street into the open courtyard
of No.1 Poultry and look for the twin
elevators. (On a sunny weekday evening
the long queue will help you find them.)
They whizz you straight up to the Coq's
roof garden with its secluded seating areas
and outside bar - a real City oasis. On a
clement day you can stand on the well-
trimmed lawn surrounded by box hedges
holding a Martini and looking down on the
Lord Mayor's gaff.

Sadly, however, the contemporary
restaurant and bar have little to offer the
discerning drinker if it's raining or cold.
Although the Coq carries some fine wines
and spirits its cocktails are mediocre and
the beers unexciting.

CORNEY & BARROW
●●●○○

10 Paternoster Square, City of London,
London, EC4M 7DX, England

Tel: +44 (0)20 7618 9520,
www.corney-barrow.co.uk
Hours: Mon-Tue 7:30am-11pm, Wed-Fri
7:30am-midnight

Type: Wine bar
Alfresco: Seating under heated canopies
Entry: Open door
Highlights: Wines
Atmosphere: Buzzy
Clientele: City types & the odd tourist
Dress code: At least collar, if not tie
Price guide: £££
Food: Modern British snacks to mains

It's a wine bar, Jim, but not as we know it.
This may be owned and operated by
Corney & Barrow, a rather old school firm
of London wine merchants, but its interior
is distinctly space age. A mixture of comfy
booths and modern tables surround the
horseshoe bar: the lamps and design
detailing would not look out of place on a
Federation Starship. Equally unusually for
a City wine bar, the feel is very loungy and
there are two private rooms, both with
huge plasma screens.

Like other Corney & Barrow bars, its
vintner's heritage is very apparent in the
extensive list of wines and champagnes.
The quality food served sees it packed with
local office workers at lunch times, as well
as out-of-place tourists fresh from
exploring the newly developed Paternoster
Square and nearby St. Paul's Cathedral.

CORNEY & BARROW
●●●●○

19 Broadgate Circle, Broadgate, City of
London, EC2M 2QS, England

Tel: +44 (0)20 7628 1251,
www.corney-barrow.co.uk
Hours: Mon-Fri 7.30am-11pm

Type: Wine bar
Alfresco: Covered balconies
Entry: Dinner bookings take preference
Highlights: Wines
Atmosphere: Relaxed
Clientele: City guys & girls
Dress code: Smart
Price guide: £££
Food: Full menu by day & bar bites by night

This is the flagship of the Corney & Barrow
wine bar chain. It overlooks Broadgate
Circle, by Liverpool Street station, which
houses an ice-skating rink in winter and
various events at other times of year.

This modern bar effectively surrounds
the circle below. The main bar is in the
centre, while two smaller satellite bars,
each with a terrace, are linked by covered
glass walkways. The interior appears to
amplify exuberant City voices, so turn your
hearing aid down if you're able.

The terraces have outside areas with
heated canopies during winter and their
windows open on warm days to add to the
al fresco feel. Suited and booted City boys
and girls flock here, especially on Thursday
evenings when it's usually packed and the
Champagne flowing.

Eight

EIGHT

● ● ● ● ○

1 Change Alley (off Cornhill, opp. The Royal Exchange), City of London, London, EC3V 3ND

Tel: +44 (0)20 7621 0808,
www.eightclub.co.uk
Hours: Mon-Fri 8am-11pm

Type:	Lounge bar/members club
Alfresco:	No
Entry:	Members & guests only
Highlights:	Service, cocktails, wines
Atmosphere:	Chilled
Clientele:	Suited & booted City types
Dress code:	At least collar if not tie
Price guide:	££££
Food:	Breakfast through to dinner

This members' retreat is hidden deep in the bowels of an office building close to the Lord Mayor's home, Mansion House. After descending several flights of stairs as if into a bunker, the interior is a pleasant surprise. It's rather like the lounge of a luxury bachelor pad, but slick enough to command girlie approval.

Brown sofas and warm tones help create a relaxing atmosphere in the main room. Beyond lies a further space with three 9-foot Brunswick championship pool tables. There is also a cinema and three private rooms, complete with self-service bars, large LCD screens and iPod decks. The club's name hints at the fact that these rooms all feature convertible poker tables.

The drinks offering kicks off with a serious champagne list featuring a selection of Dom & Krug vintages (both are available by the glass along with three other champagnes). A comprehensive wine list includes a dozen by the glass and, on our visits, cocktails from the extensive list were well made.

Ye Olde Cheshire Cheese

EL VINO

● ● ● ○ ○

47 Fleet Street (opp. Fetter Lane), London,
EC4Y 1BJ, England

Tel: +44 (0)20 7353 6786,
www.elvino.co.uk
Hours: Mon 8:30am-9pm, Tue-Fri 8:30am-
10pm

Type:	Wine bar/restaurant/off-licence
Alfresco:	No
Entry:	"All welcome"
Highlights:	Wine list
Atmosphere:	Gentleman's club goes to the pub
Clientele:	Solicitors, barristers and clients
Dress code:	Suits
Price guide:	££££
Food:	Home-cooked traditional food

El Vino was established in 1897 as a wine merchant and bar, and moved to Fleet Street in 1923. Little seems to have changed since. The small antechamber at the front of the shop still operates as an off-licence. Behind the sturdy old mahogany bar, casks of sherry still sit among shelves loaded with wine. The front section of the bar is self service while the back area offers table service; there is a restaurant in the basement.

El Vino's location naturally made it popular with members of the legal and journalistic professions. Although most of the hacks have relocated to far flung parts such as Wapping, pinstriped solicitors and barristers still pack into El Vino at lunchtime and in the evening to enjoy a swift Claret. Indeed, El Vino featured in the British TV series, 'Rumpole of the Bailey'. Immortalised as 'Pomeroy's', it was the eponymous hero's favourite bar.

El Vino has a suitably impressive wine list with a bias towards Burgundy and Bordeaux. Mobile phone use is discouraged.

YE OLDE CHESHIRE CHEESE

● ● ● ○ ○

Wine Office Court, 145 Fleet Street, City of
London, London, EC4A 2BU, England

Tel: +44 (0)20 7353 6170,
www.yeoldecheshirecheese.com
Hours: Mon-Sat 11:30am-11pm, Sun
noon-3pm

Type:	Traditional pub
Alfresco:	Standing in alley
Entry:	Open door
Highlights:	Heritage
Atmosphere:	Traditional pub
Clientele:	Tourists & office workers
Dress code:	Scruffy jeans to suits
Price guide:	££
Food:	Traditional pub grub

A pub has stood on the site of The Cheshire Cheese since 1538. Prior to that, the site was part of the guest house of a 13th century Carmelite monastery. The present pub was rebuilt after the Great Fire of 1666 but the original cellars remain.

This celebrated tavern-cum-chophouse has 132 creaking steps, which lead from the cellars to the top floor past six bars, three restaurants and a private dining room. The famous ground floor chop room is resplendent with original black oak panelling, an oak-beamed ceiling and a long oak table at which Dr. Johnson, Charles Dickens and many other famous characters have dined over the decades. It also houses the stuffed body of Polly, the pub's parrot, whose demise was reported by the BBC in 1926.

Tourists flock to see what is something of a working museum. Sadly, the drinks offering here has advanced little over the centuries and as this is a Samuel Smith's pub no drinks brands are on offer apart from the operator's.

H

G.E. CLUB

● ● ● ○

Great Eastern Hotel, Liverpool Street, City of London, EC2M 7QN, England

Tel: +44 (0)20 7618 7076,
www.geclub.co.uk
Hours: Tue-Fri noon-4pm & 6pm-2am, Sat 8pm-2am

Type:	Lounge bar/members club
Alfresco:	No
Entry:	Members & hotel guests
Highlights:	Cocktails, atmosphere
Atmosphere:	Laid-back
Clientele:	Shoreditch/funky City crowd
Dress code:	Funky casual (suits not encouraged)
Price guide:	££££
Food:	Served all hours

Conran's beautiful Great Eastern Hotel near Liverpool Street station houses this elegant members bar, which is hidden at the top of an unlikely looking staircase and behind a heavy wooden door. Leather armchairs, dark wood panelling and intimate table lamps are conducive to fat cigars, fine wines and conversation. Late week brings DJs and dancing, while the party nights are legendary.

Both classic cocktails and new creations are expertly produced. If the drinks menu doesn't appeal, then the daunting wine list from Aurora restaurant below is available. Food also comes from the kitchens of Aurora, so quality and choice is far better than offered by the average bar, while efficient table service means you don't even have to leave your seat. To gain membership and one of the coveted key tags schmooze an existing member.

Jamaica Wine House

Jamaica Wine House

Jamaica Wine House

JAMAICA WINE HOUSE
● ● ● ● ○

12 St Michael's Alley (off Cornhill), City of
London, EC3V 9DS, England

Tel: +44 (0)20 7626 9496
Hours: Mon-Fri 11am-11pm

Type: Traditional pub
Alfresco: Church garden
Entry: Open door
Highlights: Atmosphere
Atmosphere: Can be loud, always packed
Clientele: City boys & girls
Dress code: Suits
Price guide: £££
Food: Substantial sandwiches & platters

Tucked away up the medieval St Michael's
Alley is this traditional City pub, known
among local traders and brokers as the
'Jam Pot'. It stands next to St Michael, a
Wren-built church with a Hawksmoor
tower, on the site of the City's first coffee
house, which was established in 1652 and
destroyed in the Great Fire of London
sixteen years later. The pub which followed
was a haunt of Jamaican sugar, rum and
slave traders - hence the name - and was
reconstructed in 1862 in the style of a
grand Victorian public house.

Now a Grade II listed building, the
interior has been restored with a veritable
rainforest of mahogany. Panels divide the
long upstairs bar into four sections which,
apart from some hard bench seating, are
standing only. Downstairs there's more of
a restaurant/bar with plenty of chairs and
tables should you wish to eat, although
food is only available at lunchtimes.

PRISM
● ● ● ● ○

147 Leadenhall Street (@ Bishopsgate),
City of London, EC3V 4QT, England

Tel: +44 (0)20 7256 3873,
www.harveynichols.com
Hours: Mon-Fri 5pm-11pm

Type: Lounge bar
Alfresco: No
Entry: Subject to capacity
Highlights: Cocktails and wine list
Atmosphere: Hidden in the basement
Clientele: City business types
Dress code: Business suit
Price guide: ££££
Food: Caesar salad to fish & chips

This Grade One listed building, formerly
the Bank of New York, has been sensitively
converted into a fine dining restaurant and
bar. Shadowed by the vertiginous
Robocop backdrop of the Lloyds building,
the heavy Edwardian façade leads to a
marble hallway, beyond which lies the
impressive former banking hall with
columns rising to a coffered ceiling. The
tellers' desks have been replaced by a
modern bar and scarlet sofas.

Impressive though the ground level
is, I prefer the intimacy of the basement
bar. Housed in the former vaults of the old
bank, it is now a glistening subterranean
tube, filled with polished wood and leather,
rolled banquettes. All this style is
completed by great cocktails, faultless
food and an impressive wine list.

Prism is situated in the heart of the
City and so attracts suited and booted City
boys and girls. In the airy grand hall above,
they're on their best behaviour. You'll find
the atmosphere downstairs.

THE ROYAL EXCHANGE
● ● ● ● ○

The Royal Exchange, Threadneedle Street,
Bank, London, EC3V 3LR, England

Tel: +44 (0)20 7618 2480,
www.conran.com
Hours: Mon-Fri 8am-11pm

Type: Café bar & lounge bars
Alfresco: No
Entry: Subject to capacity
Highlights: Service & cocktails
Atmosphere: Refined but relaxed
Clientele: Business suited City boys & girls
Dress code: Smart (but not necessarily so)
Price guide: ££££
Food: Oysters to full meals

The Royal Exchange is a landmark building
situated in the heart of the City of London's
financial district, adjacent to the Bank of
England, the Stock Exchange and
Mansion House. Originally built in 1566 as
a bourse for the city merchants, it has
survived destruction by fire twice since it
was named by Queen Elizabeth I in 1571.

Part of the Conran empire, the Grand
Café sits smack in the centre of the
building's splendid covered courtyard,
surrounded by luxury boutiques. It's rare
to find a spare seat at the curvaceous,
polished pewter island bar, but well worth
sitting and appreciating the architecture
over a Martini if you can. (This area has a
restaurant licence, so standing at the bar
is not permitted.) Alternatively, you can
head upstairs to the more intimate twin
bars above the Colonnade shops.

Whichever bar you pick, you'll find the
same attentive service and fine
Champagnes. The impressive cocktail list
features some amazing contemporary
creations as well as the classics.

Vertigo 42

Vertigo 42

Vertigo 42

VERTIGO 42

● ● ● ● ○

Tower 42, Old Broad Street, Bank, London,
EC2N 1HQ, England

Tel: +44 (0)20 7877 7842,
www.vertigo42.co.uk
Hours: Mon-Fri noon-3pm & 5pm-10pm

Type: Lounge bar with a view
Alfresco: No
Entry: Pre-booking essential
Highlights: Champagne selection & view
Atmosphere: Quiet and relaxed
Clientele: City business types
Dress code: Business suits/smart casual
Price guide: £££££
Food: Salted almonds to charcuterie

This Champagne and seafood bar sits
atop central London's tallest building so,
after 9/11, entry rightly entails rigorous
security. You must reserve by phone: if
booking on the same day, call before noon
for lunch or before 5pm for dinner. On
arrival, you check in at the reception desk,
pass through security, feed your bags
through the X-ray machine and take the
ear-popping express lift to the 42nd floor.

The room is encircled by floor to
ceiling window bays, which offer an awe-
inspiring, panoramic view of what is, for
my money, the world's greatest capital city.
There's no beer and only a very limited
wine list, but you can choose from 30
varieties of Champagne in a range of
different bottle sizes. Then just sit, nearly
600 feet up, looking down on the slowly
revolving London Eye, while sipping
Champagne and nibbling on almonds.
That's what I call sight seeing.

THE WHITE SWAN

● ● ● ◐ ○

108 Fetter Lane, City of London, London,
EC4A 1ES, England

Tel: +44 (0)20 7242 9696,
www.thewhiteswanlondon.com
Hours: Mon-Fri 11am-11pm

Type:	Traditional/gastro pub
Alfresco:	No
Entry:	Open door .
Highlights:	Food
Atmosphere:	Relaxed
Clientele:	Lawyers & their secretaries
Dress code:	Business attire
Price guide:	£££
Food:	Gastro grub & a la carte upstairs

Formerly a down-at-heel boozer called the
Muddy Duck, this place was taken over by
the folk behind The Well in Clerkenwell in
2005. They have transformed the duck into
a swan with a serious chef, an A la carte
restaurant and a very good wine list.

With a stuffed swan over the door and
a boar's head and antlers on the walls, the
ground floor pub looks more like a hunting
lodge. The huge gilt framed mirror and
double height ceiling make it seem large
and airy. A mezzanine gallery intervenes
between this and the restaurant upstairs,
which boasts a mirrored ceiling and food
that is well above the standard of the usual
gastro pub both in quality and in price.

Prices fall as you descend the stairs
but even on the ground floor there's a
choice of 26 wines by the glass, a fair
range of beers including three ales, and a
short cocktail list.

The White Swan

The White Swan

CLAPHAM
(SW4, SW8)

ONCE PURELY RESIDENTIAL, NOW A LOCAL DESTINATION, CLAPHAM'S BUSTLING BAR SCENE COVERS ALL THE BASES – FROM PUBS, TO GASTRO PUBS, TO LOUNGES AND EVEN MEMBERS' CLUBS.

The Prince of Wales

The Abbeville

The Abbeville

THE ABBEVILLE

● ● ● ◐ ○

67-69 Abbeville Road (btwn Narbonne Ave &
Hambalt Rd), Clapham, SW4 9JW, England

Tel: +44 (0)20 8675 2201,
www.theabbeville.co.uk
Hours: Mon-Sat 11am-11pm, Sun 10am-
10:30pm

Type: Gastro pub
Alfresco: Few pavement tables
Entry: Open door
Highlights: Food, atmosphere
Atmosphere: Local boozer
Clientele: 30-something locals
Dress code: Casual
Price guide: £££
Food: Modern British gastro grub

Abbeville Road sits within a villagey,
residential area that appears miles away
from brash Clapham High Street nearby.
The Abbeville rests at the heart of this
virtual village, a true local's local that is also
a gastro pub.

The space was created by knocking
two shops together and was previously
known as Flumps. In this incarnation,
The Abbeville is a warren of small,
interconnecting rooms with two bars and
an open kitchen. Magnolia walls, dark wood
and a TV screen by the bar help create a
homely feel, while features such as a brass
kick rail and dried hops above the bar
remind you that this is a pub and not a living
room. On summer evenings drinkers spill
out onto the pavement, where they stand
and chat as if on the village green.

The pumps dispense a couple of real
ales, including Timothy Taylor Landlord,
plus a smattering of continental lagers.
Wines are also popular with the 30-
something crowd and the comprehensive
list includes a dozen by the glass.

THE COACH & HORSES

● ● ● ◐ ○

173-175 Clapham Park Road, Clapham,
London, SW4 7EX, England

Tel: +44 (0)20 7622 3815,
www.barbeerian-inns.com
Hours: Mon-Sat 11am-1pm,
Sun noon-10:30pm

Type:	Gastro pub
Alfresco:	Small front terrace
Entry:	Open door
Highlights:	Food
Atmosphere:	Relaxed
Clientele:	Mixed bag
Dress code:	Casual
Price guide:	£££
Food:	Blackboard British gastro grub

This homely little pub has survived the
bookshelf treatment to retain a traditional
tavern ambience. Dark wood tables and
chairs surround an oval island bar bristling
with hand pumps which dispense a quartet
of real ales. Watercolours of polo and
racing hang on the baize green walls and
there's a big screen lurking for sporting
events. In summer the front doors open
onto a small terrace, which, due to its
proximity to the busy main road, is far
from tranquil.

Blackboards display an eleven strong
wine list, all available by the glass, while
specials of the day bolster the printed,
neo-traditional tavern menu. Typical dishes
include beer battered cod and chips,
homemade burgers and herb crusted
Welsh lamb cutlet. The full English breakfast
is a house speciality, while traditionalists
will approve of the pickled eggs offered
alongside the more contemporary nuts
and olives.

The honest, good value food and
well-kept beers attract a mixed local crowd.

The Coach & Horses

The Coach & Horses

The Coach & Horses

THE FENTIMAN ARMS

● ● ● ◐ ○

64 Fentiman Road (corner Carroun Rd), Vauxhall, London, SW8 1LA, England

Tel: +44 (0)20 7793 9796,
www.geronimo-inns.co.uk
Hours: Mon-Sat 11am-11pm, Sun noon-10:30pm

Type:	Gastro pub
Alfresco:	Front tables & rear garden
Entry:	Open door
Highlights:	Food
Atmosphere:	Relaxed
Clientele:	Local 30-somethings, couples
Dress code:	Casual
Price guide:	£££
Food:	Blackboard British gastro grub

Cricket fans should take note of this local gastro boozer: it lies only a few good sixes from The Oval. And, for those balmy summer days when England's batting average is worth toasting, The Fentiman also boasts a sizable back garden, whose designer won a gold medal at the Chelsea Flower Show.

The interior is ye typical gastro refurb. Bookshelves, cushioned benches and eclectic second hand tables and chairs cluster around the central island bar. The floor is bare and wooden, the walls are mustard coloured and the overall feel is comfortable and on the shabby side of lived-in.

This pub's main draw, besides the garden, is the ever-changing but limited menu. Think very creative home cooking, a cross between Jamie Oliver and Delia Smith. Keith Floyd would approve of the 17 wines by the glass and the Deuchars and Greene King IPA on draught.

The 'Fentiroom' upstairs hosts a comedy night on Tuesdays and jazz on Sundays.

The Fentiman Arms

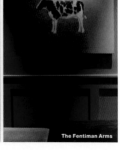

The Fentiman Arms

LOST SOCIETY
● ● ● ● ●

697 Wandsworth Road, Clapham, London,
SW8 3JF, England

Tel: +44 (0)20 7652 6526,
www.lostsociety.co.uk
Hours: Tue-Thu 5pm-1am, Fri 4pm-2am,
Sat 11am-2am, Sun 11am-1am

Type:	Lounge bar
Alfresco:	Front terrace & courtyard
Entry:	Subject to management & capacity
Highlights:	Cocktails, food & music
Atmosphere:	Relaxed
Clientele:	Local 30-somethings
Dress code:	Casual but stylish
Price guide:	£££
Food:	A la carte or mezze & platters

According to the menu, "Lost Society
endeavours to become an inspirational
drinking venue on the London bar scene. . .
Intelligent drinking, delectable dining and
bendy beats immersed within foreign
decadence." A laudable manifesto - and they
appear to be delivering.

Lost Society is set in a two storey 16th
century barn which was, from 1982 until late
last year (2005), The Tea Rooms des Artistes.
The building retains its homely feel: numerous
small, intimate rooms and spaces are
connected by alleys and stairwells (there is a
bar on each floor). The décor varies from
bohemian to oriental but is always beautifully
designed, subtly lit and atmospheric.

The manifesto quoted above appears at
the start of a very comprehensive list of both
classic and contemporary cocktails, all perfectly
rendered. Beers include Timothy Taylor Landlord
and Sierra Nevada, while the wine list caters to
all palates with eleven bins by the glass.

The most stunning aspect of this bar,
however, is its gorgeous clientele, and the
party atmosphere, fanned by DJs from 8pm
Thursday to Saturday

Lost Society

Lost Society

The Prince of Wales

THE PRINCE OF WALES

● ● ● ○ ○

38 Old Town (corner Princes Close), Old Town, Clapham, London, SW4 0LB, England

Tel: +44 (0)20 7622 3530
Hours: Mon-Fri 5pm-11pm, Sat 1pm-11pm, Sun 1pm-10:30pm

Type:	Traditional pub
Alfresco:	Tables on pavement
Entry:	Open door
Highlights:	Decor
Atmosphere:	Local boozer
Clientele:	Locals – all ages
Dress code:	Casual
Price guide:	£££
Food:	Not a place to eat

This crazy little pub trades on its acronym: 'POW.COM' is painted in large letters on the parapet and POW repeats in neon lights across the frontage. Inside, the single room is filled with curios including model planes, boxing gloves, prosthetic limbs and a bull's head. These random objects are souvenirs of the landlord's seafaring days and hang from the ceiling or cling to the walls, barely illuminated by scarlet bulbs. The music is as diverse as its surroundings and ranges from The Beach Boys to ELO.

On winter nights this is an atmospheric, warm local. Summertime pulls the crowds away from Clapham High Street to the Old Town where this becomes one of the main attractions. In warm weather the wide pavement is cluttered with tables.

The Prince of Wales may be small but it has a big personality and attracts a jolly crowd of drinkers. They enjoy a traditional pub offering that includes a couple of ales.

The Prince of Wales

The Prince of Wales

The People's Republic

So.uk

THE PEOPLE'S REPUBLIC

● ● ● ○ ○

16a Clapham Common Southside,
Clapham, London, SW4 7AB, England

Tel: +44 (0)20 7978 2691, **www.**iloveclapham.com
Hours: Mon-Wed 5pm-11pm, Thu 5pm-
midnight, Fri 5pm-2am, Sat 11am-2am,
Sun 11am-10:30pm

Type:	Lounge bar
Alfresco:	No
Entry:	Subject to management & capacity
Highlights:	Cocktails
Atmosphere:	Relaxed
Clientele:	Local 30 somethings, couples
Dress code:	Casual but hip
Price guide:	£££
Food:	Brunch, tapas & burgers

Democracy for the proletariat comes to
Clapham Common through this bar's ballot
box. Customers post nominations for new
wines, beers, cocktails, dishes and even
music and the bar takes up the most
popular. Successful nominations win prizes
but best to vote anonymously if you're
making a suggestion like "play more Britney
Spears", or you may end up in the bar's
regular email newsletter.

Behind the glass façade of what was
once Tiger Lil's restaurant lies a seventies
loft style interior with the requisite bare bricks
and exposed iron girders. Colourful,
manga-style graffiti covers the back wall,
while amber lights on the back bar and
ceiling create a warm glow. Deep, comfy
brown leather banquettes line one wall, and
high stools and tables fill the floor. Space is
left for the inevitable DJ driven shuffling late
in the week.

Confident, friendly, efficient staff help
create a laid-back atmosphere which the
young crowd appreciate. The cocktail list is
extensive and the food portions generous.

THE RAPSCALLION & THE SEQUEL

● ● ● ● ○

75 & 78 Venn Street (by and opp. cinema),
Clapham, London, SW4 0BD, England

Tel: + 44 (0)20 7787 6555 & 7622 4222,
www.therapscalliononline.com,
www.thesequelonline.com
Hours: Mon-Sat 4pm-midnight, Sun
10.30am-11.30pm

Type:	Restaurant/lounge bar
Alfresco:	No
Entry:	Subject to capacity
Highlights:	Cocktails & food
Atmosphere:	Friendly & buzzy
Clientele:	Groomed locals & trendy types
Dress code:	Designer casual
Price guide:	£££
Food:	Menu of light dishes

These two bars share the same owner and sit practically facing each other on the same Clapham side street. Rapscallion (the first of the duo) benefits from large front windows, which are thrown open in summer and make it a bright, airy restaurant-cum-bar. The aptly named Sequel (the second to open) is a low-key and fairly minimalist bar and restaurant nestling under the Clapham Picture House. Suitably enough, a large screen plays movies over the tiny but extraordinarily well stocked bar.

Each venue benefits from accomplished bartenders, attentive service and superb food. Cocktail lists include many original and stunning drinks, while Erdinger wheat beer is available on draught. The wines are varied and well priced and there is a fine selection of liqueurs and interesting spirits.

Rapscallion & Sequel offer food and drinks of a quality that negates the need for locals to trek into the West End.

SAND

● ● ● ○ ○

156 Clapham Park Road, Clapham,
London, SW4 7DE, England

Tel: + 44 (0)20 7622 3022,
www.sandbarrestaurant.co.uk
Hours: Mon-Thu 6pm-2am, Fri-Sat 6pm-
3am, Sun 6pm-2am

Type:	Lounge bar / members club
Alfresco:	Small roof terrace
Entry:	Cover charge after 9pm on Fri & Sat
Highlights:	Atmosphere
Atmosphere:	Clubby late week
Clientele:	Trendy Claphamites
Dress code:	Cool togs
Price guide:	£££
Food:	Shepherd's pie, burgers & snacks

This relaxed, multi-layered den of leather seats and low slung tables caters for a crowd drawn from the Clapham / Brixton borders. Members gain a dog tag allowing access to the upper floors where there's a second bar, a small cinema screen, pool tables and a bijou roof terrace, but non-members are restricted to downstairs.

Here the back bar is dominated by a circular Perspex hourglass (technically a two-hourglass), where the eponymous sand is reset by an elaborate cog and chain mechanism. A wall built from those patterned concrete blocks found in naff suburban gardens creates a surprisingly stylish effect.

The wine list and cocktail quality are no more than adequate, though the drinks tend to be better upstairs. There are DJs most nights and music is the main attraction, making this more of an intimate club than a bar. It could be argued that Sand is past its prime, but can still deliver a good night.

SO.UK

● ● ● ○ ○

165 Clapham High Street, Clapham,
London, SW4 7SS, England

Tel: +44 (0)20 7622 4004,
www.so-uk.co.uk
Hours: Mon-Tue 5pm-11pm, Wed-Thu
5pm-2am, Fri-Sat 5pm-2am,
Sun 5pm-midnight

Type:	Lounge bar
Alfresco:	Tables on street in summer
Entry:	Subject to management & capacity
Highlights:	Atmosphere
Atmosphere:	Intimate/relaxed
Clientele:	Young Claphamites with money
Dress code:	Not shabby
Price guide:	££££
Food:	International tapas & meze

So.uk is styled in a North African vein with Asian hints but has the atmosphere of a good house party. It is owned by a rather famous couple, the former footballer Lee Chapman and his actress wife Lesley Ash. They lived in the flat above years ago when this space was a wallpaper shop.

The sand-coloured room has a plain tiled floor and the walls are lined with comfy, built-in seating. Moroccan knick-knacks and low lighting drive the louche lounge feel: in the words of the menu, 'All tables are communal style, so please be prepared to meet new friends.' The best place to sit is the intimate raised area at the back, not least because it's en route to the toilets, allowing you to check out your fellow drinkers as they walk by.

There's a good wine selection here with 21 options by the glass and a separate 'classic wine list' for the more discerning. Cocktails are a risky option as quality varies widely according to your server. The previously all-Moroccan food menu has given way to a more international selection of tapas and meze.

Bistrotheque

CLERKENWELL & SHOREDITCH
(EC1, PARTS EC2, E2)

THE DISUSED FACTORIES IN THESE OLD INDUSTRIAL DISTRICTS GAVE WAY
FIRST TO ARTISTS, THEN TO MEDIA; AND NOW TO THOSE WITH CASH. LOFT-
STYLED, BEER-FUELLED, GOOD TIME VENUES, TRENDY PUBS PACKED WITH
POST-IRONIC FASHION PLUS THE OCCASIONAL HIGH-END LOUNGE CREATE A
LONDON DESTINATION.

BISTROTHEQUE
●●●●○

23-27 Wadeson Street (off Cambridge Heath Rd), Hackney, London, E2 9DR, England

Tel: +44 (0)20 8983 7900,
www.bistrotheque.com
Hours: Mon-Sat 5:30pm-midnight, Sun 1pm-midnight

Type: Lounge / restaurant bar
Alfresco: Covered entrance yard
Entry: No door policy
Highlights: Food & vibe
Atmosphere: Mellow
Clientele: Hip 25-45s
Dress code: Casual but very hip
Price guide: £££
Food: Great meals served upstairs

To set the scene: this former knicker factory - sorry, I can't resist, 'sweatshop' - lies down a narrow side street in the shadows of the carbuncled backside of a cash & carry warehouse. Its location, in the no man's land between Hackney and Bethnal Green, may be less than promising but Bistrotheque is an über-cool gem. So cool, in fact, that it has no signage.

Beyond the picnic tables and the roller-shutter entrance lies The Napoleon Bar, so named for its sponsor, Courvoisier cognac. The small rectangular room is dominated by an antique mahogany bar reclaimed from Otterburn Hall in Northumberland. Aptly, the columns of the mahogany back bar are crowned with carved busts of Napoleon. Small club chairs surround nine circular tables where an arty crowd appear to prefer Becks, Kronenbourg and Guinness to cognac as they prepare for the live entertainment in the Cabaret Room next door.

A full Modern British, gastro pub style menu is served upstairs in the stark, industrial dining room.

BLEEDING HEART TAVERN
●●●○○

19 Greville Street, Hatton Garden, Clerkenwell, London, EC1N 8SQ, England

Tel: +44 (0)20 7242 2056,
www.bleedingheart.co.uk
Hours: Mon-Fri 7:30am-11pm

Type: Traditional pub
Alfresco: No
Entry: If there's space
Highlights: Food
Atmosphere: Buzzy
Clientele: Very mixed
Dress code: Office attire predominates
Price guide: £££
Food: Full restaurant menu

The gruesome name of this little pub comes from the legend of Lady Elizabeth Hatton, who entered into an alliance with the Devil. Apparently she failed to meet her side of the bargain and one night in 1646 Satan took revenge. The next morning a stable lad found her heart still pumping blood over the cobblestones of the yard behind the inn. Bleeding Heart Yard, as it was unsurprisingly renamed, became famous thanks to Dickens - Little Dorrit and Mr Plornish lived in a house at the far end. A Bleeding Heart Tavern was first recorded in this version of 1746: this version, although newer, retains the name.

Like its sister restaurant behind, this small place with its bare brick and mahogany interior is noted for its food. It also boasts an atmospheric basement dining room with farmyard illustrations and an open kitchen.

Wines are great value and the full list boasts some 450 bins but 'The Full English' breakfast with Suffolk bacon is unmissable.

CANTALOUPE
●●●●○

35-42 Charlotte Road, Shoreditch, London, EC2A 3PD, England

Tel: +44 (0)20 7729 5566,
www.cantaloupe.co.uk
Hours: Mon-Fri 11am-noon, Sat noon-midnight, Sun noon-11.30pm

Type: Lounge / restaurant bar
Alfresco: No
Entry: No door policy
Highlights: Food & vibe
Atmosphere: Mellow
Clientele: Hip 20-40
Dress code: Casual, grungy
Price guide: ££
Food: Reasonable tapas

Rough and ready, but in a sophisticated, fashionably Shoreditch kinda way, Cantaloupe was the first bar to open in this hip part of town and since November 1995 it has set the style for many others.

Scruffy old leather sofas, ramshackle wooden tables and benches sit on a worn, red painted plywood floor in a converted warehouse. Scaffolding boards make up the back bar and a garage door is opened when busy to reveal the newest area and a second bar.

The open kitchen turns out some very respectable food to soak up the beer which remains the core drink. Some interesting wines and spirits are advertised on the blackboards scattered around the walls, while cocktails are cheap, if not brilliant. Easygoing and friendly, this is a classic Ditch venue.

CARGO

●●●◐○

Kingsland Viaduct, 83 Rivington Street,
Shoreditch, London, EC2A 3AY, England

Tel: +44 (0)20 7739 3440,
www.cargo-london.com
Hours: Mon-Thu noon-1am, Fri noon-3am,
Sat 6pm-3am, Sun noon-midnight

Type:	Café bar/nightclub
Alfresco:	Yard
Entry:	Expect to pay cover charge
Highlights:	Live music, atmosphere
Atmosphere:	Pumpin'
Clientele:	Hoxton crowd
Dress code:	Casual/grungy
Price guide:	££
Food:	Mediterranean/Latin 'street food'

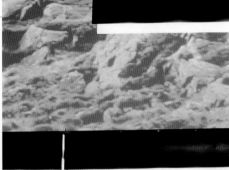

Three high, bare brick railway arches have been knocked together to create this 600 capacity live music venue. Arch 1 houses a restaurant serving Mediterranean and Latin American 'street food' at communal tables large enough to seat twelve. Windows overlook an outside patio area with driftwood seating and bamboo filled planters.

Arch 2 houses the bar, which features freestanding Douglas fir drinking stations and a raised lounge area. The short cocktail list offers a range of choices but beer and spirits with mixers are the mainstay here. Beers range from Czech lagers to German wheat beer to Old Speckled Hen.

Arch 3 has a great sound system that's put to good use by a nightly succession of bands and DJs from across the musical spectrum. Cargo is popular with the young Shoreditch arts and media crowds, and travelling hipsters attracted by the music and the vibe.

Cargo

Bistrotheque

Cargo

CELLAR GASCON

● ● ● ○ ○

59 West Smithfield, Smithfield, London, EC1A 9DS, England

Tel: +44 (0)20 7600 7561
Hours: Mon-Fri noon-midnight, Sat 6pm-midnight

Type:	Wine bar
Alfresco:	No
Entry:	Busy early evening
Highlights:	Wines and food
Atmosphere:	Dark & slightly moody
Clientele:	Suited city boys & girls
Dress code:	Smart (but not required)
Price guide:	£££
Food:	French tapas-style dishes

This tiny adjunct to the Michelin-starred Club Gascon next door is a hybrid of classic French wine bar, Clerkenwell exposed-brick style emporium and Pullman dining car, arched ceiling and all.

As the name would suggest, Cellar specialises in the wines and cuisine of South West France. Knowledgeable, French staff let you sample some of the huge selection of bins (nearly 30 are available by the glass) until you find one you like, which won't take very long. Some rare and unusual bottles, as well as a fine list of Cognac and Armagnac, will please spirit enthusiasts, while gourmets can sop up the booze with Gascon style tapas-style dishes, including pâtés, cured meats and seafood.

Weekday lunchtimes and early evenings see the Cellar filled with suited city types but after 9pm and at weekends the place returns to its natural state: a wonderfully atmospheric French wine bar.

THE COACH & HORSES

● ● ● ○ ○

26-28 Ray Street, Clerkenwell, London, EC1R 3DJ, England

Tel: +44 (0)20 7278 8990,
www.thecoachandhorses.com
Hours: Mon-Fri 11am-11pm, Sat 6pm-11pm, Sun noon-3pm

Type:	Gastro pub
Alfresco:	Bench pavement seating & covered garden
Entry:	Open door
Highlights:	Food
Atmosphere:	Relaxed
Clientele:	Local office escapees
Dress code:	Suits to scruffy jeans
Price guide:	£££
Food:	Chalkboard snacks plus full menu

This unprepossessing looking Victorian boozer lies at the bottom of Back Hill on Ray Street in the backwaters of Clerkenwell. The wood panelled dining room and small bar show the merest hints of gentrification from workaday boozer. Nondescript wooden tables, comfortable but unremarkable padded chairs and a boarded up fireplace hardly shout made over. No matter, score one of the window seats with a view up Back Hill and be prepared for something special - the food.

The Coach and Horses is a critically acclaimed gastro pub with an impressive daily changing menu, plus far from ordinary snack foods, on the chalkboard. The wine and beer offering is also pretty special with sixteen wines by the glass on a broad list and three real ales on draught plus a good range of lager.

Regulars include Guardian hacks and pretty young trendies from local PR agencies. Unlike many gastro pubs, the Coach and Horses takes bookings but early week you're usually OK to drift in.

THE DOVETAIL

● ● ● ○ ○

9 Jerusalem Passage (btwn St. John's Sq & Aylesbury St), Clerkenwell, London, EC1V 4JP, England

Tel: +44 (0)20 7490 7321,
www.belgianbars.com
Hours: Mon-Fri noon-11pm, Sat 6pm-11pm, Sun noon-3pm

Type:	Contemporary pub
Alfresco:	Open front in summer
Entry:	Most welcome
Highlights:	Belgian beer selection
Atmosphere:	Convivial
Clientele:	Suits, media & 30 somethings
Dress code:	Casual
Price guide:	£££
Food:	Belgian beer sausages and burgers

Clerkenwell has a religious past. In 1730 a Carthusian Monastery was founded here. Although it is long gone, some of its buildings remain on Charterhouse Square and are now pensioners' alms-houses. St John's Square, off Clerkenwell Road, is the site of the medieval Priory of The Knights of the Order of St John of Jerusalem. Its gateway, rebuilt in 1504, still stands at the southern end of the square and Jerusalem Passage lies at the opposite side of the square. Hidden up this narrow alley, which was originally paved with stones brought back from the Holy Land, is the Dovetail.

The Dovetail's interior is basic. Its slate floor, wooden tables, gothic chairs and reclaimed pews herald the appropriately monastic beer theme. The 100 strong list of beers is exclusively Belgian: 14 are available on draught. The Dovetail is rightly a place of pilgrimage for Belgian beer lovers, as well as a relaxed local for young media types.

The Coach & Horses

THE EAGLE

●●●○○

159 Farringdon Road, Farringdon, London,
EC1R 3AL, England

Tel: +44 (0)20 7837 1353
Hours: Mon-Sat noon-11pm, Sun noon-
5:30pm

Type:	Gastro pub
Alfresco:	Pavement tables
Entry:	Open door
Highlights:	Food
Atmosphere:	Relaxed
Clientele:	Hacks, suits, locals, tourists
Dress code:	Suits to worn jeans
Price guide:	£££
Food:	French-orientated menu

London's first gastro-pub is still going
strong. To call it 'popular' is an under-
statement – lunchtimes and evenings see
the place stuffed with visiting foodies, staff
from nearby new media companies and
hacks from the Guardian next door.

A 'no bookings' policy operates and
trying to get a table is like trying to get a
tube seat at rush-hour. Sharing tables is
inevitable and, to be honest, part of the
place's charm. Both food and furnishings
are unpretentious and no nonsense. The
chefs work in a cramped, open kitchen
space which is a continuation of the bar,
and so are the focal point of the
experience, almost a performance piece.

There's little to choose from beer wise
but the sensible wine list offers six by
the glass.

THE FOX PUB & DINING ROOM

●●●○○

28 Paul Street (corner Scrutton St),
Shoreditch, London, EC2A 4LB, England

Tel: +44 (0)20 7729 5708
Hours: Mon-Fri noon-10pm

Type:	Traditional/gastro pub
Alfresco:	Small roof terrace
Entry:	Open door
Highlights:	Food
Atmosphere:	Workaday
Clientele:	Designers / office workers
Dress code:	Casual
Price guide:	£££
Food:	Warm salt beef sandwiches, full menu upstairs

This tiny Victorian pub has been given the
merest of makeovers and furnished with
reclaimed tables and chairs cleared from a
deconsecrated church. The tables wobble
and the chairs are rickety but, strangely, that
adds to its scruffy charm. Nattering graphic
designers, achingly hip new media folk and
the odd out of place suit sink pints and
create a warm, buzzy atmosphere.

The Fox is an offshoot of the original
gastro-pub, The Eagle in Clerkenwell, and
the first floor dining room has something
of a reputation. With its rug covered
wooden floor, antique mirrored walls,
candelabras, mismatched tables and
chairs, and even mismatched crockery, it
has a wonderfully rustic feel. Service can
be lackadaisical but somehow that suits
the place.

Few seem aware of the small roof
terrace off the dining room, which is open
to drinkers during the summer months. The
Wells Bombardier is always in great
condition and there's a dozen wines by
the glass.

GREAT EASTERN DINING ROOM & BELOW 54

●●●○○

54-56 Great Eastern Street (@ Charlotte Rd),
Shoreditch, EC2A 3QR, England

Tel: +44 (0)20 7613 4545,
www.greateasterndining.co.uk
Hours: Mon-Wed noon-midnight, Thu-Sat
7.30pm-1am

Type:	Lounge / restaurant bar
Alfresco:	No
Entry:	Most welcome
Highlights:	Atmosphere
Atmosphere:	Convivial
Clientele:	New media/fashion/music/creatives
Dress code:	Designer, cool casual
Price guide:	£££
Food:	Pan-Asian meals or dim sum

In Shoreditch terms, this bar is positively
geriatric. It dates back to the mid-90s
when the area was still an urban desert
and is the elder sister of E&O over in
Notting Hill. The ground floor is divided
between the bar and the excellent
restaurant. The two very different spaces
are separated by a stairway which leads
down to the basement club, Below 54
(which opens later in the week).

Crinkly glass windows preserve
patrons' privacy, although the panes of
one side window are left clear to tantalise
passers-by with the flickering flames from
the gas fire. During the day this bright, airy
lounge serves as a relaxed meeting place
for graphic designers and new media
bods who drop in for a meal, snacks or
just a drink. Evenings are noisier and
busier with the odd suit wandering up from
the city but the same relaxed, friendly
atmosphere prevails.

The Fox

The Fox

The Fox

Green & Red

GREEN & RED BAR & CANTINA

●●●●◐

51 Bethnal Green Road, Shoreditch,
London, E1 6LA, England

Tel: +44 (0)20 7749 9670,
www.greenred.co.uk
Hours: Mon-Fri 5pm-1am, Sat noon-1am,
Sun noon-1am

Type:	Lounge bar & steakhouse
Alfresco:	No
Entry:	Subject to management & capacity
Highlights:	Tequila, food, atmosphere, cocktails
Atmosphere:	Chilled to rocking
Clientele:	Shoreditch twats & discerning cool
Dress code:	Stylishly scruffy
Price guide:	££££
Food:	Authentic Mexican/Jaliscan cuisine

Rather than a reference to the Mexican flag,
this bar takes its name from its location:
practically opposite the top end of East
London's famous Brick Lane, at the point
where Redchurch Street meets Bethnal
Green Road.

The building initially looks uninspiring,
but you'll find a homely bar with more than a
hint of Mexican cantina behind that expanse
of window. Head downstairs and you're in for
a further surprise: a space several times the
size of upstairs with ample secluded corners
and another two bars. While upstairs is always
chilled and relaxed, come the end of the week
the basement simply goes off with DJs fuelling
the madness.

This is London's foremost tequila bar,
with a huge range of rare and limited 100%
agave tequilas. These feature prominently in
the excellent cocktail list which includes gems
such as the Sage & Pineapple Margarita.

The food is authentic Mexican, majoring
on recipes from Jalisco state. Tasty mains
come with freshly made corn tortillas, refried
beans, shredded cabbage and house salsas
so you can make your own tacos.

Green & Red

Green & Red

The Light

JERUSALEM TAVERN

● ● ● ○ ○

55 Britton Street, Clerkenwell, London, EC1M 5UQ, England

Tel: +44 (0)20 7490 4281,
www.stpetersbrewery.co.uk
Hours: Mon-Fri 11am-11pm

Type: Traditional pub
Alfresco: Pavement tables
Entry: Open door subject to capacity
Highlights: St Peter's ales
Atmosphere: Relaxed & friendly
Clientele: City boys & girls
Dress code: Business suits to tatty jeans
Price guide: ££
Food: Proper grub & sandwiches

This tiny pub is sub-divided by partitions glazed with small, Georgian windows. It has a Dickensian feel and looks as though it has been this way for centuries but, although the building dates back to 1720, it has been a pub for less than a decade, and was previously a coffee house.

Now the building is the London shop window for the excellent Suffolk brewery St Peter's. Their whole range is here, including fruit beers like Cinnamon & Apple, Elderberry or Lemon & Ginger, more traditional ales such as Winter Ale or Porter and the popular Golden Ale which is perfect for those who think they prefer the likes of Stella. Many of the beers are on draught. The rest are served from the brewery's distinctive green oval bottles.

The scruffy ale fanciers who flock to the Jerusalem Tavern from far and wide compete for limited seating with suited city boys and girls. All share an appreciation of the relaxed atmosphere and St Peter's beers.

THE LIGHT

● ● ● ● ○

233 Shoreditch High Street (btwn Worship & Gt Eastern St), London, E1 6PJ, England

Tel: +44 (0)20 7247 8989,
www.thelighte1.com
Hours: Mon-Wed noon-midnight, Thu-Fri noon-2am, Sun noon-10.30pm

Type: Lounge/restaurant/members bar
Alfresco: Courtyard, lawn & roof terrace
Entry: Subject to management & capacity
Highlights: Roof terrace on a summer's evening
Atmosphere: Warehouse party
Clientele: City boys & girls, Hoxton posse
Dress code: Business suits to Hoxton grunge
Price guide: ££££
Food: Snacks served all day in downstairs bar

This 10,000 sq. ft brick building was once an electricity generating station and in its day provided power for the lighting in nearby Liverpool Street and Bethnal Green stations. The industrial feel has been maintained along with original exposed timber, steel girders and ceramic faced bricks. The ground floor houses a 300-capacity bar and an 85-seater restaurant, the first floor an 180 capacity members bar. There's a roof terrace and a street-level area with a lawn for seasonal drinking.

Downstairs on weekdays you'll find City boys and girls mixing with Hoxtonites. At weekends eastenders replace the City folk. The suit-free members lounge upstairs attracts a more chilled crowd.

There's a fair range of wines on offer, but beer appears most popular: the range includes bottles of flavoursome Union. Cocktails aren't big here but there are at least two bartenders who hold their own well and can cater for most requests.

LOUNGELOVER

● ● ● ● ○

1 Whitby Street (off Club Row), Shoreditch, London, E2

Tel: +44 (0)20 7012 1234,
www.loungelover.co.uk
Hours: Tue-Sat 6pm-midnight, Sun noon-6pm

Type: Lounge bar
Alfresco: No
Entry: Subject to space
Highlights: The look of the interior & clientele
Atmosphere: Chilled & mellow
Clientele: Arty, music & media
Dress code: Casual, way-out, hip
Price guide: ££££
Food: Served all hours

Loungelover's location in a former butcher's warehouse on a grungy, cobbled Shoreditch back street sets the scene for what looks like a scrap merchant's yard filled with the hoard of a kleptomaniac. In fact both the multitude of chandeliers and the taxidermy, antiques and bric-a-brac they illuminate were assembled by the trio of antiques dealers who also own Les Trois Garçons, a highly respected and equally unique nearby restaurant.

The drinkers are as diverse and unusual as the décor ranging from arty, media types to young bankers and solicitors who have moved into the area due to its proximity to the City. The cocktail list with its many original concoctions is also inimitable.

Loungelover would be an unusual venue to find in any location, but in London's East End, a short walk from the curry houses of Brick Lane, it is bizarre and truly superb.

MATCH EC1

●●●○○

45-47 Clerkenwell Road, Clerkenwell,
London, EC1M 5RS, England

Tel: +44 (0)20 7250 4002,
www.matchbar.com
Hours: Mon-Sat 11am-midnight

Type: Lounge bar
Alfresco: Pavement tables in summer
Entry: Subject to space rather than dress
Highlights: Cocktails
Atmosphere: Chilled
Clientele: City, pre-club, media & plain nice people
Dress code: Anything goes – suits to jeans
Price guide: £££
Food: Sausages, tortillas, wraps, tapas etc.

Back in 1997 I spent a night barhopping
with a former lawyer called Jonathan
Downey who told me of his plans to open
a lounge bar in Clerkenwell. Well, he did.
Such a good thing was Jonathan on to that
he now has a chain of such bars and a list
of 'best bar' awards tucked under his belt.
The original Clerkenwell Road Match
branch has sofas and tables at street level,
surrounding a sunken, stone-floored 'pit',
which houses the bar. When it's busy, it's
not dissimilar to feeding time at the zoo and
best watched from above. Details of the
stylish décor such as the railings and sofas
are repeated in the newer Match Bars,
which are bigger and possibly better than
the original.

The superb cocktail list is filled with
original creations now much copied by
other bars, which unfortunately usually fail
to mimic the quality of service and
ingredients found at Match.

YE OLDE MITRE TAVERN

●●●○○

1 Ely Court (btwn Ely Place & Hatton Garden)
Farringdon, London, EC1N 6SJ, England

Tel: +44 (0)20 7405 4751,
www.yeoldemitre.co.uk
Hours: Mon-Fri 11am-11pm,
Sat-Sun closed

Type: Traditional pub
Alfresco: Standing in alleyway
Entry: Open door
Highlights: Heritage, ales
Atmosphere: Traditional pub
Clientele: Legals, jewellers, tourists & office workers
Dress code: Scruffy jeans to suits
Price guide: ££
Food: Toasted sandwiches, pies, sausages

This little pub is one of London's best-kept
secrets, lurking down the narrow alley that
links Hatton Garden and Ely Place. It was
originally built in 1546 as servants' quarters
for the Bishop of Ely, whose palace stood
on the eponymous Place – a mitre, for your
reference, is the tall, deeply cleft hat
bishops wear. The building became a
prison and then a hospital before being
rebuilt in 1772.

This is one of London's most
picturesque pubs. When admiring it from
the alleyway, look up and you'll see a stone
mitre from the bishop's gatehouse in the
pub's wall. Inside are two small, dark
panelled rooms. In the tall, deeply cleft hat
a cherry tree Elizabeth I once danced
around preserved behind glass.

Three regular cask ales plus one
guest beer mean this pub tends to appeal
to mature ale drinkers. The quaintness and
heritage attracts tourists.

THE PEASANT

●●●○○

240 St. John Street, Clerkenwell, London,
EC1V 4PH, England

Tel: +44 (0)20 7336 7726,
www.thepeasant.co.uk
Hours: Mon-Sat noon-11pm,
Sun noon-6pm

Type: Gastro pub
Alfresco: Patio attached to restaurant
Entry: Subject to capacity
Highlights: Food
Atmosphere: Relaxed local boozer
Clientele: Suits to cool Clerkenwell
Dress code: Suits to designer shabby
Price guide: £££
Food: Tapas, sharing platters & single dishes

London is awash with gastro-pubs and
Clerkenwell's Peasant is one of many
neighbourhood pubs in a similar vein.
Unusually for the genre, it feels like a
boozer with good food, rather than a
restaurant with beer fonts.

We have the brothers Gregory and
Patrick Wright to thank for funkifying and
gastrofying this old pub. It was once the
George & Dragon, as is obvious from the
interior, where a tiled fresco depicts the
saint slaying the monster. Other original
features, including a mosaic floor and a
very solid looking mahogany bar, combine
well with warehouse-style lighting, plain
red walls and funky beats. Seating is of the
functional oaken kind, while the bare wood
tables are typical.

A la carte dining is offered upstairs
and food also features highly in the
downstairs pub. The drinks list continues
to improve with real ale, English cider and
some interesting bottled Belgian beers on
offer. The folk of Clerkenwell are lucky to
have such a local on their doorstep.

THE PRINCESS

● ● ● ● ○

76 Paul Street (@ Willow St), Shoreditch,
London, EC2A 4NE, England

Tel: +44 (0)20 7729 9270
Hours: Mon-Fri 12:30pm-11pm,
Sat 5pm-11pm, Sun noon-5pm

Type:	Gastro pub
Alfresco:	No
Entry:	Open door
Highlights:	Food
Atmosphere:	Relaxed
Clientele:	Suited city types to Shoreditch twats
Dress code:	Suits to jeans
Price guide:	£££
Food:	Superb Mediterranean led menu

This Victorian back street boozer has been
given a new lease of life by two young Aussie
expats, Zim Sutton and Andrew Veevers.

Downstairs retains some of its
workaday charm. Fittings such as the pub's
original 'Princess Royal' mirror blend with
contemporary design touches such as
wallpaper covered in charging horses. The
beer offering is uninventive with two
traditional British ales on draught and a
pretty mundane selection of draught and
bottled lagers.

However, the real draw here lies up the
spiral staircase: a small, chic dining room
with big picture windows, a fireplace and
florid wallpaper to match the outside
signage. Smart upholstered chairs surround
neat wooden tables, a far cry from the
salvaged furniture traditional to the genre.

The Mediterranean influenced menu
is of fine dining standard but served in pub-
size portions. The broadly based wine list
is categorised by flavour profile and offers
something to suit most palates and
pockets, including nine by the glass.

The Princess

Match EC1

Match EC1

THE PROPHET

● ● ● ○ ○

5-11 Worship Street (@ Tabernacle Street),
London, EC2A 2BP, England

Tel: +44 (0)20 7588 8835,
www.lewisandclarke.com
Hours: Mon-Wed 10am-11pm, Thu-Fri
10am-midnight

Type: Gastro / contemporary pub
Alfresco: No
Entry: Open door
Highlights: Food
Atmosphere: Relaxed
Clientele: Suited City boys & girls
Dress code: Suits
Price guide: £££
Food: Modern British snacks & meals

The boundaries between pub, bar and
restaurant are increasingly blurred and with
its modern look and loft-style interior, not
to mention the open kitchen and extensive
food menu, it is not immediately clear what
to call this place.

To further confuse the issue, the
space is divided into several rooms and
uses a mixture of styles. The main room
houses the kitchen and bar counter, and
combines industrial ceramic tiles with bare
brick walls, exposed wooden floors and
salvaged tables and chairs. The Red
Room, so named for its burgundy walls,
feels like a dining room, while the far Black
Annex looks like a club chill-out space.
Late night towards the end of the week,
when the music and tempo are turned up,
it feels like one too.

The Prophet is not all design and no
substance. The food offering is substantial
and can be great, while the wine list
touches many bases and offers nearly
thirty bins by the glass. The draught beer
range includes the likes of Leffe plus two
cask ales for us traditionalists.

ST. JOHN BAR

● ● ● ● ○

26 St. John Street, Smithfield, London,
EC1M 4AY, England

Tel: + 44 (0)20 7251 0848,
www.stjohnrestaurant.co.uk
Hours: Mon-Fri 11am-11pm,
Sat 6pm-11pm

Type: Gastro bar
Alfresco: No
Entry: Open door policy
Highlights: Food and wine
Atmosphere: Friendly & informal
Clientele: 30-somethings in the know
Dress code: Business suits to scruffy jeans
Price guide: ££
Food: Honest, tasty snacks listed on blackboards

The entrance to St John is matter-of-fact:
two sets of swing doors lead into a white
painted room. Its past as a smokehouse
serving the nearby Smithfield Meat Market
is evidenced by the racks above the bar
area, while the friendly staff wear white
jackets and aprons not unlike those of
market porters. Old, industrial-style lights
hang from the high ceiling and their bare
bulbs guarantee bright surroundings
whether or not the sun is shining through
the skylights.

The stark interior, concrete floor and
simple wooden tables and chairs make a
surprisingly welcoming gastro heaven,
helped by the smell of fresh bread from the
open bakery. The adjoining restaurant is
famous for its meat dishes and the bar
snacks live up to this reputation, although
snacks such as anchovy toast and Welsh
Rarebit are also on offer.

Drinkers are well served with two ales
and a serious cider on draught, as well as
a grown-up wine list and an excellent
selection of digestives.

SOSHO

● ● ● ● ○

2a Tabernacle Street, Shoreditch, London,
EC2A 4LU, England

Tel: + 44 (0)20 7920 0701,
www.matchbar.com
Hours: Mon 11.30am-1am, Tue-Wed 11.30am-midnight,
Thu 11.30am-1am, Fri 11.30am-3am, Sat 7pm-3am

Type: Lounge bar
Alfresco: No
Entry: Cover charge may apply
Highlights: Cocktails
Atmosphere: Varies from day to day
Clientele: City, Shoreditch crowd
Dress code: Business suits to Shoreditch grunge
Price guide: £££
Food: Sausages, tortillas, wraps, tapas, burgers etc.

Sosho, the third of Jonathan Downey's
Match bars, repeats the winning formula
of top quality drinks and exposed
brickwork. In this South Shoreditch venue
they have even managed a 3am licence
(entry charges may apply). A former
photographic studio, the site has been
coolly converted. The old skylights remain
while a host of second-hand leather sofas
and Match's trademark slatted screens
have been added in.

Sosho benefits from Match's superb
cocktail list. Many drinks are in-house
creations, now copied by numerous other
bars. The spirits selection is impressive
and you'll also find some bottled beers
such as Union, though nothing on
draught. For private dos, there's a separate
room downstairs with its own bar.

The odd location, between
Shoreditch, Old Street and the City, draws
a range of stray Hoxtonites and
adventurous All Bar One escapees. On
weekends the place morphs into a DJ-led
party venue.

WILLIAM IV

● ● ● ○ ○

7 Shepherdess Walk (corner Micawber St.),
Hoxton, London, N1 7QE, England

Tel: +44 (0)20 3119 3012
Hours: Mon-Wed noon-11pm, Thu-Sat
noon-midnight, Sun noon-10:30pm

Type: Gastro pub
Alfresco: No
Entry: Open door
Highlights: Food
Atmosphere: Relaxed
Clientele: Local media types
Dress code: Casual, hip
Price guide: ££££
Food: Traditional British grub

Top interior designer Shaun Clarkson
co-owns this previously forgotten, back street
corner boozer and he's had the decorators
in. They've applied gallons of creamy off-white
paint to the walls, the ceiling and even the
furniture. The hue is bright enough to lift the
traditional dowdy, dark wooden walls and
furnishings but soft enough to lend the room
a cosy, almost farmhouse kitchen feel, helped
by the two long, chunky communal tables
and the open log fireplace. The joanna in the
corner adds an appropriately East End touch,
while the imposing portrait of William IV over
the fireplace creates a sense of history. Other
details include grey velvet drapes and glass
cabinets filled with stuffed birds, topped by a
collection of pewter pots, mugs and trophies.

Proper British dishes such as 'pork
sandwiches with apple sauce' are typical of
this gastro pub's daily changing menu, also
available in the dining room upstairs. There's
a couple of ales (Black Sheep and Flowers
IPA) and a short, none too exciting wine list
with six by the glass.

Young trendies from local media and
design agencies drink alongside original
locals, who still regard this as their
corner boozer.

Sosho

Sosho

COVENT GARDEN
(WC2)

THE CAPITAL'S TOURIST MECCA – THINK STREET
PERFORMERS, COVERED MARKETS, GIFT SHOPS
AND MUSICALS – HAS A FEW GEMS HIDDEN AMID
THE BRANDED DROSS AND MID-MARKET BISTROS.
ON SUMMER SATURDAYS THE PLACE JUST HEAVES.

The Seven Stars

ALBANNACH & DOON

● ● ● ● ○

66 Trafalgar Square, London, WC2N 5DS,
England

Tel: +44 (0)20 7930 0066, **www.**albannach.co.uk
Hours: Mon-Wed noon-1am, Thu-Sat
noon-3am, Sun noon-midnight (Doon
opens at 5pm Mon-Sat)

Type:	Lounge bar / restaurant
Alfresco:	No
Entry:	Few restrictions
Highlights:	Whisky list, cocktails
Atmosphere:	Lacking
Clientele:	Post-work crowd
Dress code:	Smart casual
Price guide:	££££
Food:	Contemporary Scottish dishes & plates

Whether it's the location, the lighting, its
polished, almost new-built, look or the way
the balustraded mezzanine restaurant juts
out into the room, the double-height main
area of this Scottish-themed bar and
restaurant feels rather like the bar of a
corporate hotel. The very contemporary
design fails to tame its antlers and tartan.

Albannach's soul is buried in the
catacomb below. Now named 'Doon' (as
in 'doon'stairs), this basement bar is more
intimate and moody, thanks to warm
lighting and a low ceiling. The five booths
tunnelled into the back wall are perfect for
half a dozen mates to hide away.

But, whichever floor you find yourself
on, it's the drinks offering which makes this
place special. The selection of Scotch malt
whiskies must be one of the best in the
country and a team of very able and
enthusiastic bartenders use whisky as a
base for many of the classic and contemporary cocktails offered here.

BEDFORD & STRAND

● ● ● ● ◑

1 Bedford Street (just off The Strand), Covent
Garden, London, WC2E 9HH, England

Tel: +44 (0)20 7836 3033
Hours: Mon-Sat noon-midnight

Type:	Wine bar
Alfresco:	No
Entry:	Open door
Highlights:	Wines, food & cocktails
Atmosphere:	Friendly/relaxed
Clientele:	Local office workers
Dress code:	Office attire
Price guide:	£££
Food:	Charcuterie & cheese to full meals

In what sounds like an Enid Blyton story, five
friends from the drinks industry took over what
was a down-at-heel, rather grim, basement
wine bar. Bedford & Strand is the result and they
have stratospherically improved the 80s original.

The still rather dowdy entrance and
staircase lead down to a large single room
dominated by a 15 metre zinc-topped bar
backed by a wall of wine and spirits. In front of
this a bare board floor is dotted with classic
French café-style tables and chairs. The
magnolia room is divided by glazed panels and
illuminated by 1930s green enamelled lamps.

One of the 'Boozy Five' was once an
Oddbins buyer and his knowledge and
contacts are evident in the excellent wine list
which includes seven house wines listed as
'honest', 'decent' and 'good'. Classic and,
aptly, wine based cocktails are also
outstanding. Leffe Braun and draught Grolsch
keep beer drinkers refreshed, while you can
choose between snacks from the hors
d'oeuvres counter or the à la carte menu.

This is a truly outstanding, very
reasonably priced offering with great service.

Bedford & Strand

CAFÉ PACIFICO

● ● ● ○

5 Langley St, Covent Garden, London, WC2H 9JA, England

Tel: +44 (0)20 7379 7728,
www.cafepacifico-laperla.com
Hours: Mon-Sat noon-11.45pm,
Sun noon-10.45pm

Type: Mexican restaurant & bar
Alfresco: No
Entry: Subject to capacity
Highlights: Tequilas & cocktails
Atmosphere: Friendly/relaxed
Clientele: Office workers to tourists
Dress code: Wear what you like
Price guide: £££
Food: Mexican

This Mexican bar and restaurant opened in February 1982 and its aged, worn décor helps add an air of authenticity. You know you're in a themed restaurant in Covent Garden, but you can almost believe it's Mexico, particularly with enough Tequila from the vast range stocked here.

The twelve metre bar contributes hugely to both décor and ambience and over it have passed more than three million Margaritas, as well as some damn fine Vanilla Daiquiris. There are probably more Mexican beers available here than anywhere else in London. Indeed, it was here that the likes of Sol and Corona were first sold in the UK.

Café Pacifico remains a family-owned, fun-packed institution that doesn't take itself too seriously.

Café Pacifico

Café Pacifico

Café Pacifico

THE COVE BAR

●●●◐○

1 Piazza, Covent Garden Market, Covent
Garden, London, WC2E 8HB, England

Tel: +44 (0)20 7836 7880
Hours: Mon-Sat 11am-11pm,
Sun noon-10.30pm

Type:	Traditional pub
Alfresco:	Heated roof terrace
Entry:	Via staircase from pasty shop
Highlights:	Beers, pasties & roof terrace
Atmosphere:	Relaxed & friendly
Clientele:	Those in the know & lucky tourists
Dress code:	Casual
Price guide:	££
Food:	Superb pasties

The West Cornwall Pasty Company's
London outlet is on the very north west
corner of Covent Garden Market, directly
opposite the Dr. Martens store. This great
little shop sells traditional Cornish and
flavoured pasties, clotted cream teas and
similar West Country fare. The Cove Bar
above is a real hidden treasure. Besides
pasties, they offer superb Cornish ales
such as Betty Stogs and Ice Blond. For
those who are misguided enough not to
like real ale there's also lager, wine and
spirits on offer.

The Cove Bar consists of several
attic-like rooms with bare floorboards and
exposed brickwork, furnished with old
leather chairs, heavy wooden stools and
pirate memorabilia. A few steps lead up to
the small roof terrace. The balcony
overlooks the market and the area where
buskers perform in front of Saint Paul's
Church, making it an ideal place to enjoy
a pint and a pasty while being entertained.

The Cove Bar

The Cove Bar

DETROIT

● ● ● ● ○

35 Earlham Street, Covent Garden, London,
WC2 9LD, England

Tel: +44 (0)20 7240 2662,
www.detroit-bar.com
Hours: Mon-Fri 5pm-midnight, Sat 6pm-midnight

Type:	Lounge bar
Alfresco:	No
Entry:	Open to all subject to space
Highlights:	Cocktails
Atmosphere:	Very laid back
Clientele:	Youngish office and hipsters
Dress code:	Casual and relaxed
Price guide:	£££
Food:	Spring rolls, fried calamari, bruschetta

Detroit is housed in a cavernous warren of rooms in a basement close to Covent Garden's Seven Dials. The interior and, come to that, some of the drinkers look like something out of a Star Wars movie: Detroit attracts a very esoteric and interesting crowd.

In its time Detroit has been home to some of London's best-known bartenders and the ever-evolving list bears evidence of this. The narrow shelves of the back bar groan with a truly superb range of bottles, the palette from which talented bartenders produce truly outstanding cocktails. The food is also surprisingly good.

Detroit is best midweek when it has a relaxed lounge atmosphere. Weekends can be hectic with a DJ driven buzz. Find yourself a dark corner and a cocktail menu, and try something new.

GORDON'S WINE BAR

● ● ● ◐ ○

47 Villiers Street (@ Watergate Walk), Charing
Cross, London, WC2N 6NE, England

Tel: +44 (0)20 7930 1408,
www.gordonswinebar.com
Hours: Mon-Sat 11am-11pm, Sun noon-10pm

Type:	Wine bar
Alfresco:	Pavement by Embankment Gardens
Entry:	Villiers St or side entrance on Watergate Walk
Highlights:	Wines & atmosphere
Atmosphere:	Almost Dickensian
Clientele:	Bohemians & after work crowd
Dress code:	Casual to suits
Price guide:	£££
Food:	Homemade pies to wonderful cheeses

Gordon's, London's oldest wine bar, was established by Arthur Gordon in 1890. But the Gordon family who have owned the bar for generations are not actually related to the original Arthur. The name was a happy coincidence.

In the 1680s the building was home to the diarist Samuel Pepys. Later (around 1820), it was used as a warehouse by a firm of seed dealers. This came to an abrupt end when, in 1864, the Thames was embanked, leaving the warehouse landlocked. (The gardens next door, where patrons drink on summer evenings, enclose a water gate. The steps from this used to lead directly to the river.)

The wooden walls of the basement room are covered in faded historical newspaper cuttings. Beyond lies a tunnel-like cellar, illuminated by flickering candles and furnished with rickety, ancient tables. The age-encrusted ceiling is low enough to induce a stoop. Little has changed here in over a century. There's no music, beer or spirits – just good wine and atmosphere.

LA PERLA

● ● ● ● ○

28 Maiden Lane (Bedford St. end), Covent
Garden, London, WC2E 7JS, England

Tel: +44 (0)20 7240 7400,
www.cafepacifico-laperla.com
Hours: Mon-Sat noon-11pm,
Sun noon-10.30pm

Type:	Mexican restaurant & bar
Alfresco:	No
Entry:	Usually space
Highlights:	Margaritas & tequila
Atmosphere:	Relaxed & friendly
Clientele:	City boys, tourists & Margarita lovers
Dress code:	Business suits to grunge
Price guide:	£££
Food:	Mexican

La Perla is the sister venue of Café Pacifico, London's oldest Mexican restaurant. It first opened in Paris in 1988 and this Covent Garden branch (along with outlets in Fulham and Fitzrovia) followed.

The Mexican restaurant theme is enhanced by nautical design featuring sport fishing and surfing. A fantasy mural of La Perla's mermaid dominates the airy, skylit dining room. However, the action and indeed most of the drinking takes place by the front bar. People come from all over town to squeeze into this narrow space and be barged by folk wanting to get through to the restaurant. Cheese-drenched nachos are washed down with superb Margaritas and other cocktails based on the house specialities of rum and Tequila. The fridges are crammed with ice-cold Mexican beers.

The unsophisticated nature of this place attracts a broad cross-section of society. City boys, sassy Latina babes and home-from-home Americans all enjoy the La Perla spirit.

LIGHT BAR

● ● ● ● ○

St. Martins Lane Hotel, 45 St. Martin's Lane,
Covent Garden, London WC2N 4HX, England

Tel: +44 (0)20 7300 5599,
www.morganshotelgroup.com
Hours: Mon-Sat 5.30pm-3am, Sun
5.30pm-10.30pm (hotel residents midnight)

Type:	Lounge bar
Alfresco:	No
Entry:	Members & hotel guests only
Highlights:	Cocktails, atmosphere
Atmosphere:	Kitchen at a great party
Clientele:	Media, music, fashion
Dress code:	High fashion
Price guide:	££££££
Food:	Sushi served Tuesday to Saturday

Ian Schrager opened St. Martins Lane Hotel in October 1999 amid a blaze of publicity. The original Light Bar that lay at the end of the Starck designed lobby was noted for being full of celebs, being impossible for mere mortals to access and for not having a bar! It was a bar without a bar! Waitresses took your order and a hidden bartender created your drink.

The new look Light Bar still sits at the end of the hotel's lobby, between Asia de Cuba and Tuscan restaurants. And, yes, it still has the waitress service and the hidden bar screened from view by a cabinet of antique glassware, but there's now also a very visible second bar in the middle of the room. The wobbly high chairs that used to line the room have been replaced by the eponymous light filled ceiling shafts are still there, as are the celebs, great cocktails and the door policy.

LOBBY BAR

● ● ● ● ○

One Aldwych Hotel, 1 Aldwych, London,
WC2B 4R, England

Tel: +44 (0)20 7300 1070,
www.onealdwych.com
Hours: Mon-Sat 9.30am-11pm,
Sun 10am-10.30pm

Type:	Lounge/hotel bar
Alfresco:	No
Entry:	No door policy
Highlights:	Cocktails
Atmosphere:	Relaxed
Clientele:	Theatre lovers, business and hotel guests
Dress code:	Smart
Price guide:	££££
Food:	Sausages, dim sum, sushi etc.

The lobby of the boutique hotel One Aldwych is no common foyer and its bar is no ordinary lobby bar. This airy grand hall with its double-height ceiling and tall arched windows oozes class. Centre stage on the polished floor is a vast sculpture by André Wallace of a hunched man rowing what appears to be a bath tub. Around this are well-spaced chairs, low tables and impressive flower arrangements.

This opulence is nothing compared to the delights contained within the extensive but simply presented drinks list. Wonderfully unique cocktails using ingredients such as saffron infused gin, wine, Port and fresh fruits are mixed and served to your table by friendly, professional staff.

Situated in central theatreland, the Lobby Bar attracts the pre- and post-show crowd, local business types and glamorously wealthy hotel guests. All in all, a bar with the service and grandeur that befits a hotel of this quality.

LOWLANDER BEER CAFÉ

● ● ● ● ○

36 Drury Lane (corner of Dryden Street),
Covent Garden, London, WC2B 5RR, England

Tel: +44 (0)20 7379 7446,
www.lowlander.com
Hours: Mon-Sat 11am-midnight, Sun
11am-10.30pm

Type:	Contemporary pub
Alfresco:	No
Entry:	Relaxed door policy
Highlights:	Beers, service and snacks
Atmosphere:	Warm & friendly
Clientele:	Local office/those in the know
Dress code:	Suits to jeans
Price guide:	£££
Food:	Deli snacks and full meals

This beerhall-styled pub is based on the grand cafés of Holland and Belgium, particularly two celebrated Brussels bars, La Mort Subite and the Falstaff. Polished chrome fonts line the long, zinc, pewter rimmed counter while the back bar features a towering display of wine and bottled brews. Rows of long, narrow, dark wooden tables are mounted on tracks, which enable them to be moved but prevent annoying wobbles. The walls are lined with leather banquettes and benches.

There's a choice of fourteen draught and forty bottled Belgian and Dutch beers, all listed by category on the extensive menu. Headings include pilsner, blonde, golden ale, Trappist, abbey, amber and wheat beers, while taster trays of three beers (3 x 1/3 pint) are available for those who wish to explore. Other highlights include the friendly table service, flavoured Belgian Jenever, Dutch Genever, interesting wines (13 by the glass) and a 'deli menu'. It is only the clientele that sometimes disappoints.

THE PORTERHOUSE

● ● ● ● ○

21-22 Maiden Lane, Covent Garden,
London, WC2E 7NA, England

Tel: +44 (0)20 7379 7917,
www.porterhousebrewco.com
Hours: Mon-Wed 11am-11pm, Thu-Sat
noon-11:30pm, Sun noon-10:30pm

Type:	Contemporary pub
Alfresco:	No
Entry:	Open door
Highlights:	Beer range
Atmosphere:	Buzzy
Clientele:	Eclectic
Dress code:	Casual
Price guide:	£££
Food:	Oysters, filled panini, chips, Irish stew etc.

This contemporary pub on the south side
of Covent Garden probably has more
bottled beers than any other pub or bar in
London. It's a huge place, covering some
13,500 square feet and laid out over
several levels with galleries. Rivet covered
steel, copper pipes and brass fittings
create a feel a little like an old steam ship.
The centrepiece is a 200 year old Irish clock
rescued from Gortnahoe Town Hall.

An informative beer menu lists some
180 of the world's best brews as well as
Porterhouse's own nine unpasteurised
draught offerings, brewed by the Irish
owners in Dublin. All, including their three
stouts, can be tried as part of sampler trays.
A separate food menu offers traditional Irish
dishes from beef and stout or Oyster Stout
sausages and mash through to Dublin Bay
oysters and Irish smoked salmon.

Live music Wednesday through to
Saturday ensures a good atmosphere. The
size means that, even when crowded (which
it usually is), there are so many hidden corners
that there's seemingly always a free table.

The Seven Stars

The Seven Stars

THE SEVEN STARS

● ● ● ◐ ○

53a Carey Street, London, WC2A 2JB,
England

Tel: +44 (0)20 7242 8521
Hours: Mon-Fri 11am-11pm,
Sat noon-8pm

Type: Traditional pub
Alfresco: Stone balustrade of the law courts
Entry: Open door but limited space
Highlights: Food, atmosphere
Atmosphere: Warm, friendly local
Clientele: Barristers, lawyers & clerks
Dress code: Business attire
Price guide: £££
Food: Sandwiches to traditional British pub meals

Imbibing here could be described as drinking in 'Queer Street', a phrase for being in financial trouble (for all our non-Brit readers) which apparently derives from the bankruptcy courts which stood here for many years. Built in 1602, this ancient boozer was originally known as The League of Seven Stars, after the seven provinces of the Netherlands, and some of its first customers were Dutch sailors who settled in the area around that time. It survived the Great Fire of 1666 and is now a Grade II listed building.

The pub faces the back of the Royal Courts of Justice and its small rooms combine to form a space no longer and only a little wider than a railway carriage. The narrow Elizabethan stairs to the toilets are so steep that it's not uncommon to see barristers crawling up them on all fours, a few pints of the excellent ale selection the worse for wear or not. Food comes down from the kitchen in a hoist clad in mullioned glass which resembles an old British phone box.

The Seven Stars

The Seven Stars

Morgan Arms

EAST END
& DOCKLANDS
(E1, E3, E14)

ONE OF THE CAPITAL'S MOST DIVERSE AND DEVELOPING AREAS, AS TRENDIES AND MONEY SPREAD OUTWARDS FROM SHOREDITCH, THIS LARGE LOCALE IS SCATTERED WITH HISTORIC PUBS, HIP BARS AND CASUAL, FRIENDLY LOCALS. PARTS STILL RETAIN THEIR GANGLAND EDGE.

Big Chill Bar

BIG CHILL BAR

● ● ● ◑ ○

The Old Truman Brewery, Dray Walk, 91 Brick Lane, London, E1 6QL, England

Tel: +44 (0)20 7392 9180, **www.**bigchill.net
Hours: Mon-Sun noon-midnight

Type:	Music bar
Alfresco:	Front terrace (covered in winter)
Entry:	Open door
Highlights:	Atmosphere
Atmosphere:	An indoor festival
Clientele:	Fun loving folk
Dress code:	Cool casual
Price guide:	£££
Food:	Sandwiches, burgers, salads etc.

The former Truman Brewery on Brick Lane is now a rambling complex of studios, shops and offices which has helped add yet more diversity to this famous East End street. The Big Chill Bar is set on a side lane which leads into the heart of the brewery.

Like the eponymous festival, the Big Chill is mostly about music – warm background stuff by day and pumping DJ sets by night. The interior design is utilitarian with rugged furnishings crafted from tree trunks, bare concrete floors and exposed brickwork softened by walls covered in pleated fabric and ceilings draped in theatrical metallics.

The chalkboard wall behind the long bar lists popular cocktails and a short but considered wine list including nine by the glass. The draught and bottled beer range exceeds expectations, while snacks are available until 11pm - so no need to leave the party for one of the nearby curry houses.

This very funky bar in an equally funky part of London attracts a suitably cool audience.

Big Chill Bar   Big Chill Bar

BROWNS RESTAURANT & BAR

● ● ● ○ ○

Hertsmere Road, West India Quay,
Docklands, London, E14 8JJ, England

Tel: +44 (0)20 7987 9777,
www.browns-restaurants.com
Hours: Mon-Wed 11am-10pm, Thu-Sat
11am-11pm, Sun 11am-9:30pm

Type: Lounge bar & restaurant
Alfresco: Dockside & secluded side terraces
Entry: Open door
Highlights: Nothing exceptional but done well
Atmosphere: Relaxed
Clientele: Office escapees
Dress code: Business attire to casual
Price guide: £££
Food: Casual bar snacks & formal dining

West India Quay, as its name suggests,
was once home to ships bringing cargo
from the Caribbean and Browns is housed
in a former sugar warehouse, built in the
early nineteenth century by prisoners of
war. Interestingly, its low ceilings are due
to the fact that sugar could only be stacked
to a height of eight feet.

The floor of the ground level restaurant
has been cut away to reveal the bar below.
Descend the stairs and you'll discover that
what initially appears a dark, subterranean
space actually looks out onto a secluded
side terrace. Browns' usual colonial style
is sensitively incorporated into this historic
space. Wicker chairs and magnolia meld
with exposed joists, iron supporting piers
and bare brick walls hung with framed
sepia prints.

Browns offers a sensible range of
imported draught beers, a cocktail list
centred around the classics, a very
affordable wine list with 17 by the
glass and even afternoon tea or
coffee. Bar snacks range from soup of the
day to antipasti.

Browns

Browns

COMMERCIAL TAVERN
● ● ● ○ ○

142 Commercial Street, Spitalfields,
London, E1 6NU, England

Tel: +44 (0)20 7377 8455
Hours: Mon-Sat 5pm-11pm, Sun noon-
10:30pm

Type: Contemporary pub
Alfresco: Pavement bench tables
Entry: Open door
Highlights: Interior design & ale
Atmosphere: Warm & friendly
Clientele: Cool Shoreditch set
Dress code: Cool casual
Price guide: £££
Food: English bistro from Sept 06

The rounded frontage of this old Victorian corner pub makes it something of a landmark on Commercial Street. It is said that the Elephant Man once lived in the caverns below. But whatever the truth of that, recent years have seen its conversion from a very traditional old boozer to a quirky, flamboyant, gay-friendly, modern pub. The place may still be titled a 'tavern' and still stock draught ale on hand pump but its theatrical interior is more bordello than boozer.

Baby blue hues cover the walls and even the furniture. A cluster of half a dozen chandeliers adorns one part of the high ceiling while framed mirrors look down from another. Aeroplane wallpaper leads upstairs to another couple of rooms, both graced with centrepiece lights. This is where you'll find Rad and his cocktail bar. The ground floor bar offers three ales on draught, including the excellent Brains SA. Unusually, the wine list has an English bias.

THE GUN
● ● ● ● ○

27 Coldharbour, Blackwall, Isle of Dogs,
London, E14 9NS, England

Tel: +44 (0)20 7515 5222 , **www**.thegun
docklands.com **Hours:** Mon-Fri 11am-
midnight, Sat 10:30am-midnight, Sun
10:30am-4:30pm & 6pm-9:30pm

Type: Gastro pub
Alfresco: Riverside terrace
Entry: Open door
Highlights: Food, wine & terrace
Atmosphere: Warm & friendly
Clientele: Young professionals
Dress code: Business attire to casual
Price guide: ££££
Food: Mediterranean-influenced modern British

The site of a public house for over 250 years, The Gun's rear terrace looks across the Thames to the Millennium Dome on the opposite bank. This Grade II listed early 19th century pub takes its name from the cannon fired to celebrate the opening of the West India Import Docks in 1802. It allegedly hosted Lord Nelson's secret assignations with Lady Hamilton.

This is a foodie pub and the front room with its beautiful old carved oak bar and oak floor is mainly given over to linen covered tables. Behind this lie two cosy snugs, the Red Room with Chesterfield sofas and wingback leather armchairs, and the Gun Room with an original Georgian bullseye fireplace plus a collection of antique rifles and pistols.

Impressive cuisine is matched by a 100 bin wine list and three traditional cask ales but the rear terrace with views across the river is reason enough to visit.

HAWKSMOOR
● ● ● ● ○

157 Commercial Street, Spitalfields,
London, E1 6BJ, England

Tel: +44 (0)20 7247 7392,
www.thehawksmoor.com
Hours: Tue-Wed 5pm-12am, Thu-Fri 5pm-
1am, Sat noon-1am, Sun noon-10:30pm

Type: Lounge bar & steakhouse
Alfresco: No
Entry: Open door
Highlights: Cocktails, food
Atmosphere: Chilled
Clientele: Varied
Dress code: Whatever
Price guide: £££
Food: Steaks & freshly prepared salads

This cocktail bar and steakhouse takes its name from the celebrated 18th century architect, Nicholas Hawksmoor, who designed the magnificent Christ Church, Spitalfields, further down Commercial Street.

Quality furnishings distinguish the plain interior: vintage black Series Seven chairs, handmade sofas and reclaimed Burmese teak tables, chrome and glass deco-style coffee tables, and even a pair of rare high-backed Oxford chairs from St Catherine's College, Oxford. The bar counter is made of twelve-foot long slabs of teak from a 1930s dancehall in Hull.

A superb range of bourbons graces the back bar and the informative cocktail list also has an American slant. An extensive selection of different Juleps and Sours are listed with historical references. The wine list includes some phenomenal super Tuscans and a number of fantastic Spanish wines. Be sure to try the rosé.

Quality cuts of meat cooked on a charcoal grill and a selection of freshly prepared salads underpin the food menu but it's the triple cooked chips that steal the show.

HAWKSMOOR JULEP
BY NICK STRANGEWAY

AVAILABLE @ HAWKSMOOR

Glass: Julep cup
Garnish: Sprig of mint, sprig of thyme, gooseberries
& lemon twist. Serve with very short straws.
Method: MUDDLE leaves with syrup, half the gin
and the puree. Fill glass with cracked ice, STIR well,
add the rest of the gin then more cracked ice. STIR
again and keep adding ice until the glass is full.

35ml Beefeater gin
15ml Gooseberry and lemon thyme puree
10ml Thyme syrup
dash Orange bitters
3-4 Mint leaves
3-4 Lemon balm leaves

Morgan Arms

L'OASIS

● ● ● ◐ ○

237 Mile End Road, Stepney, London, E1 4AA, England

Tel: +44 (0)20 7702 7051,
www.loasisstepney.co.uk
Hours: Mon-Sat noon-11pm,
Sun noon-10:30pm

Type:	Contemporary/gastro pub
Alfresco:	No
Entry:	Open door
Highlights:	Food
Atmosphere:	Relaxed
Clientele:	Doctors, nurses and locals
Dress code:	Casual
Price guide:	££
Food:	Traditional British on chalkboard

In November 2000 John Clearly, a down to earth Eastender, and his business partner cum chef, Alan Mattibbi, took over a sorry old Victorian boozer and gutted it. They set out to create an eating and drinking oasis in the then otherwise bereft East End and naturally named their new venture L'Oasis. It is!

The long, rectangular room is plainly decorated with partly panelled walls and bare floorboards. Wooden tables line both sides and the bar is at the back. John won't have any mucking about in his bar. He's after pleasant regulars who'll appreciate the well kept ales (Timothy Taylor Landlord & Adnam's Broadside), the wide choice of lagers, the incredibly reasonably priced wines and the homely British comfort food. Hence L'Oasis attracts a slightly older, considered clientele who appreciate this quiet, civilised bar on the hectic Mile End Road.

MORGAN ARMS
● ● ● ● ○

43 Morgan Street (corner Coborn Rd), Bow,
London, E3 5AA, England

Tel: +44 (0)20 8980 6389,
www.geronimo-inns.co.uk
Hours: Mon-Thu noon-11pm, Fri-Sat
noon-midnight, Sun noon-10:30pm

Type:	Gastro pub
Alfresco:	Side terrace
Entry:	Open door
Highlights:	Food
Atmosphere:	Warm & friendly
Clientele:	Young professionals
Dress code:	Casual
Price guide:	£££
Food:	Mediterranean influenced modern British

Gastro pubs are a phenomenon particular
to posh and upwardly mobile areas and the
fact that this excellent example lies just
off Mile End Road in Bow is testament to
the continuing gentrification of the East
End. Indeed, nearby Tredegar Square has
been described in the press as "The
Cockney Eaton Square".

This old corner boozer sits among
Victorian terraced houses. Inside is pure
gastro pub with comfy sofas mixed with
old wooden tables, chairs, the odd
butcher's block and a smattering of
modern art. The splendid old oak bar
counter is topped with chunky carved
arches, making it almost altar-like. Behind
this is an open kitchen and a brightly
decorated dining room with doors onto a
decked patio.

The Mediterranean influenced modern
British food served here is excellent and a
good wine list plus Adnam's and Landlord
keep the drinks flowing up to par. The no
bookings policy may persuade some to aim
for an early arrival.

PROSPECT OF WHITBY
● ● ● ○ ○

57 Wapping Wall (opp. Wapping Hydraulic),
Wapping, London, E1W 3SH, England

Tel: +44 (0)20 7481 1095
Hours: Mon-Fri 11:30am-3pm & 5:30pm-
11pm, Sat 11:30pm-11pm, Sun noon-
10:30pm

Type:	Traditional pub
Alfresco:	Small riverside terrace
Entry:	Usually room for all
Highlights:	Heritage
Atmosphere:	Quiet and relaxed
Clientele:	Locals & tourists
Dress code:	Anything goes – casual
Price guide:	££
Food:	Ploughman's, pies and steaks

Built around 1520, the original pub on this East
London site was a haunt for smugglers and
thieves. Appropriately named the Devil's Tavern,
it was rebuilt in 1777 after a fire and renamed the
Prospect of Whitby, taking its new and more
salubrious name from a coal carrying coaster
whose moorings lay close by.

This claims to be London's oldest riverside
pub and past regulars include Samuel Pepys,
Charles Dickens, the writer Samuel Johnson and
the painter Joseph Turner. Another famous
customer was George Jeffreys, known as
'Hanging Judge Jeffreys,' and a hangman's
noose still dangles over the Thames from the
gallows behind the pub. In more recent times the
restaurant upstairs has been patronised by such
luminaries as Kirk Douglas and Princess Margaret.

A couple of traditional ales are offered but
the reason to visit the Prospect is the chance to
step back into history. It is hard to tell which is more
ancient: the pewter-topped counter, the ceiling
beams or the worn flagstone floor. The best spot,
however, is outside, on the small riverside terrace
where picnic tables settle under an old
weeping willow.

TOWN OF RAMSGATE
● ● ● ○ ○

62 Wapping High Street, Wapping, London,
E1W 2PN, England

Tel: +44 (0)20 7481 8000
Hours: Mon-Sat noon-11pm, Sun noon-
10:30pm

Type:	Traditional pub
Alfresco:	Riverside rear terrace
Entry:	Open door
Highlights:	Heritage
Atmosphere:	Friendly local
Clientele:	Locals & tourists
Dress code:	Casual
Price guide:	££
Food:	Traditional pub grub

Dating from the time of the Wars of The
Roses, this 15th century pub is the oldest
on the River Thames. It is also where the
notorious Judge Jeffries sentenced
hundreds of local people to death in the
17th century. They were hung on the
gallows behind the pub, guilty or not.
Legend has it that the Judge was captured
here as he prepared to flee to France and
taken to the Tower of London.

The Town of Ramsgate is a narrow
pub that stretches to the river: its small rear
terrace backs directly onto the Thames,
although the view is limited. The interior
has been much amended over the years
but remains very traditional with panelled
walls and dark stained wooden furnishings.

Three well kept traditional ales are
joined by continental imports such as
Leffe. However, the menu is all British with
ploughman's lunch, steak & kidney pie and
bangers & mash. The history and style of
this place attracts a few tourists but it
remains very much a locals' pub.

FULHAM & CHELSEA
(SW3, SW5-6, SW10)

HOME TO HIGH EARNERS AND INHERITED WEALTH, FULHAM AND CHELSEA OFFER A THRIVING, OCCASIONALLY EVEN BRAYING SCENE. STEER CLEAR OF THE HUBBUB OF THE BEACH, THE NIGHTLIFE STRIP ON THE FULHAM ROAD, AND OPT INSTEAD FOR COSIER, LOCAL PUBS AND BARS.

Lots Road

THE ADMIRAL CODRINGTON

● ● ● ● ○

17 Mossop Street (opp. Leverett Street),
Brompton, London, SW3 2LY, England

Tel: +44 (0)20 7581 0005,
www.longshotplc.com
Hours: Mon-Sat 11:30am-midnight, Sun
noon-10:30pm

Type: Gastro pub
Alfresco: Side patio with heaters
Entry: Open door
Highlights: Food
Atmosphere: Conservatively relaxed
Clientele: Sloane set
Dress code: Smart casual
Price guide: ££££
Food: Snacks to full menu

In this pub's seventies and eighties heyday it attracted the rich and beautiful of Chelsea plus Fergie, Andrew and the then Lady Diana Spencer. While today's young royals appear to favour racier haunts, the Chelsea hoorays still flock here.

The main room of the 'Cod', as it's known by regulars, is dominated by a square island bar. This is surrounded by mismatched sofas and standing drinkers planning their next safari. The Cod is noted for its food and the separate, more formal dining room has a long line of tables in front of a banquette covered in embroidered thistles that runs the length of the room. The best tables are the three intimate booths hidden beside the open kitchen. Daylight floods the room though a large roof light.

While a couple of ales lead an unremarkable beer offering, the French and New World dominated wine list is lengthy with over twenty available by the glass. The Cod is not a cheap bet for dinner, but patrons here would hate to be considered 'cheap'.

AMUSE BOUCHE

● ● ● ● ○

1 Parsons Green Lane, Parsons Green,
London, SW6 4JA, England

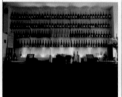

Tel: +44 (0)20 7371 8517
Hours: Mon-Sun noon-11pm

Type: Champagne bar
Alfresco: Small back yard
Entry: Open door
Highlights: Well priced champagne
Atmosphere: Buzzy
Clientele: Slightly Sloaney
Dress code: Smart casual
Price guide: ££££
Food: List of canapés inc. mini-burgers

This out and out champagne bar sits practically opposite Parsons Green tube, a testament to the area's gentrification, and its walls are covered in champagne-themed quotes from the likes of Francis Bacon and Napoleon Bonaparte.

The main front room is white and open. Plush, comfortable high chairs covered in chocolate brown leather line the bar and the tables opposite it. An intimate back room with burgundy walls leads onto the small back yard and there is a private function room upstairs.

The champagne selection offers a choice of 26 by the bottle and eight by the glass. The theme continues in the cocktail list, which includes ten champagne-based mixes, best avoided in our experience. Beer lovers are advised to give this place a wide berth but, with a bottle of the house champagne a mere £20, why come for anything else?

Amuse Bouche is buzziest early evening when it attracts a good looking crowd of affluent young professionals on their way home from work.

APARTMENT 195

● ● ● ● ○

195 King's Road (above Henry J Beans),
Chelsea, London, SW3 5ED, England

Tel: +44 (0)20 7351 5195,
www.apartment195.co.uk
Hours: Mon-Sat 4pm-11pm, Sun 4pm-
10:30pm

Type: Members lounge bar
Alfresco: No
Entry: Members have priority
Highlights: Cocktails
Atmosphere: Homely
Clientele: Well dressed & affluent
Dress code: Smart casual (no trainers)
Price guide: ££££
Food: Canapés and snacks

The listed building which houses Henry J Beans also plays host to this three room 'apartment', a homely drinking den complete with its own all-female staff in sexy uniforms. The lounge is full of leather sofas and an open fire burns in winter; the salon is ideal for hosting a dinner party; the TV room shows old movies and sport. Altogether a man's dream - home from home.

The burnished copper, star encrusted bar, salvaged from Criterion in Piccadilly, takes centre stage in the lounge. Here the girls, led by manager Charlotte Voisey, mix an interesting array of classic and bespoke cocktails which are delivered with style.

The thirty-something clientele are predominantly Chelsea locals, so are both well-heeled and well-dressed.

THE ATLAS
● ● ● ● ○

16 Seagrave Road, Fulham, London, SW6 1RX, England

Tel: +44 (0)20 7385 9129,
www.theatlaspub.co.uk
Hours: Mon-Sat 11am-11pm,
Sun noon-10:30pm

Type: Gastro / contemporary pub	
Alfresco: Secluded yard at side	
Entry: Open door	
Highlights: Food	
Atmosphere: Relaxed	
Clientele: Exhibition escapees & Fulham set	
Dress code: Business suits to very casual	
Price guide: £££	
Food: Full Mediterranean-led menu	

The Atlas lies near the top of Seagrave Road, a side road practically opposite the Earls Court 2 exhibition centre. It is handily located, if you are visiting or exhibiting, next to the main car park.

Formerly a Truman's pub, the names of old beers can still be seen in gold lettering around the top of the varnished panelling that lines the pub's walls. Little of the interior has changed over the years and the Atlas retains a workaday appearance with bare wooden floorboards and mismatched old tables and chairs.

A kitchen visible through the hatch above the rear fireplace and a blackboard menu hint at gastro pub credentials. Brothers Richard and George Manners bought this place after serving their apprenticeship at the celebrated Eagle in Farringdon. The daily changing Mediterranean menu represents excellent value for money and can be washed down with a good choice of wines (14 by the glass) and several draught ales, including Deuchars Caledonian IPA.

THE BUILDERS ARMS
● ● ● ● ○

13 Britten Street (Sydney St & Chelsea Green), Chelsea, London, SW3 3TY, England

Tel: +44 (0)20 7349 9040,
www.geronimo-inns.co.uk
Hours: Mon-Sat 11am-11pm, Sun noon-10:30pm

Type: Gastro pub	
Alfresco: Pavement tables in summer	
Entry: Open door	
Highlights: Wine, food, atmosphere	
Atmosphere: Very homely, relaxed	
Clientele: Youngish, affluent locals	
Dress code: Sloaney casual	
Price guide: £££	
Food: Modern British fare served from 4pm	

The Builders lies tucked away in an imposing Georgian building among the posh residential streets between the Fulham and King's Roads. It is surprisingly cosy, with comfy leather sofas, wooden floors, bookshelves, low lighting, a flickering fire and even the odd visiting black Labrador. Black and white photos of punters and staff adorn the warm panelled walls, boldly contrasted with several large Dali prints. Many gastro pubs feel more like a restaurant, but the Builders has retained a true local pub feel.

The clientele is an upscale crowd of mainly 30-somethings, drawn in part by the modern British menu. Typical dishes include 'twice baked stilton soufflé' and 'slow roasted baby back ribs' as well as old favourites such as steak & chips and Sunday roast.

Blackboards over the bar list a good wine selection with 19 by the glass, while there is a choice of three ales (including Deuchars IPA) for those simply after a pint in a cosy pub.

THE BUTCHER'S HOOK
● ● ● ● ○

477 Fulham Road (@ Moor Park Rd), Fulham, London, SW6 1HL, England

Tel: +44 (0)20 7385 4654
Hours: Mon-Sun 11am-midnight

Type: Gastro pub	
Alfresco: No	
Entry: Open door	
Highlights: Food	
Atmosphere: Relaxed	
Clientele: Local foodies & match day fans	
Dress code: Casual	
Price guide: £££	
Food: Simple snacks to full modern British menu	

This new, stylish gastro pub lies practically opposite Chelsea's Stamford Bridge ground and is where the football club was founded back in 1905, although in those days the pub was named The Rising Sun.

Pale blue walls contrast with rustic bare brick, exposed floorboards and old, mismatched wooden tables and chairs. A high, communal centre table breaks up the space and adds to the conviviality. The overall effect is slick and modern yet warm and atmospheric.

The kitchen is visible through a couple of wall hatches and its food has quickly put the Butcher's on the map. The menu ranges from simple snacks such as Welsh Rarebit to an interesting and diverse full modern British menu. It's worth considering pre-ordering the special, slow cooked shoulder of lamb, which requires 48 hours notice.

An excellent wine list includes seventeen wines by the glass and a good few sherries and ports. There is a good variety of beers, including two cask ales.

ECLIPSE
● ● ● ○ ○

111/113 Walton Street, Chelsea, London,
SW3 2PH, England

Tel: +44 (0)20 7581 0123,
www.bareclipse.com
Hours: Mon-Fri 5.30pm-late, Sat-Sun
2pm-late

Type:	Lounge bar
Alfresco:	No
Entry:	Subject to management & capacity
Highlights:	Atmosphere
Atmosphere:	Chelsea house party
Clientele:	Locals/Chelsea set
Dress code:	Designer casual
Price guide:	££££
Food:	Sushi

This Chelsea bar is the original version of
what is now a chain of five high end
cocktaileries. Still a cosy little place,
Eclipse used to be not much bigger than
a large cupboard, but its capacity has
doubled since it was knocked through into
next door. Part of its charm was always the
intimacy enforced by its meagre
proportions and the extension has not
destroyed this. Indeed, the second room
with its snug corners is at least as warm as
the first.

Eclipse is rarely empty. Local boys
and girls flock here for the cocktails, the
friendly service, the fun atmosphere or just
to get close to each other. The bar team
knock out some great drinks, of which the
Watermelon Martini is the most popular. A
list of fine crus will please lovers of bubbly
and, while Eclipse has no kitchen, sushi is
available courtesy of the restaurant a few
doors away.

THE FARM

● ● ● ○ ○

18 Farm Lane, Fulham, London, SW6 1PP, England

Tel: +44 (0)20 7381 3331,
www.thefarmfulham.co.uk
Hours: Mon-Sat 11am-11pm, Sun noon-10:30pm

Type:	Gastro pub
Alfresco:	No
Entry:	Open door
Highlights:	Food
Atmosphere:	Relaxed
Clientele:	Local 20 somethings, couples
Dress code:	Casual but stylish
Price guide:	£££
Food:	Full modern British menu

Hidden in the residential back streets of Fulham, The Farm is part pub, part bar and part restaurant. The central bar breaks up the main area into two distinct lounge areas. The left houses small booth areas and two open fires while the right is more loungy with low slung box sofas and another fireplace.

Both the lounges and the bar counter are generally busy, so the size and airiness of the dining area tucked away behind the bar come as something of a surprise.

Both décor and drinks are modern. A good range of beer and wine is supplemented by a surprisingly good spirits selection and even a short cocktail list.

The bar attracts a cross-section of locals. The young outnumber the old at weekends, when the more mature appreciate the dining room and particularly the Sunday roast.

KOSMOPOL

● ● ● ○ ○

138 Fulham Road, Chelsea, London, SW10 9PY, England

Tel: +44 (0)20 7373 6368,
www.kosmopol.co.uk
Hours: Mon-Sun 6pm-midnight

Type:	Lounge bar
Alfresco:	No
Entry:	Subject to capacity - no rope
Highlights:	Cocktails
Atmosphere:	Chilled to party
Clientele:	Local 20-40 somethings
Dress code:	Designer casual
Price guide:	££££
Food:	From Wok Wok nearby

Swede Fredrik Olsson fronts this tiny, two level bar which he named after a place back home in Gothenburg. The ground floor is loungy and simply decorated with plum suede banquettes and low seats around small glass tables. The basement hosts a second bar with cosy alcoves, which transforms into a mini-club later in the evening when a party atmosphere prevails.

Fredrik is something of a celebrity among London's bartending fraternity and has roped in many of his friends, all very experienced bartenders, to man the bars. Understandably, the focus is on cocktails. Popular drinks include the Watermelon Smash, Passion Fruit Martini and Swedish Spring Punch but classics are also well made, even when the bar is packed.

One design detail is worth a mention, chaps. The mirror above the urinals in the blokes' toilet is, in fact, a two-way mirror, so all passers-by can see the look of relief on your face as you pee.

LOTS ROAD DINING ROOM
● ● ● ● ○

114 Lots Road, Chelsea, London, SW10 0RJ,
England

Tel: +44 (0)20 7352 6645
Hours: Mon-Sat noon-11pm, Sun noon-
10:30pm

Type:	Gastro pub
Alfresco:	No
Entry:	Open door
Highlights:	Food
Atmosphere:	Relaxed & friendly
Clientele:	Media, Chelsea set, pre-606 club
Dress code:	Business suits to tatty jeans
Price guide:	£££
Food:	Modern British gastro grub

In a previous life, this corner site near the
entrance to Chelsea Harbour was a rather
tatty Firkin pub. But fashions change and
today it is a rather good example of the
gastro pub genre. A lounge area at one
end features original varnished, panelled
walls and reclaimed leather sofas.
Opposite lies a small dining area with
tables set in front of a fire engine red back
wall. Between these two spaces sweeps
a curved, zinc topped bar fronted by
reclaimed church benches and chairs and
chunky wooden tables.

A stylish, well educated young crowd
are drawn here by the modern British menu
which has strong Mediterranean accents.
Bread is served in cake tins while the
condiments come in tin buckets. The wine
list is short but considered and beers
include a couple of cask ales.

THE PHOENIX
● ● ● ● ○

23 Smith Street (corner Woodfall St), Chelsea,
London, SW3 4EE, England

Tel: +44 (0)20 7730 9182,
www.geronimo-inns.co.uk
Hours: Mon-Sat 11am-11pm, Sun noon-
10:30pm

Type:	Gastro pub
Alfresco:	Three pavement tables
Entry:	Open door
Highlights:	Food
Atmosphere:	Relaxed
Clientele:	30-something Sloanes
Dress code:	Casual but fashionable
Price guide:	£££
Food:	Tapas to substantial meals

Yet another previously down-at-heel
boozer in a good part of town has received
the gastro treatment. The smoke-stained
interior of this back street corner pub has
given way to a plush, designer living room
effect with comfy sofas, modern art and
rugs over old wooden floorboards. A
collection of vases lines the open shelves
that separate the pub proper from the rear
dining room. The clientele has also
changed and 30-something Sloanes
playing Connect 4 have replaced the old
men and their dominoes.

Modern British gastro fare with a
Mediterranean bias is a big part of the draw
here. You can snack on tapas in the bar or
enjoy a more leisurely meal in the dining
room. The wine list is arranged by style and
offers some well selected bins, including
18 by the glass. Beers include Bitburger
and Leffe on draught, while cask ale
drinkers will appreciate Sharps Doom Bar
from Cornwall and that mainstay, Fuller's
London Pride.

THE PIG'S EAR
● ● ● ● ●

35 Old Church Street (off the King's Road),
Chelsea, London, SW3 5BS, England

Tel: +44 (0)20 7352 2908,
www.thepigsear.co.uk
Hours: Mon-Sat noon-11pm, Sun noon-
10:30pm

Type:	Gastro pub
Alfresco:	No
Entry:	Open door, but gets packed
Highlights:	Food
Atmosphere:	Relaxed
Clientele:	30-something Sloanes
Dress code:	Designer casual
Price guide:	££££
Food:	Full gastro menu

For our foreign readers I should explain that
to 'make a pig's ear' of something is
normally colloquial British for 'mess up'.
Here, however, a pig's ear means a pig's
ear and £1 will buy you one to chew on.

Thankfully, the food menu extends to
far more appetising dishes and this is
deservedly a gastro pub of some note. You
can eat in the busy bar but I recommend
reserving a table in the cosy side room or
the charming panelled dining room on the
first floor.

The place has real character and the
walls are covered in old film posters and
other paraphernalia. This is the heart of
residential Chelsea and so unsurprisingly
the clientele is somewhat Sloaney, but it
gets so busy that a great atmosphere
is guaranteed.

The excellent food is matched by a
good wine list which includes 18 by the
glass. Alternatively enjoy a pint of Pigs Ear
real ale, brewed by the old Uley Brewery
in Gloucestershire.

The Pig's Ear

The Pig's Ear

The Phoenix

SPANISH TAPAS
(all £5)

* Spanish meats
* Marinated
   vegetables
* chilli & garlic
   tiger prawns
(all with grilled bread
& dressed leaves)

SHARPS
DOOM BAR

ADNAMS
BITTER

The White Horse

THE SALISBURY TAVERN
● ● ● ○ ○

21 Sherbrooke Road (@ Dawes Rd), Fulham, London, SW6 7HX, England

Tel: +44 (0)20 7381 4005,
www.thesalisbury.co.uk
Hours: Mon-Sat 11am-11pm, Sun noon-10:30pm

Type:	Gastro / contemporary pub
Alfresco:	No
Entry:	Open door
Highlights:	Food
Atmosphere:	Buzzy local
Clientele:	30-something City boys & girls
Dress code:	Casual
Price guide:	£££
Food:	Modern British gastro grub

This may be the sister pub to Chelsea's Admiral Codrington but it is very different in scale, clientele and atmosphere. The Cod is a thoroughly upmarket affair and even when full of Sloane revellers retains a certain decorum. The Salisbury attracts a good number of commuting City boys and girls who appear, after a couple of bottles of champs, to think decorum is the person their mate is trying to shag.

The Salisbury is divided into a sizable bar and a separate restaurant. After a complete refurbishment in April 2005, both continue to look good. The bar's colour scheme is best described as Mediterranean: several shades of red cover the walls and the plentiful soft furnishings, while panelling and book shelves conceal secluded booths.

The dining room is bright and airy, especially in summer when the glass roof is retracted to offer an almost alfresco dining experience. A full modern British menu is supplemented by all day bar bites, while the short but comprehensive wine list includes some seriously fine wines.

TUGGA
● ● ○ ○ ○

312-314 King's Road, Chelsea, London, SW3 5UH, England

Tel: +44 (0)20 7351 0101,
www.tugga.com
Hours: Mon-Sun 5:30pm-midnight

Type:	Restaurant / lounge bar
Alfresco:	Front opens onto street
Entry:	Subject to capacity
Highlights:	Cocktails
Atmosphere:	Relaxed to party
Clientele:	Chelsea boys and girls
Dress code:	Designer casual
Price guide:	£££
Food:	Modern Portuguese tapas

Tugga is apparently the slang term for a Portuguese national, the local equivalent of the English expression 'Brit'. Three young 'Tuggas' have clubbed together to open this King's Road restaurant and lounge.

With its open frontage and bold décor, Tugga looks very welcoming. Beyond the bar area, which is almost à la fresco in summer, is the dining space. Think Austin Powers meets Paul Smith and you won't go far wrong. Striped banquettes sit against psychedelic floral wallpaper and glowing filament bulbs illuminate the candy-striped tables. I looked forward to sampling what had been billed as 'modern Portuguese tapas' but found the dishes disappointing.

The basement bar is more sober and club-like in style with plum coloured walls, a suspended ceiling impregnated with tiny twinkling bulbs, and a shiny grey resin floor. A small alcove at the back lined with sofas so deep that they resemble beds provides an intimate spot to relax after some mischief on the dancefloor (DJs play nightly).

The all Portugese wine list includes ten wines by the glass and the Latin inspired cocktail menu features a number of drinks which produce impressive results from non-obvious combinations.

THE WHITE HORSE
● ● ● ● ○

1-3 Parsons Green, (north corner of green), Parsons Green, Fulham, London, SW6 4UL, England

Tel: +44 (0)20 7736 2115,
www.whitehorsesw6.com
Hours: Mon-Sat 11am-11pm, Sun noon-10:30pm

Type:	Traditional / gastro pub
Alfresco:	Beer garden / front terrace
Entry:	Subject to capacity
Highlights:	Beers, food
Atmosphere:	Busy / bustling
Clientele:	Locals & those in the know
Dress code:	Suits to tatty jeans & T-shirts
Price guide:	£££
Food:	Good changing menu

This famous old coaching inn in Parsons Green, West London, is something of a Mecca for beer lovers. The clips on the impressive line up of fonts are ever-changing with guest ales from breweries all over the country. Due to the efforts of the manager, Mark 'Dorberman' Dorber, you can be sure that each will be served at its peak.

If real ale is not your thing then The White Horse also boasts a bewildering range of bottled beers, including just about every Trappist brew produced. The pub also caters for the local Parsons Green set and so is perhaps better known by its nickname 'The Sloaney Pony'.

Both audiences crowd in to this pub and make the most of the rather good food available. The menu recommends beers to match each dish but if you prefer wine there's an excellent wine selection. The outside terrace and regular barbecues make this a great place to head on a summer evening.

GREENWICH & BLACKHEATH
(SE3, SE8 & SE10)

SITTING PRETTY ON A CURVE OF THE THAMES, GREENWICH'S MARKET, PARK, TALL SHIPS AND HISTORY DRAW TOURISTS AND FAMILIES ALIKE. IT'S THE WELL-HEELED LOCALS WHO SUPPORT A SCENE WHICH RUNS FROM STYLISH EATERIES TO GASTRO AND HISTORIC PUBS.

The Greenwich Union

ADMIRAL HARDY

● ● ● ○ ○

7 College Approach (by north entrance to market), Greenwich, London, SE10 9HY

Tel: +44 (0)20 8858 6452,
www.admiralhardy.co.uk
Hours: Mon-Sat 11am-11pm, Sun 12pm-10:30pm

Type:	Traditional pub
Alfresco:	No
Entry:	Open door
Highlights:	Proximity to market
Atmosphere:	Relaxed
Clientele:	Tourists & locals
Dress code:	Casual
Price guide:	£££
Food:	Gastro pub fare and open sandwiches

Thomas Hardy was Nelson's friend and Flag Captain, and commanded HMS Victory at the Battle of Trafalgar in 1805. He became Governor of Greenwich Hospital in 1834 and is buried in the mausoleum just beside the west wing of the Museum. In spirit, at least, he remains a Greenwich local.

Like The Coach & Horses (also featured), the Admiral Hardy looks onto Greenwich Market. The frontage looks out on the busy roundabout of College Approach while its rear doors, which are thrown open in summer, offer views of the market's north-east corner.

The Admiral Hardy dates from 1830, although its interior is much more recent. The old sofas make parts of it feel more New York lounge than traditional Greenwich pub. However, boozer it was and boozer it remains, providing up to three real ales, plenty of locals and a generally good buzz.

The Coach & Horses

THE COACH & HORSES

● ● ● ○ ○

13 Greenwich Market (southwest corner of market), Greenwich, London, SE10 9HZ

Tel: +44 (0)20 8293 0880
Hours: Mon-Sat 11am-11pm, Sun 11am-10:30pm

Type:	Traditional / gastro pub
Alfresco:	Under market roof
Entry:	Open door
Highlights:	Proximity to market
Atmosphere:	Relaxed
Clientele:	Tourists & local traders
Dress code:	Casual
Price guide:	£££
Food:	Mediterranean-influenced gastro grub

Like the Admiral Hardy, this pub lies on the edge of Greenwich's famous covered market. Originally established as a general produce market in 1737, it is now open Thursday to Sunday only and specialises in antiques, collectibles, arts and crafts.

The Coach is set within the market square, looking out over the stalls on the south-west corner: the bench tables outside are under the market's canopy. Windows on two sides make it bright and airy, a bonus for the local artists who use the walls as a gallery from which to sell their work. An open fire and a combination of old leather sofas and mix-and-match chairs and tables make this a cosy spot after a spot of winter shopping. In summer, be sure to arrive early to bag one of the market tables.

Despite gastrification this remains a very traditional boozer and there are always at least two ales on draught. The daily changing menu has a Mediterranean influence, although roasts tend to dominate on Sundays. Parents will be pleased to note that babies and children are welcome until 9am.

The Coach & Horses

The Coach & Horses

THE CUTTY SARK

● ● ● ○ ○

5 Ballast Quay (off Lassell St.), Greenwich,
London, SE10 9PD, England

Tel: +44 (0)20 8858 3146
Hours: Mon-Sat 11am-11pm, Sun noon-
10:30pm

Type: Traditional pub
Alfresco: Riverside picnic tables
Entry: Open door
Highlights: Location
Atmosphere: Relaxed
Clientele: Locals & tourists
Dress code: Casual
Price guide: ££
Food: Home-made pies & "up-market" bar food

Situated beyond the old power station, this
riverside pub is a fair way downstream from
the eponymous tea clipper which lies
marooned in the heart of Greenwich. The
present building, which is thought to date
from 1805, replaces an earlier pub called
the Green Man, which is believed to have
been built in 1695. It was called the Union
until 1954 when the name was changed
to honour the arrival of the Cutty Sark in
Greenwich.

The black and white façade, a first floor
listed building is dominated by a first floor
bow window which juts out over the
pavement, offering views of the Thames
and the Dome. The interior features heavy
beams, bare floorboards, bare brickwork,
a flagstone floor and old ships' lanterns.

With four traditional British ales on
draught, eight wines by the glass and a
good spread of wholesome pub grub, this
historic pub offers more than just a
commanding position.

THE GREENWICH UNION

● ● ● ● ○

56 Royal Hill, Greenwich, London, SE10
8RT, England

Tel: +44 (0)20 8692 6258,
www.greenwichunion.co.uk
Hours: Mon-Fri 11am-11pm, Sat 10am-
11pm, Sun 10am-10:30pm

Type: Local / gastro pub
Alfresco: Front terrace & long rear garden
Entry: Open door
Highlights: Beer & food
Atmosphere: Relaxed
Clientele: Locals & beer aficionados
Dress code: Very casual
Price guide: £££
Food: Mediterranean led all day menu

While the tourists visiting Greenwich climb
the hill to the Royal Observatory, beer
lovers ascend the quiet, residential Royal
Hill to this cosy little pub owned by the
Greenwich-based Meantime Brewery.

Behind the narrow, red brick façade,
The Union is a quaint little pub. Traditional
flagstone floors and wood-panelled walls
contrast with orange décor and modern
art. Beyond the bar is a long, narrow
conservatory which leads to an equally
slender beer garden with bench seating.

Meantime are noted for their excellent
and varied range of lager style beers and all
are served here, including the eponymous
Union, a dark lager in the old Viennese style.
Before choosing your pint, ask for a few
tasters - or if you're really indecisive, order
the sample tray. There are also six wines by
the glass and even the fruit juices are freshly
squeezed and unpasteurised.

A reasonably priced, Mediterranean
led menu appears to encourage local
mothers with pushchairs to make that trek
up the hill.

ZERODEGREES

● ● ● ● ○

28-31 Montpelier Vale, Blackheath,
London, SE3 0TJ, England

Tel: +44 (0)20 8852 5619,
www.zerodegrees-microbrewery.co.uk
Hours: Mon-Sat noon-midnight, Sun noon-
10:30pm

Type: Contemporary brew pub
Alfresco: Few tables on pavement
Entry: Open door
Highlights: Beer & pizza
Atmosphere: Local pub
Clientele: Locals & beer aficionados
Dress code: Very casual
Price guide: £££
Food: Excellent pizza & pasta

A florists turned restaurant bang opposite
Blackheath houses this microbrewery. The
industrial interior is scented with wood
smoke from the pizza ovens in the open
kitchen and dominated by stainless steel
brewing equipment. Amid nautical steel
stairwells and gantries, chairs and comfy
modern sofas sit on a brown tiled floor.

The pizza is great but the five
distinctive beers brewed here are even
better. There's a Golden Pilsner, an
American-style Pale Ale, a Brown Ale, a
regularly changing Special and a Wheat
Ale, which alternates between American,
Belgian and German styles. Zerodegrees
has picked up a number of accolades and
is carving out a name for itself among beer
aficionados. Although the wine list is not
extensive, the selections are great value.

Zerodegrees has become a popular
destination with young local professionals. Its large screen makes it a superbly
atmospheric place to head for big sporting
occasions.

The Greenwich Union   Zero Degrees

The Greenwich Union

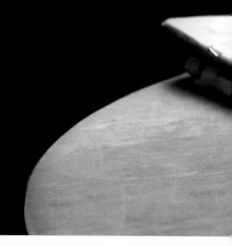

HAMPSTEAD
& KENTISH TOWN
(NW3, NW5-6, NW8)

NO LONDON SUMMER IS COMPLETE WITHOUT A STROLL ACROSS
HAMPSTEAD'S ROLLING HEATH AND A PINT IN ONE OF ITS PRETTY PUBS
– SOME OF THEM THREE OR FOUR CENTURIES OLD. FOR A SLICE OF THE
COUNTRY IN THE HEAT OF THE CITY, IT TAKES SOME BEATING.

The Washington

BLACK LION
● ● ● ○ ○

274 Kilburn High Road, Kilburn, London, NW6 2BY, England

Tel: +44 (0)20 7625 1635,
www.blacklionguesthouse.com
Hours: Mon-Fri noon-midnight,
Sat 11am-midnight, Sun noon-11:30pm

Type:	Gastro pub
Alfresco:	No
Entry:	Open door
Highlights:	Food & interior
Atmosphere:	Relaxed
Clientele:	Old soaks & young locals
Dress code:	Casual
Price guide:	££££
Food:	Modern international

The Black Lion is a substantial, late Victorian gin palace, complete with twelve guest rooms above. It is known for its splendid interior and status as Kilburn's original gastro pub.

The ornate, grade II listed interior has been recently restored. Moulded plasterwork adorns the walls and ceiling of the main bar, decked out in green and burgundy with flamboyant gold detailing. The large windows and plain wooden bar and furnishings save the room from being gaudy, while the large panelled dining room with its high ceiling, roof light and original open fireplace is more subdued. Flickering candles throughout help make the vast space feel cosy.

The daily changing menu is served from 6pm weekdays and from lunchtime at weekends. It combines international influences with unusual produce such as ostrich fillets and wild boar. While this is the main attraction and the pub various awards, the Black Lion remains at heart a traditional boozer.

FREEMASONS ARMS
● ● ● ● ○

32 Downshire Hill (corner Willow Rd), Hampstead, London, NW3 1NT, England

Tel: +44 (0)20 7433 6811,
www.freemasonsarms.co.uk
Hours: Mon-Sat 11am-11pm,
Sun noon-10:30pm

Type:	Gastro pub
Alfresco:	Large patios & terraces
Entry:	Open door
Highlights:	Skittles, garden & food
Atmosphere:	Somewhat lacking
Clientele:	30-something Hampsteadites
Dress code:	Casual but not scruffy
Price guide:	£££
Food:	Pizzas, burgers, grilled meat & fish

Rebuilt in 1933, this vast pub sits among equally palatial residential properties at the south-western edge of Hampstead Heath. Like many of its neighbours it boasts large, landscaped gardens complete with water features - perfect for catching the last rays and a pint after a summer stroll on the heath.

The Freemasons open-plan, bright interior is as manicured as its borders, to the extent that its soul has been largely designed away. However, with small leather armchairs and the odd sofa scattered about, it is comfortable enough.

A sizeable part of the pub is set aside for diners and, while the menu offers some more adventurous dishes, comfort foods such as pizza, pasta and steaks appear the culinary mainstay. The wine selection is a cut above average (16 are available by the glass) and, although a few ales are on hand pump, the beer and spirits selection lacks many special interest offerings for the discerning.

The last thing you'd expect to find in such a designer pub is the country's last public London Skittles alley, in the basement. To play visit www.londonskittles.co.uk.

THE HILL
● ● ● ● ○

94 Haverstock Hill (opp. Steeles Rd), Belsize Park, London, NW3 2BD, England

Tel: +44 (0)20 7267 0033,
www.geronimo-inns.co.uk
Hours: Mon-Wed 4pm-11pm, Thu-Sat noon-midnight, Sun 12:30pm-11pm

Type:	Traditional pub / gastro pub
Alfresco:	Large, tree shaded garden
Entry:	Open door
Highlights:	Garden & food
Atmosphere:	Relaxed
Clientele:	Cross-section of locals
Dress code:	Casual
Price guide:	£££
Food:	Salt & pepper squid to bangers & mash

This old Victorian boozer was a landmark on the hill between Chalk Farm and Belsize Park tube stations long before its gentrification made it trendy. Formerly the 'Load of Hay', it sits next to what was once the famous 'gym on the hill', where boxers including Muhammad Ali trained.

Today, The Hill's interior style is faded French boudoir. The walls are pastel green, with rococo detailing picked out in gilt, while velvet chairs, gilded mirrors and crystal chandeliers add to the baroque feel. The equally plush, almost formal, French-style garden rises up the hill and is shaded by trees.

Food is an important part of the offer and, while not at the top of the gastro pub pile, this is well above your average boozer. The beer selection is less than notable but there's a respectable range of wines including many by the glass.

The Hill is surprisingly quiet during the day. It comes into its own when the sun sets.

The Hill

Freemasons Arms

The Holly Bush

The Holly Bush

THE HOLLY BUSH

● ● ● ● ○

22 Holly Mount, (off Holly Hill), Hampstead, London, NW3 6SG, England

Tel: +44 (0)20 7435 2892,
www.hollybushpub.com
Hours: Mon-Sat noon-11pm, Sun noon-10:30pm

Type: Gastro pub
Alfresco: Few seats at front
Entry: Open door
Highlights: Food & old interior
Atmosphere: Traditional pub
Clientele: Locals of all ages & walks
Dress code: Office attire to jeans & T-shirts
Price guide: £££
Food: Homemade sausage rolls to organic dishes

The Holly Bush Tavern was established in May 1807, when the stables to a house built for the painter George Romney some nine years earlier were leased to a Thomas Lovelock "for the purpose of being converted at his expense into a public house".

It takes its name from the surrounding area, Holly Hill, which was famous for its holly groves right up until the 1940s. Local laundresses hung their washing over the bushes, and so the hill was known as Cloth Hill during the eighteenth century.

The ground floor houses a labyrinth of cosy, wood panelled rooms and there is a more formal dining room upstairs. Original features like etched glass windows, oak floors, pressed tin ceilings, gas lamps and high back settles add to the olde worlde feel.

Organic lamb, beef, Orkney salmon and wild game, plus gourmet sausages, head the food menu. The quality beer offering is topped by four regular and one guest ale.

THE JUNCTION TAVERN

● ● ● ● ○

101 Fortess Road (corner Lady Somerset Rd),
Tufnell Park, London, NW5 1AG, England

Tel: +44 (0)20 7485 9400,
www.junctiontavern.co.uk
Hours: Mon-Sat noon-11pm, Sun noon-
10:30pm

Type: Gastro pub
Alfresco: Shaded garden
Entry: Open door
Highlights: Food & ales
Atmosphere: Relaxed
Clientele: Cross-section of locals
Dress code: Casual
Price guide: £££
Food: Daily changing lunch & dinner menus

The glass frontage of The Junction shouts
gastro pub and its stainless steel kitchen
and dining tables are plainly visible to
passers-by. This central open kitchen and
the bar that backs onto it divide the pub in
two. The front may be restaurant, but the
back is out & out old boozer. The traditional
rear lounge has its own bar counter
bristling with real ale pumps and leads via
a modern conservatory to an attractive
back yard packed with picnic tables and
shaded by trees.

The food is excellent and both the
lunch and dinner menus change daily.
Bookings are taken for the front dining
room only but you're welcome to eat in the
pub, conservatory or garden.

Drinkswise, The Junction's offering is
well above your usual boozer. The wine list
includes ten bins by the glass and there
are always at least four traditional ales on
draught, including one that changes
weekly.

The Junction Tavern

The Junction Tavern

The Junction Tavern

Spaniards Inn

The Salt House

LORD PALMERSTON

● ● ● ● ○

33 Dartmouth Park Hill (corner Chetwynd Rd), Dartmouth Park, London, NW5 1HU

Tel: +44 (0)20 7485 1578,
www.geronimo-inns.co.uk
Hours: Mon-Sat noon-11pm, Sun noon-10:30pm

Type:	Gastro pub
Alfresco:	Front terrace & rear garden
Entry:	Open door
Highlights:	Food & atmosphere
Atmosphere:	Very chilled
Clientele:	Local bohemians
Dress code:	Casual
Price guide:	££££
Food:	Moorish/Mediterranean-led modern British

Named after the nineteenth century Prime Minister and father of 'gunboat diplomacy', the Lord Palmerston is an imposing Victorian pub, halfway up the steep Dartmouth Park Hill.

On a sunny day you may never make it past the large front terrace, which is a great place to sit and watch the world go by. Inside comprises a main room, dominated by the curved bar but offering some cosy corners, the Chapel, a converted stable, and an attractive conservatory which looks out onto a small, shady garden. There is a function room upstairs.

The menu is written on the blackboard above the open fireplace in the main bar. It changes daily for lunch and dinner and I can vouch for its quality. This place is too casual to take reservations, but there's plenty of room.

The excellent food is complemented by a serious wine offering with some twenty wines available by the glass. There are usually at least three real ales on draught, a good selection of premium spirits and even some interesting sherries.

THE OLD BULL & BUSH

● ● ● ● ○

North End Road (by Hampstead Way), Golders Green, London, NW3 7HE, England

Tel: +44 (0)20 8905 5456,
www.thebullandbush.co.uk
Hours: Mon-Sat 11am-11pm, Sun noon-10:30pm

Type:	Gastro pub
Alfresco:	Large front patio
Entry:	Open door
Highlights:	Food
Atmosphere:	Relaxed
Clientele:	Locals of all ages
Dress code:	Casual
Price guide:	£££
Food:	Pizzas, burgers, grilled meat & fish

This Grade II listed pub dates back to 1721 when what was then a farmhouse was granted a licence to sell ale. During Edwardian times its lavish gardens made it popular but national recognition came to this London landmark in the 1920s when music hall star Florrie Ford had a hit with 'The Old Bull & Bush'. All together now: "Come, come, come and make eyes at me - down at the Old Bull and Bush."

The structure of the present day pub derives substantially from extensive rebuilding in 1924. Earlier this year new owners further refurbished the pub and introduced a stronger food offering, modern interior design and the inevitable partly open kitchen. Thankfully the low ceiling and some period features, among them the etched mirrors on the back bar, have been retained.

Food is of the comfort variety and matched by a reasonable wine list with 16 by the glass. Three ales lead an otherwise pretty mainstream beer and spirits offering.

THE SALT HOUSE

● ● ● ○ ○

63 Abbey Road (corner Belgrave Gardens),
St John's Wood, London, NW8 0AE, England

Tel: +44 (0)20 7328 6626
Hours: Mon-Sat noon-11pm, Sun noon-
10:30pm

Type: Gastro pub
Alfresco: Patio at front
Entry: Open door
Highlights: Food (on a good day)
Atmosphere: Relaxed
Clientele: Upmarket locals
Dress code: Upscale casual
Price guide: £££
Food: Mediterranean influenced menu

This pub sits on the famous Abbey Road,
close to the EMI studios where The Beatles
recorded many albums, most famously the
eponymous 1969 LP whose cover
features the pedestrian crossing outside
the studio building. It is perhaps not
surprising that this pub became the Abbey
Road Pub & Dining Room for a short time
before reverting to its previous incarnation,
The Salt House.

This is a sprawling place with a small
front bar, a dining room, an upstairs room
and a large, partly decked and covered
terrace. The décor throughout is warm and
appealing. The interior woodwork is
particularly effective: generations of paint
have been partially burnt off and the
results varnished.

Like the name, owners have come
and gone and so has this pub's reputation
for food. On a good day meals can still be
great, although my last visit was very
disappointing. A not terribly inspiring drinks
selection includes ten wines by the glass
and a couple of real ales. Locals still enjoy
this place but it is no longer the destination
it once was.

SPANIARDS INN

● ● ● ● ○

Spaniards Road, Hampstead Heath,
London, NW3 7JJ, England

Tel: +44 (0)20 8731 6571
Hours: Mon-Sat 11am-11pm, Sun noon-
10:30pm

Type: Traditional pub
Alfresco: Large attractive garden
Entry: Open door
Highlights: History & beer
Atmosphere: Relaxed
Clientele: Heath walkers & locals
Dress code: Casual
Price guide: £££
Food: Traditional pub meals & snacks

It's hard to miss Spaniards Inn when driving
along the road that cuts through Hampstead
Heath. Its white, weatherboarded buildings
jut out into the road, causing a traffic
bottleneck as the space between the pub
and the 18th century toll keeper's cottage is
so tight. Both buildings are listed so drivers
will continue to yield for the foreseeable.

Originally built in 1585 as a country house
for the Spanish ambassador, this did not become
a pub until the mid 18th century when two (also
Spanish) brothers took over the property.

Several cosy rooms lie off the saloon bar,
each oak panelled with low ceilings and old
wooden settles - one is tiny, too small to seat even
ten people comfortably. Upstairs is a charming
panelled room with creaking floorboards. The
large garden, where John Keats heard the
nightingale's song which inspired his famous ode,
boasts plenty of tables and greenery.

Traditional meals and pub snacks are
served here, alongside one of the best beer
selections in Hampstead including up to five
ales and some interesting Belgian bottled
brews. The wine selection is also extensive.

TOAST

● ● ● ◑ ○

50 Hampstead High Street (above tube
station), Hampstead, London, NW3 1QG

Tel: +44 (0)20 7431 2244,
www.toastnw3.com
Hours: Mon-Sat 11am-midnight, Sun 11am-
10:30pm

Type: Restaurant / lounge bar
Alfresco: No
Entry: Open door
Highlights: Food & cocktails
Atmosphere: Changes according to time
Clientele: 30-something locals
Dress code: Not dressy
Price guide: £££
Food: Scones to "global fusion" snacks & mains

Toast is tucked away above Hampstead
tube station, which, incidentally, is the
deepest station on the entire Underground
network. (It opened in 1907 and marked
the completion of the Charing Cross,
Euston & Hampstead Railway, now part of
the Northern line.)

The glass doorway to Toast is just to
the right of the station entrance, and the
staircase leads up to a 1970s styled room
with chocolate brown leather banquette
seating and nicotine coloured polished
plaster walls. Arched windows offer
panoramic views of the street outside.

It's rare that you find a lounge bar over
a tube station, but it's even rarer to find one
which serves clotted cream scones and
afternoon tea. That's the great thing about
Toast: it really does cater for the local
community, morphing from brunch
restaurant to cocktail lounge bar as day
turns to night. The food is honest, the
cocktails are of a good standard and the
service friendly and efficient. What
lucky locals.

The Washington

THE WASHINGTON
● ● ● ● ○

50 Englands Lane (corner Primrose Hill Road), Belsize Park, London, NW3 4UE

Tel: +44 (0)20 7722 8842
Hours: Mon-Sat noon-11pm, Sun noon-10:30pm

Type:	Contemporary / gastro pub
Alfresco:	No
Entry:	Open door
Highlights:	Food
Atmosphere:	Buzzy local
Clientele:	Young & upwardly mobile
Dress code:	Fashionably casual
Price guide:	£££
Food:	Modern British fare

The Washington is an old, back street pub with a lively atmosphere driven by a sympathetic refurbishment, gastrofication and the young and upwardly mobile. However, this corner pub remains a community boozer and still welcomes old men in for pints of ale.

Original Victorian features - the splendid tiled entrance, carved mahogany bar counter, ornate ceiling, and etched glass and mahogany panels - contrast with some very contemporary lighting and comfy sofas. The panels and central bar divide the large space and create secluded corners.

A chalkboard over the bar lists a good wine selection (with 20 by the glass). Draught beers include three ales and a couple of more interesting brews among the selection of European lagers. For the peckish there are light dishes such as goat's cheese and red onion tart through to substantial meals such as steak & ale pie with all the trimmings or vegetarian gnocchi.

The Washington

The Washington

THE WELLS

● ● ● ○ ○

30 Well Walk (corner Christchurch Hill), Hampstead, London, NW3 1BX, England

Tel: +44 (0)20 7794 3785,
www.thewellshampstead.co.uk
Hours: Mon-Sun noon-11pm

Type:	Gastro pub
Alfresco:	Front & side terraces
Entry:	Open door
Highlights:	Food
Atmosphere:	Relaxed
Clientele:	Local young professionals
Dress code:	Casual but not shabby
Price guide:	££££
Food:	Full restaurant menu & snacks

In the late 17th century, the village of Hampstead Wells, as this area was then, became fashionable after its waters were declared medicinal and its air beneficial to health. The Wells and the village Well Walk on which it stands honour the area's spa past.

With its grand Georgian façade The Wells stands out gracefully from the quaint houses that surround it. So the starkly modern interior with its black tiled walls and plush furnishings can come as something of a shock to first time visitors. This look continues upstairs in the three intimate dining rooms.

Although there is a good drinks offering, with real ales, plenty of wines and even a cocktail list, The Wells seems predominantly about food. The area reserved for drinkers at the front of the pub is small, but more importantly the décor has over-sanitised the place and removed its pub character.

I'd recommend eating here but book a table upstairs.

The Wells

The Wells

HIGHGATE & ISLINGTON
(N1, N5, N7, N19, N6)

THE GASTRO PUB IS LONDON'S BIGGEST THING FOR YEARS AND
ISLINGTON ITS SPIRITUAL HOME. AND, IF CHAMPAGNE SOCIALISTS AND
MEEJA BUNNIES AREN'T YOUR THING, YOU CAN ALWAYS HEAD FOR PRETTY
HIGHGATE VILLAGE AND ITS OH-SO-COUNTRY PUBS.

The Duke of Cambridge

THE ALBION
● ● ● ○ ○

10 Thornhil Road (btwn. Albion Mews & Richmond Av.), Barnsbury, London, N1 1HW, England

Tel: + 44 (0)20 7607 7450
Hours: Mon-Sat 11am-11pm,
Sun noon-10:30pm

Type:	Traditional pub
Alfresco:	Front terrace, rear garden
Entry:	Open door
Highlights:	Rear garden
Atmosphere:	Relaxed
Clientele:	Locals of all ages
Dress code:	Casual to suits
Price guide:	£££
Food:	Snacks to plates

Once upon a time Barnsbury was a tiny hamlet a short walk away from the village of Islington. Things have changed and Islington is now London to the core yet, while Barnsbury is also metropolitan, it retains a country air. Here sits the Albion, an ivy-clad Georgian coaching inn that would look quite at home among fields and farms. In summer, drinkers lounge at the outside picnic tables as if on the edge of the village cricket pitch.

The large interior with exposed beams and loud carpet is sub-divided into smaller, intimate spaces which have not been redecorated for some time. By far the best part of this pleasant pub is its secluded rear garden, shaded by vine-entwined trellises and trees.

THE BARNSBURY
● ● ● ● ○

209-211 Liverpool Road, Islington, London, N1 1LX, England

Tel: +44 (0)20 7607 5519,
www.thebarnsbury.co.uk
Hours: Mon-Sat noon-11pm, Sun noon-10:30pm

Type:	Local / gastro pub
Alfresco:	Walled garden
Entry:	Open door
Highlights:	Food
Atmosphere:	Relaxed
Clientele:	All manner of Islingtonians
Dress code:	Whatever
Price guide:	£££
Food:	Full modern British menu

The Barnsbury lies on a B-road in Islington that is thoroughfare enough to drive passing trade but sufficiently far into residential Islington to escape the youthful exuberance that plagues Upper Street.

More restoration than refurbishment, this neglected Victorian boozer reopened in November 2002. Stripped oak panelling, fireplaces and other period details have been retained but are now emphasised by an altogether brighter interior. The centrepiece is the island bar with its cut glass goblet chandeliers designed by Giles Gough. The work of a different young London artist is displayed every three months.

A good beer selection includes three traditional ales, one a guest ale that changes monthly. But food and wine is where The Barnsbury excels with a full modern British menu accompanied by a carefully chosen international wine list, featuring fifteen wines by the glass and as many organic bins. French doors lead to a secluded walled garden for alfresco summer dining.

The Barnsbury

THE BULL

● ● ● ● ○

13 North Hill, Highgate, London, N6 4AB, England

Tel: +44 (0)845 456 5033,
www.inthebull.biz
Hours: Mon 5pm-11pm, Tue-Sat 11am-11pm, Sun 11am-10:30pm

Type:	Gastro pub
Alfresco:	Front patio
Entry:	Open door
Highlights:	Food
Atmosphere:	Chilled
Clientele:	Local professionals
Dress code:	Relaxed
Price guide:	££££
Food:	Full modern British menu

Highgate is well served by pubs but the superb modern British food makes The Bull stand out. Like many of the nearby taverns, it has been here since the days when horse drawn coaches passed by on the main route to London. Substantially rebuilt in 1906, The Bull dates back to 1765, but the Grade II listed building has been so well spruced up that it looks almost new.

On the ground floor is the open plan, austerely decorated dining room with polished wooden tables, chunky candles and a coal fire in the cast iron grate. Expect to enjoy anything from foie gras with wilted rocket, jerusalem artichoke and devilled sauce to goat's cheese risotto with chicken livers, scallops, cauliflower puree and parsnip salad.

The pub proper on the first floor is more relaxed with floor to ceiling windows, an open fire, a cherry wood bar and an original American pool table.

The Bull has two real ales on draught, Timothy Taylor and Highgate IPA (the latter is actually made in Walsall). It also has a cocktail menu and a broad wine list with 14 by the glass.

CHARLES LAMB
● ● ● ○ ○

16 Elia Street (corner Quick St.), Islington,
London, N1 8DE, England

Tel: +44 (0)20 7837 5040,
www.thecharleslambpub.com
Hours: Mon-Wed 4pm-11pm, Thu-Sun
noon-11pm

Type: Gastro pub
Alfresco: Few picnic benches outside
Entry: Open door
Highlights: Food, beers & atmosphere
Atmosphere: Relaxed
Clientele: Locals of all ages
Dress code: Casual to suits
Price guide: £££
Food: Snacks to substantial meals

The street on which this pub stands is named Elia, after the pen name used by the essayist Charles Lamb when he contributed to The London Magazine in the late 18th and early 19th centuries. This corner local was built in 1839 and originally named the Prince Alfred, but after its recent refurbishment and gastrofication was appropriately renamed for Elia's creator.

Inside, this quaint little pub has an almost cottagey feel with a light stripped pine floor and creamy walls. The bar takes up much of the lounge area: the adjoining room is filled with pine topped tables reserved for diners.

Whether you're here for a snack or a full meal, you will appreciate the standard of the food. Drinkers are also well served with more regularly changing real ales, an interesting wine list (including 14 by the glass) and bottled brews from Breton Cider to Liberty Ale. Unusually for a pub, the back bar line-up includes gems such as Punt E Mes.

Well chosen background music and a friendly crowd from local offices and homes ensure a cordial atmosphere.

THE DRAPER'S ARMS
● ● ● ● ○

44 Barnsbury Street (btwn Liverpool Rd &
Thornhill Rd), Islington, London, N1 1ER, England

Tel: +44 (0)20 7619 0348,
www.thedrapersarms.co.uk
Hours: Mon-Sat 11am-11pm, Sun noon-
10:30pm

Type: Gastro pub
Alfresco: Rear garden with heaters
Entry: Open door
Highlights: Food
Atmosphere: Relaxed
Clientele: Local young professionals
Dress code: Straight from the office to jeans
Price guide: £££
Food: Full modern European menu

The Draper's Arms was opened in November 2001 by two partners (Paul McElhinny, the manager, and Mark Emberton, the chef) who refurbished a disused, derelict, double-fronted Georgian building at the north end of Lonsdale Square. Although well-hidden in the back streets of N1, it is worth searching out.

Step over the trapdoors as you enter (don't worry, they're safe) and into a parlour-like room with salmon pink walls, leather sofas, bookshelves, mirrors and fireplaces. Walk around the bar, pass under the mirrored sloping ceilings and open the doors onto a gem of a secluded garden with heaters and a natty awning which opens when rain threatens.

On the first floor lies a more formal yet wonderfully atmospheric dining area with red bucket seats and Wedgwood blue walls. The food is exceptional with the starters particularly appealing. An international wine list with 23 wines by the glass and three traditional ales on draught also helps mark The Drapers as more gastro than boozer.

THE DUKE OF CAMBRIDGE
● ● ● ○ ○

30 St. Peter's Street (corner Danbury St),
Islington, London, N1 8JT, England

Tel: +44 (0)20 8986 5384,
www.sloeberry.co.uk
Hours: Mon 5pm-11pm, Tue-Sat noon-
11pm, Sun noon-10pm

Type: Gastro pub
Alfresco: No
Entry: Open door
Highlights: Food
Atmosphere: Relaxed
Clientele: Affluent locals & organic foodies
Dress code: Casual
Price guide: ££££
Food: Organic

Since it opened in December 1998, this old boozer on a rat run off an Islington back road has been a foodie destination as the nation's first totally organic pub.

It's not just the food that's organic: the beers are organic, the many wines are organic - even the vodka, gin and cola are organic.

Named for a famous Victorian philanthropist, this pub dates back to 1861 and although it's been gastrified and extended with a conservatory dining area, it retains that old local charm. Eco-warriors and young professionals pack the place, attracted by the twice daily changing menu and local atmosphere.

After eating and drinking here several times I have to report that the quality of both service and food is mixed and the organic beers are disappointing.

The Duke of Cambridge

THE FLASK
● ● ● ○ ○

77 Highgate West Hill, Highgate Village,
London, N6 6BU, England

Tel: +44 (0)20 8348 7346,
Hours: Mon-Sat 11am-11pm, noon-
10:30pm

Type:	Gastro pub
Alfresco:	No
Entry:	Open door
Highlights:	Food
Atmosphere:	Relaxed
Clientele:	Affluent locals
Dress code:	Casual
Price guide:	£££
Food:	Great organic food

Highgate has more than its fair share of old pubs but this one, which dates back to the early 18th century, is one of the oldest, and probably the best known. Its name heralds from the days when visitors en route to Hampstead springs would call in here to buy a flask in which to carry the healing water home.

The Flask is especially busy in the summer within the partially covered and secluded forecourt is packed with drinkers. On such evenings it's not unusual for an orderly queue to run from the bar to the door.

But this ancient place, with its low ceilings, wooden floors and panelling, is best enjoyed in the winter: the many interconnecting tiny rooms come in to their own as snug places to huddle, chat and bask by log fires. This is also the right time of year to appreciate the pub's well-kept real ales, lengthy wine list and homely comfort food – especially the Sunday roasts.

THE HOUSE
● ● ● ● ○

63-69 Canonbury Road (@ Halton Rd),
Islington, London, N1 2DG, England

Tel: +44 (0)20 7704 7410,
www.inthehouse.biz
Hours: Mon 5pm-11pm, Tue-Sat noon-
11pm, Sun noon-10:30pm

Type:	Gastro pub
Alfresco:	Street-side patio
Entry:	Open door
Highlights:	Food
Atmosphere:	Can be loud
Clientele:	Local yuppies
Dress code:	Casual
Price guide:	££££
Food:	Regarded full menu plus snacks

The House sits on its own triangular traffic island in the part of Islington known as Canonbury, a mere five minutes walk from Highbury Corner. Not so many years ago this was just another forgotten backstreet boozer, but an award winning menu built around British produce has made The House something of a destination.

Although the exterior of The House looks like a pub, the inside feels more like a restaurant, albeit with a large bar area. However, a pub it is, and to prove it there's Adnams ale on draught. The décor is clean and bright with stripped wooden floors, white walls, and comfy sofas and armchairs. The dining area hosts old mismatched chairs and wooden tables, some with crisp white cloths, in front of an open hatch kitchen. Framed photographs of the staff adorn the walls and make for a pleasant, homely touch.

The broad wine list offers fifteen wines by the glass and even a number of cocktails. There is a cognac trolley and tables can be booked.

THE MARQUESS TAVERN
● ● ● ● ○

32 Canonbury Street (btwn Arran Walk & Douglas
Rd), Canonbury, Islington, London N1 2TB, England

Tel: +44 (0)20 7354 2975,
Hours: Sun-Thu noon-11pm,
Fri-Sat noon-midnight

Type:	Gastro pub
Alfresco:	Small front patio with picnic benches
Entry:	Open door
Highlights:	Food & beers
Atmosphere:	Relaxed
Clientele:	Locals of all ages
Dress code:	Casual to suits
Price guide:	£££
Food:	Weekday evenings & weekend lunchtimes

Canonbury Street is villagey and picturesque. Quaint old houses face the narrow park which traces the course of the New River, designed by Sir Hugh Myddleton, that began supplying fresh water to London in 1613. The Marquess, a splendid, neoclassical pub with soaring, fluted Corinthian plasters sits proudly in this tranquil setting.

The pub was built in the 1850s and plenty of late Victorian wood panelling remains but old leather sofas, stripped wood floorboards and liberally applied white emulsion mark the change from its previous incarnation as workaday boozer to gastro pub. In the back dining room rows of tables sit under a high ceiling and blackboards list appealing dishes, wines and aperitifs. A small side room houses a bar billiards table.

The high standard of the traditional English dishes on the food menu is matched by a drinks offering which includes up to six real ales (due to a tie most are Young's), over forty malt whiskies and bottled beers, plus a rounded wine list with a dozen by the glass.

The Marquess Tavern

THE NORTH STAR

● ● ● ● ○

188-190 New North Road, Islington, London, N1 7BJ, England

Tel: +44 (0)20 7354 5400,
www.northstarbar.co.uk
Hours: Mon-Fri noon-11pm, Sat 4pm-11pm, Sun noon-11pm

Type: Gastro pub
Alfresco: Rear terrace
Entry: Open door
Highlights: Food
Atmosphere: Relaxed - busy at weekends
Clientele: Locals
Dress code: Casual
Price guide: £££
Food: Mediterranean influenced modern British

Positioned on what is both a cut-through and a no-man's-land between Hoxton and Upper Street, over the years many an entrepreneur has tried their luck at making this difficult venue work. However, the Gainsborough Studios development has brought a new set of locals and the present owners appear to have succeeded. The Moroccan drapes and gilded furniture from its previous incarnation 'Babushka' have gone and the place now has a clean, simple, gastro pub feel with prints of 1950s American cars on the walls. The small padded basement remains and is a great space if you're in a group. Out back there's a small terrace with an awning in case of rain.

Cocktails are cheap and can be well made. There's no ale but a reasonable wine list with ten by the glass. While the drinks offering may not be special the food is far above that of the average pub.

THE NORTHGATE

● ● ● ● ○

113 Southgate Road (corner Northchurch Rd), Islington, London, N1 3JS, England

Tel: +44 (0)20 7359 7392
Hours: Mon-Fri 5pm-11pm, Sat noon-11pm, Sun noon-10:30pm

Type: Gastro pub
Alfresco: Front terrace
Entry: Open door
Highlights: Food
Atmosphere: Relaxed
Clientele: Locals & gastronauts
Dress code: Casual
Price guide: £££
Food: Nibbles & full restaurant menu

Formerly a strip joint called the Dog & Dumplings, this old boozer has been taken stratospherically upmarket and given an altogether posher moniker. The Northgate's vast interior is pure pub at the front but as you move back towards the open kitchen, the feel is much more like a restaurant. The décor is clean and bright yet the pick 'n' mix wooden tables and chairs contribute towards the homely feel. Food is served throughout although you can only book tables in the restaurant.

The modern British menu changes daily and offers diverse choices from noodles to pork fillet or seared tuna. The bar has a selection of wines to suit most tastes, including thirteen by the glass plus sherry and dessert wines. A fair range of beers is topped by three traditional British cask ales.

The Northgate sits in a somewhat down-at-heel part of Islington but attracts young professional types who are moving into the area. Recommended for a hearty meal or just a pint.

OQO

● ● ● ● ○

4-6 Islington Green, Islington, London, N1 2XA, England

Tel: +44 (0)20 7704 2332
Hours: Sun-Wed noon-11pm, Thu-Sat noon-midnight

Type: Lounge bar & restaurant
Alfresco: No
Entry: Subject to management & capacity
Highlights: Cocktails, food
Atmosphere: Buzzy
Clientele: Local 20 & 30 somethings
Dress code: Designer casual
Price guide: £££
Food: Chinese tapas and Cantonese dim sum

Leafy Islington Green helps shield this stylish Chinese tapas and cocktail bar from the mayhem that surrounds many of the more mass market venues on Upper Street.

The long, narrow, interior is ultra-modern designer cool, with black floor, black walls and a forty foot long black granite bar counter that stretches from the lounge area to the open kitchen. Glowing filaments and a backlit, woodgrain bar front give warmth to the otherwise austere room, while a trio of circular images of food and drink behind the bar stylishly reflect the three letters of its name.

While the classic and contemporary cocktails offered here are judiciously made, the Chinese tapas and Cantonese dim sum are the highlight. Enjoy a casual snack at one of the white cube tables or head to the more formal dining area secluded at the rear.

THE ROSEMARY BRANCH
● ● ● ○ ○

2 Shepperton Road (@ Southgate Rd), Islington,
London, N1 3DT, England

Tel: +44 (0)20 7704 2730,
www.rosemarybranch.co.uk
Hours: Mon-Thu noon-11pm, Fri-Sat noon-
midnight, Sun noon-10:30pm

Type:	Traditional pub
Alfresco:	Tables on pavement
Entry:	Open door
Highlights:	Atmosphere, beer & food
Atmosphere:	Buzzy local
Clientele:	Locals & media types
Dress code:	Casual
Price guide:	££££
Food:	British & international starters & mains

When it was first built this Victorian pub
was renowned for its music hall, where
Charlie Chaplin is said to have once
appeared. In the mid-19th century, the
Rosemary Branch Gardens behind are
said to have rivalled the Vauxhall Pleasure
Gardens as a source of entertainment.
Since then the surrounding area has
changed much but despite the ugly
housing estates the Regents Canal still
runs under the Rosemary Branch Bridge
opposite the pub.

Refurbished by its present owners in
1992, the Rosemary Branch has a homely
shabbiness with stuffed fish over the bar
and huge model planes hanging from the
ceiling. All manner of productions are still
staged in the theatre upstairs. This very
traditional, cosy boozer has character and
atmosphere. Locals come to enjoy the
Monday night music quiz, a good selection
of ale and wines plus modern British fare.

ST JOHN'S
● ● ● ● ○

91 Junction Road (btwn Brookside Rd & St
Johns Grove), Tufnell Park, London, N19 5QU

Tel: +44 (0)20 7272 1587
Hours: Mon-Sat 11am-11pm, Sun noon-
10:30pm

Type:	Gastro pub
Alfresco:	No
Entry:	Open door
Highlights:	Food
Atmosphere:	Chilled, friendly
Clientele:	Moneyed Highgate, trendy Archway blend
Dress code:	Casual
Price guide:	£££
Food:	Modern British gastro grub

The heavy, castle-like doors of St. John's
are not exactly welcoming, but inside lies a
warm, friendly locals' pub frequented by an
unpretentious crowd of moneyed Highgate
and trendy Archway types. Odd
lampshades, which look like they have been
salvaged from an old people's home, lend
a cosy, homely ambience to this slightly
shabby boozer.

But St John's is much more than just
an old boozer and hidden behind the bar is
a large, art-strewn dining room. Chandeliers
hang from the high ceiling of this
atmospheric converted church and chesterfield sofas sit around an open fireplace.

Wholesome modern British gastro grub
is preceded by complimentary chunks of
tasty, home-baked bread. A sensibly
selected and priced wine list includes twelve
by the glass. Beer lovers will find a choice of
European brews plus three ales on draught.

St John's can sometimes be a victim
of its own success as bar staff and kitchen
struggle to satisfy patrons.

THE SOCIAL
● ● ● ○ ○

33 Linton Street (@ St. Mary St), Arlington
Square, Islington, London, N1 7DU, England

Tel: +44 (0)20 7354 5809,
www.thesocial.com
Hours: Mon-Fri 5pm-11pm, Sat noon-
11pm, Sun noon-10:30pm

Type:	Gastro pub / lounge bar
Alfresco:	No
Entry:	Small cover charge some nights
Highlights:	Music, food
Atmosphere:	Dependent on night
Clientele:	Locals, media & musos
Dress code:	Casual
Price guide:	£££
Food:	Full modern British menu

This out-of-the-way old man's pub used
to be called The Hanbury Arms. Then
Heavenly Recordings (the record label
behind the Social in W1 and Nottingham)
bought it and made it so fashionable that
new media types travel miles to eat and
drink here. Like the other Socials, this is
music led and DJs puncture the silence
most Wednesdays, Fridays, Saturdays
and Sundays. Early in the week it has more
of a quiet, informal, restaurant feel.

This substantial boozer has three-
quarter panelled walls, which give more
than a hint of what it was like
pre-gastrofication and help the down-to-
earth feel. Downstairs has the look of a
typical pub-restaurant mélange but
upstairs with its fashionably shabby sofas
is out and out lounge. The drinks selection
is only adequate but the food and
atmosphere can be superb.

KENSINGTON & SHEPHERDS BUSH
(W6, W8, W12, W14)

KENSINGTON IS WHERE THE YOUNG, POSH AND PRIVILEGED LIVE, LOUNGE AND PLAY, AND A HANDFUL OF EXPENSIVE CLUBS AND BARS DRAW LEGGY FILLIES AND THEIR CHINLESS BEAUX. SHEPHERDS BUSH ATTRACTS A MORE DIVERSE CROWD, THANKS TO MORE FEASIBLE PRICES AND THE NEARBY BBC.

The Ealing Park Tavern

ABINGDON

● ● ● ● ○

54 Abingdon Road (@ Abingdon Villas),
Kensington, London, W8 6AP, England

Tel: +44 (0)20 7937 3339
Hours: Mon-Sat 12:30pm-11pm, Sun
11am-10:30pm

Type: Gastro pub
Alfresco: Pavement tables
Entry: Open door
Highlights: Food
Atmosphere: Relaxed
Clientele: Moneyed locals, ladies who lunch
Dress code: Designer casual
Price guide: £££
Food: Superb mains to simple snacks

The Abingdon is tucked away in a posh
residential neighbourhood between
Kensington High Street and the nice end
of the Earls Court Road. As befits its
location, it is a distinctly upmarket affair
and a far cry from your traditional boozer.

The bright, loungy interior is warmly lit
and modern with comfy couches and
leather banquette seating. However, it is
the modern European menu which attracts
the moneyed locals and ladies who lunch.
The most desirable of the three dining
areas is a row of high booths under a
skylight and you may want to request one
when making your booking.

There are no draught ales to be found
in this pub and indeed few beers.
Customers drink wine and champagne,
and the fifteen international wines by the
glass are reasonably priced considering
the area.

THE ANGLESEA ARMS

● ● ● ● ○

35 Wingate Road (corner Wellesley Rd),
Chiswick, London, W6 0UR, England

Tel: +44 (0)20 8749 1291
Hours: Mon-Sat 11am-11pm, Sun noon-
10:30pm

Type: Gastro pub
Alfresco: Tables at front
Entry: Open door
Highlights: Food
Atmosphere: Relaxed
Clientele: Trendy locals (& kids)
Dress code: Casual
Price guide: £££
Food: Great modern British gastro grub

One of the first and best-known of
London's gastro pubs. The Anglesea Arms
has the look and feel of a country pub.
Wooden logs crackle in the fireplace of the
main dark panelled room where an old
clock on the wall has been stuck at ten to
twelve for years. The décor is slightly
shabby but in a welcoming, homely way.

The rear dining area with its mustard
yellow walls, skylights, well-worn tables
and colourful mural has a village hall feel.
The small open kitchen is famous for its
food and the menu is chalked up on a large
blackboard. There is barely room for forty
diners, and all are accommodated on a
first come first served basis so it pays to
be early.

The wine list struggles to fill one side
of A4 laminated paper but offers a choice
of 16 wines by the glass. All bins are good
and well priced, while the draught beers
include two traditional ales.

BUSH BAR & GRILL

● ● ● ● ○

45a Goldhawk Road (btwn Wells & Woodger
Rds), Shepherd's Bush, London, W12 8QP

Tel: +44 (0)20 8746 2111,
www.bushbar.co.uk
Hours: Mon-Sat noon-midnight,
Sun noon-6pm

Type: Restaurant/lounge bar
Alfresco: Front terrace
Entry: Can get busy on Fridays
Highlights: Cocktails, wines, food
Atmosphere: Relaxed
Clientele: Locals
Dress code: Smart casual
Price guide: £££
Food: Full restaurant menu

Blink and you'll miss this place: the narrow
entrance, set within a row of shops, looks more
like an alley leading to a carpark. But this slick
dining room belies its implausible location in
an otherwise dingy corner of Shepherds Bush.

The spacious converted dairy was once
a bar called the Blob Shop. Now the restaurant
takes up much of the warehouse space,
which has been brightened up with colourful
walls, although the paint on the underside of
the industrial roof is a little drab. The food is
indeed a big draw here. The attractively priced
lunch and early evening set menu pulls in both
after-workers and the Elle Deco reading,
Champagne quaffing locals.

Drinkers congregate at one end, lining
the bar and filling the raised seating area which
is fitted out with comfy banquettes. The
polished concrete bar with its beautiful curving
front hosts an impressive range of illuminated
spirits and serves a good selection of
well-made cocktails. The place is part owned
by wine merchant and restaurateur John Armit,
and he has provided a decently priced wine
list, with fourteen offered by the glass.

↑ **Beefeater Dry Martini**

↚ Method: Stir vermouth with ice and strain to discard excess, leaving the ice coated with vermouth. POUR Beefeater over vermouth coated ice, STIR and strain into a chilled glass.

Stop

↑ Glass: Martini
↑ Garnish: Olive or Lemon zest twist
↑ ¾ measure Dry Vermouth
← 2 ½ measures Beefeater

N
R
S
L

THE CUMBERLAND ARMS
●●●●○

29 North End Road, Hammersmith,
London, W14 8SZ, England

Tel: +44 (0)20 7371 6806,
www.thecumberlandarmspub.co.uk
Hours: Mon-Sat noon-11pm,
Sun noon-10:30pm

Type: Gastro pub
Alfresco: Side patio with picnic tables
Entry: Open door
Highlights: Food
Atmosphere: Relaxed
Clientele: Locals & exhibition goers
Dress code: Casual
Price guide: £££
Food: Mediterranean-influenced gastro grub

The owners of this pub seem to like their establishments within stumbling distance of a large exhibition hall. The Atlas lies in the shadows of Earls Court and this sister pub is pretty much opposite Olympia.

The Cumberland sits like a royal blue, flower covered gatehouse at the entrance to a small park. Well established trees shade the picnic tables on the large side patio. The interior design follows the spruced-up boozer school of bare wood tables and floors, and dark varnish covers just about everything except the magnolia walls and mock-Victorian light fittings.

Like The Atlas, The Cumberland has been gastrofied. Chalkboards and printed sheets offer a Mediterranean-led menu. But exhibition goers come here to be watered as well as fed and a draught beer selection that includes Broadside, Deuchar's IPA and Pride is bolstered by a sensible wine list including some 14 bins by the glass.

THE DOVE
●●●○○

19 Upper Mall (Furnival Gdns),
Hammersmith, London, W6 9TA, England

Tel: +44 (0)20 8748 5405
Hours: Mon-Sat 11am-11pm, Sun noon-10:30pm

Type: Traditional pub
Alfresco: Riverside terrace
Entry: Open door
Highlights: History, Fuller's ales
Atmosphere: Can get crowded
Clientele: Mixed crowd of locals
Dress code: Casual
Price guide: ££
Food: British fare (fish & chips, spotted dick)

The back terrace of this 17th century pub looks directly over the river close to Hammersmith Bridge, making it a favourite viewpoint for the Oxford and Cambridge Boat Race. Celebrities who have enjoyed a pint here include Graham Greene and Ernest Hemingway. William Morris lived next door and James Thomson, who wrote Rule Britannia, lived and died upstairs.

The Dove is hidden down a quiet, narrow alleyway so can be tricky to find. Follow the path upriver on the north bank from Hammersmith Bridge, cross the small park and take the alley on the far side that runs parallel with the river.

The bar on the right as you enter is the smallest in Britain at 1.27 x 2.39 metres (4'2" x 7'10" feet). But old wooden chairs, stools and benches, plus the requisite low ceiling, black wood panelling and open fire, do not make its traditional interior picturesque.

Be sure to try one of the four draught ales from the Fuller's brewery just down the road.

THE EALING PARK TAVERN
●●●●○

222 South Ealing Road, Ealing, London, W5 4RL, England

Tel: +44(0)20 8758 1879
Hours: Mon 5pm-11pm, Tue-Sat 11am-11pm, Sun noon-10:30pm

Type: Gastro pub
Alfresco: Large walled garden
Entry: Open door
Highlights: Food, real ale
Atmosphere: Relaxed
Clientele: All manner of locals
Dress code: Casual
Price guide: £££
Food: Tapas & Modern British

When this huge old Victorian boozer, then called the Penny Flyer, was built in 1885, the Arts and Crafts movement was in full swing, a style reflected in its oak panelled interior to this day. Much else has changed and the large, airy lounge now houses a bar topped with 26 metres of zinc, plus the conventional mix of old leather sofas and mismatched tables and chairs.

Gastrofication is more evident on the right side of the pub, which now houses two dining areas overlooked by a wide open kitchen. So well regarded is the modern British food that you're advised to book ahead. If you're only after a snack, then chalk boards in the bar area offer tapas.

Drinks match the high standard of the food with a bold, well-priced, forty-strong wine list that includes fifteen by the glass. There's also a good range of lager and five traditional ales accompanied by well considered tasting notes.

Happily it's still common to find a regular hunched over a pint of Guinness and a paper among the young professionals that flock here.

The Ealing Park Tavern

The Ealing Park Tavern

HAVELOCK TAVERN

● ● ● ◐ ○

57 Masbro Road (corner Irving Road),
Brook Green, London, W14 0LS, England

Tel: +44 (0)20 7603 5334,
www.thehavelocktavern.co.uk
Hours: Mon-Sat 11am-11pm,
Sun noon-10:30pm

Type:	Gastro pub
Alfresco:	Tables in front & at rear
Entry:	Open door
Highlights:	Food
Atmosphere:	Relaxed
Clientele:	30-something trendies & foodies
Dress code:	Casual
Price guide:	£££
Food:	Modern British gastro fare

The Havelock is a corner pub set in the
residential streets behind the Olympia
exhibition halls. It first opened in 1932 when
two shops, one a wine merchants, were
knocked together. It wasn't until 1996,
however, when The Havelock was converted
into one of West London's first gastro pubs,
that this place became a destination.

Foodies were shocked when a serious
fire on 31st August 2005 left it closed for
over ten months. Thankfully all is now back
to normal and great food is once again being
served in this relaxed, unpretentious pub.

The eclectic menu changes twice
every day with at least one starter and one
main course for vegetarians. Draught
offerings include three ales and the varied
wine list of a dozen reds and a dozen
whites is bolstered by the specially selected
red and white 'Wines of the Times'. These
are usually the best bet.

Be warned, neither bookings nor credit
cards are accepted and the place is
constantly packed with locals, so arrive early
and with cash to avoid disappointment.

Scarsdale

Scarsdale

SCARSDALE

●●●●○

23a Edwardes Square (corner Earls Walk), Kensington, London, W8 6HE, England

Tel: +44 (0)20 7937 1811
Hours: Mon-Sat noon-11pm,
Sun noon-10:30pm

Type:	Traditional / gastro pub
Alfresco:	Front patio with heaters
Entry:	Open door
Highlights:	Food, atmosphere
Atmosphere:	Warm, friendly local
Clientele:	Smart Kensington set
Dress code:	Casual but not shabby
Price guide:	£££
Food:	Good food served all day

The Scarsdale has a picture postcard Georgian façade with trailing ivy, hanging baskets and window boxes brimming with flowers, and sits facing the lush gardens of Edwardes Square, creating a wonderful village pub feel. This continues inside, where the atmosphere is warm and friendly, and locals natter over a meal or just a drink. The décor is rustic yet grand with etched windows, bare wooden tables, an olive green, Tudor-style moulded ceiling and musty orange walls.

Both the square and the pub were built in 1812 by Louis Changeur, a speculative French builder. These days this is a very well t'do area and regulars at the Scarsdale answer to names like Sebastian, Julian and Dominic. How many other pubs have chalk boards offering a champagne selection including Dom Perignon and walls lined with spent champagne bottles?

The open kitchen serves good, hearty, meat oriented meals while the international wine list is also a cut above the average and includes sixteen wines by the glass. There are four well kept traditional ales to choose from.

THE WINDSOR CASTLE

● ● ● ● ○

114 Campden Hill Road (corner Peel Street),
Kensington, London, W8 7AR, England

Tel: +44 (0)20 7243 9551,
www.windsor-castle-pub.co.uk
Hours: Mon-Sat 11am-11pm,
Sun noon-10:30pm

Type:	Traditional pub
Alfresco:	Rear walled garden
Entry:	Open door
Highlights:	Sausages & garden
Atmosphere:	Relaxed
Clientele:	Old school (public)
Dress code:	Casual but not scruffy
Price guide:	£££
Food:	Noted range of sausages & mash

The Windsor Castle was built around 1835
on the brow of a hill and in those times the
eponymous castle was visible from its
upper windows. Once a stopping off point
for farmers taking their livestock to market
at Hyde Park, today this is one of London's
poshest pubs. Its renowned sausage and
mash and well kept ales attract upmarket
locals, while its rear, ivy covered, walled
garden ensures its popularity in summer.

The left side of this olde-worldy pub
is divided into three by wooden panelling
that is said to have been salvaged from a
ship. It is rumoured that the bones of
Thomas Paine (author of 'The Rights Of
Man') are buried in the cellar. When he died
in 1809, the social reformer William
Cobbett had his bones shipped from
America to England. But Cobbett died
before he could entomb them in his
planned memorial and his son gave
Paine's skeleton to The Windsor Castle's
landlord to settle a drinking debt.

The Windsor Castle

The Windsor Castle

KNIGHTSBRIDGE & BELGRAVIA
(SW1–SW7)

THOUGHT THE BRITISH CLASS SYSTEM WAS DEAD? THINK AGAIN. AMID THE GORGEOUS STUCCO OF THESE OH-SO-POSH DISTRICTS NESTLE SOME WONDERFUL OLD PUBS, SOME STILL WITH THE SCREENS ONCE USED TO SHIELD THE SIPPING GENTRY FROM THE SUPPING HOI POLLOI.

The Anglesea Arms

THE AMERICAN BAR

● ● ● ○ ○

The Stafford Hotel, St James's Place, St James's, London SW1A 1NJ, England

Tel: +44 (0)20 4493 0111,
www.thestaffordhotel.co.uk
Hours: Mon-Sat 11am-11pm, Sun 11am-10.30pm

Type: Hotel/lounge bar
Alfresco: Tables in Blue Bell Yard
Entry: Via hotel lobby or Blue Bell Yard
Highlights: Service, old-school ambience
Atmosphere: Quiet gentleman's club
Clientele: Mature, American, regimental
Dress code: Gents required to wear jackets
Price guide: ££££
Food: Snacks to full meals

Blue Bell Yard is a quiet cobbled mews off busy St James's Street. At the end of this, past a line of 18th century stables, lies the back of The Stafford Hotel and the entrance to its American Bar. Once inside, the bustle of St James's is quickly forgotten. The walls of the small room are plastered with hundreds of autographed celebrity photographs while the ceiling is hung with a colourful collection of club ties, baseball caps, hard hats and model aeroplanes.

The bartenders in their green jackets look rather like Wimbledon umpires but competently deal with requests for any classic cocktail. There's a serious wine cellar below and a superb selection of whiskies and other spirits stashed around the tiny corner bar. An old hand pump dispenses Thwaites Bitter, an ale made by the Lancashire, family-controlled brewery that owns the Stafford.

This quiet, wonderfully old-fashioned bar is a favourite of American visitors and regimental types.

THE ANGLESEA ARMS

● ● ● ● ○

15 Selwood Terrace, South Kensington, London, SW7 3QG, England

Tel: +44 (0)20 7373 7960,
www.capitalpubcompany.com
Hours: Mon-Sat 11am-11pm, Sun noon-10:30pm

Type: Traditional pub
Alfresco: Front terrace with bench seats
Entry: Open door
Highlights: Food, real ale
Atmosphere: Relaxed, informal
Clientele: South Ken set
Dress code: Casual
Price guide: £££
Food: Finger snacks to full meals

This wonderfully traditional old pub hasn't changed that much since it was built in the late 1820s on the site of a market garden owned by the Mr Selwood who lent his name to the road on which it stands. Not long after, Charles Dickens moved into No.11 Selwood Terrace and later D.H. Lawrence resided at No.9.

Today the pub's neighbours are captains of industry and their trustafarian children so this local continues to enjoy patronage by a select crowd of regulars.

On summer's evenings the large front terrace with its bench tables is an obvious attraction. Inside, the Anglesea Arms is charming with a bare wooden floor, dark mahogany panelling and framed prints, padded leather benches, pews and spindle chairs. Some of the panelled partitions which divide the room still have panes of original etched glass. There's also a cosy dining room to the rear.

Good traditional pub fare is supplemented by more modern dishes such as pan fried haloumi with caper salad. Happily there are six changing cask ales to choose from and a fair wine list including a dozen by the glass.

AURA KITCHEN & BAR

● ● ● ● ○

48-49 St James's Street (corner of Piccadilly), London, SW1A 1JT, England

Tel: +44 (0)20 7499 9999,
www.the-aura.com
Hours: Mon-Fri noon-3am, Sat 7pm-3am
(non-members must leave after 11.30pm)

Type: Restaurant bar/nightclub
Alfresco: No
Entry: Members only after 11.30pm
Highlights: The energy
Atmosphere: DJ led party
Clientele: City boys, Essex girls and gorgeous models
Dress code: Glamorous
Price guide: £££££
Food: Oysters, pâté etc.

Hidden in a basement beneath Caviar House lies a restaurant and bar lined with deep plum leather banquettes and mirrors. Two chandeliers that previously adorned Claridge's ballroom hang from the ceiling, while murals compete for wall space with the films projected over the bar.

The concept behind Aura echoes that of Amsterdam's famous Supper Club - once diners have finished their dessert, the lights are dimmed, the music turned up and the restaurant transformed into a club. Even the tables here are lowered by hydraulics to a height befitting that of a club rather than a dining room.

If you're drinking at the bar early in the evening you're bound to feel like you're missing out as others dine at the long tables. However, the drinks are good and once the lights are dimmed and the non-members ushered out, the party kicks off. Expect meagrely clad girls and cash-rich City boys.

BLUE BAR

● ● ● ● ○

The Berkeley Hotel, Wilton Place,
Knightsbridge, London, SW1X 7RL, England

Tel: +44 (0)20 7201 1680,
www.the-berkeley.co.uk
Hours: Mon-Sat 4pm-1am, Sun 3pm-midnight

Type: Lounge/hotel bar
Alfresco: No
Entry: Subject to capacity, hotel guests have priority
Highlights: Bling factor
Atmosphere: Quietly pretentious
Clientele: Media, business & celebs of all ages
Dress code: Can be casual, must be expensive
Price guide: ££££
Food: Modern tapas - bite sized (but gorgeous)

Turn left as you enter the Berkeley Hotel lobby and you'll find yourself in the aptly named Blue Bar. Although it is tiny, with only 50 seats, no one could accuse it of being understated. Cherubs and floral woodcarvings drip from the ceiling and surround the fish-eye mirrors on the beach hut blue walls, while a white onyx bar and black crocodile print leather floor add a further touch of loucheness.

Among the exquisite décor highly skilled bartenders in white jackets serve some excellent classic cocktails and some of their own creations. Should the tasty nibbles provided with each drink not hit the spot, slightly more substantial 'modern tapas' are available.

This five star venue attracts five star money, so expect cosmetically challenged ladies of leisure perusing the impressive Champagne list (vintage wines can cost a grand a pop). There are also a good few young professionals who heard that Madge dropped by once.

CALMA LOUNGE & SHUMI BAR

● ● ● ◐ ○

23 St. James's Street, Piccadilly, London,
SW1A 1HA, England

Tel: +44 (0)20 7747 9380,
www.shumi-london.com
Hours: Mon-Fri noon-1am,
Sat 6.30pm-1am

Type: Lounge bar
Alfresco: No
Entry: Subject to capacity
Highlights: Cocktails
Atmosphere: Mellow
Clientele: Suited St James's boys & girls (25-45)
Dress code: Smart
Price guide: ££££
Food: Finger food. Restaurant upstairs.

Housed within the celebrated Economist building, the first 1960s building to be listed, is this bar and restaurant, perhaps best known among the London drinks fraternity as the former home of Che, a venue whose bar team were at the front of the capital's cocktail culture for years.

Sadly good things don't last for ever and in the summer of 2003 the site was taken over by Steamroller Restaurants, which is owned by Geoffrey Moore (son of Roger Moore) and Jamie Barber, and also owns Hush. You'd think James Bond's involvement in a cocktail bar would ensure success, but much of Shumi's street-level bar was re-launched in September 2004 as Calma Lounge.

Things look good today. The cocktails, split between classic and contemporary, are well made. The bar snacks are tasty (especially the deep fried risotto balls, or arancini). And the well-to-do young things of St James's appear to be flocking here once more.

Blue Bar

The Ebury

THE EBURY

● ● ● ● ○

11 Pimlico Road, Pimlico, London, SW1W 8NA, England

Tel: +44 (0)20 7730 6784,
www.theebury.co.uk
Hours: Mon-Sat noon-11pm,
Sun noon-10:30pm

Type:	Gastro pub
Alfresco:	No
Entry:	Subject to capacity
Highlights:	Food
Atmosphere:	Relaxed (apart from music)
Clientele:	Office types, upmarket locals
Dress code:	Office wear to casual
Price guide:	££££
Food:	Impressive full menu

As pub names go, The Ebury sounds plummy – and indeed it's hardly your average Dog & Duck. Not only the upmarket location but the serious food offering sets it apart.

The interior is dominated by brown and dark wood. Frisbee-style hanging lights, large rectangular windows with curved corners, and a wall decorated in flames of the style used on seventies custom cars create a seventies feel. Tables and very comfy brown leather chairs for diners dominate the space. Drinkers are relegated to small, loungy areas on either side of the bar: the area under the sweeping, restored oak staircase is the cosiest.

Drinkswise, there's no real ale on offer and an unexciting range of draught lagers. However, there's a well-executed cocktail list and a wine list sensibly arranged by flavour profile and offering one or two wines by the glass under each category.

The music is often heavy, beat-driven and completely inappropriate.

The Ebury

The Grenadier

THE FIFTH FLOOR BAR

● ● ● ● ○

5th Floor, Harvey Nichols, 109-125
Knightsbridge, London, SW1X 7RJ, England

Tel: +44 (0)20 7201 8771,
www.harveynichols.com
Hours: Mon-Sat 11am-11pm,
Sun noon-6pm

Type: Lounge/restaurant bar
Alfresco: No
Entry: Express lift from Sloane or Seville Sts
Highlights: People watching
Atmosphere: Buzzy
Clientele: Shoppers, tourists, businessmen
Dress code: Couture casual/business suits
Price guide: ££££
Food: Caviar, canapés & snacks

The Fifth Floor Bar lies atop the preferred
department store of Sloanes and Chelsea
girls but has its own entrance by express
lift from Sloane or Seville Street. By day it
is a whitewashed haven for moneyed and
style conscious shoppers who pop in for
a respite and sip cocktails alongside
business folk engaged in informal
meetings. By night things hot up as the
"regulars" arrive, for this is a pick-up joint
of some repute.

The interior adheres to a clinical style.
Windows overlooking Knightsbridge relieve
the monotony of two of the sterile white
walls, while the third has large plasma
screens showing bar-friendly TV on either
side of the entrance to the space-age
restaurant next door.

I'm a sucker for island bars and Fifth
Floor's white, marble topped, horseshoe
bar sits centre stage. Here the sophisticated
bar staff and interesting clientele provide plenty
of theatre. Visit in the afternoon and try one
of the imaginative cocktails or splash out
on the impressive Champagne list.

THE GRENADIER PUB

● ● ● ○ ○

Wilton Row (off Wilton Crescent),
Knightsbridge, London, SW1 7NR, England

Tel: +44 (0)20 7235 3074
Hours: Mon-Sat noon-11pm, Sun noon-
10:30pm

Type: Traditional pub
Alfresco: One bench outside
Entry: Open door
Highlights: Beers, Bloody Mary & heritage
Atmosphere: Relaxed
Clientele: Local residents & businessmen
Dress code: None but expect suits
Price guide: £££
Food: Chips, nachos, sausage & mash

The Grenadier is hidden away at the end of
an exclusive mews. Unsurprisingly given its
name and the red sentry box outside, the
pub has its military history: it was originally a
mess for the Duke of Wellington's officers.
The Iron Duke came here for a last drink
before the battle of Waterloo in 1815 and,
although the building became a pub three
years later, his portrait still stands above the
fireplace and a stone from his mounting block
remains in the yard. Prints of Guardsmen and
other military memorabilia adorn the walls,
while the ceiling is covered with money sent
by customers from around the world.

Well kept real ale is still served across the
original pewter-topped counter and
competition-winning Bloody Marys are made
to a secret recipe passed from licensee to
licensee. This delightful little pub even has its
own ghost - an officer who was caught
cheating at cards and died after being flogged,
and comes to pay his respects in September.
The Grenadier is also a haunt for Madonna
who once held a post-gig party here.

LIBRARY BAR

● ● ● ● ○

Lanesborough Hotel, Hyde Park Corner,
Mayfair, London, SW1X 7TA, England

Tel: +44 (0)20 7259 5599,
www.lanesborough.com
Hours: 11am-11pm daily (residents only
after 11pm)

Type: Lounge/hotel bar
Alfresco: No
Entry: Subject to capacity
Highlights: Cocktails, wines, spirits
Atmosphere: Refined
Clientele: Rich, famous and trying to be
Dress code: Smart (jacket not required)
Price guide: £££££
Food: Good food served all hours

This intimate and atmospheric bar,
panelled in mahogany in the style of an old
library, is a classic hotel bar. Bizarrely,
though, the room might once have been
an operating theatre. For the building that's
now the Lanesborough Hotel dates back
to 1719 and was formerly St George's
Hospital. (The hotel is named after a
country house that once stood on the site.)

Although the hotel only opened in
1991, the bar fits neatly into the tradition
of London's crusty private clubs, although
some young and beautiful people mingle
with the fat old bankers. This refined
clientele soak up the atmosphere and sip
Martinis from frozen cut crystal
glasses while the pianist plays in the
corner. Skilled bartenders wear suits to
rival those of the guests en route to or from
black-tie dinners.

MANDARIN BAR
● ● ● ◐ ○

Mandarin Oriental Hotel, 66 Knightsbridge,
Knightsbridge, SW1X 7LA, England

Tel: +44 (0)20 7235 2000,
www.mandarinoriental.com
Hours: Daily 11am-2am

Type:	Lounge bar
Alfresco:	No
Entry:	No obvious door policy
Highlights:	Glassware
Atmosphere:	Refined & pretentious
Clientele:	Guests, City types & the wealthy
Dress code:	Business suits & Prada darlings
Price guide:	££££
Food:	Oriental platters

The Mandarin Oriental hotel was built in
1889 but was only recently restored to its
former grandeur. With this refurbishment
came the opulent Mandarin Bar which lies
at the back left side of the grand marble-
lined lobby.

This is, however, no ordinary bar. All
the bottles are stored behind frosted glass
so when you order a drink your bartender
disappears into a futuristic pharmacy,
reappearing minutes later with your pre-
scription in hand – usually well mixed and
beautifully presented. It's strange being at
a bar that hasn't got a parade of bottles to
tempt your fancy and some might miss the
theatre of watching a bartender mix a drink.

Occasional jazz duos entertain
wealthy hotel guests who order a drink at this
bar by young successful city types and
gorgeous socialites. The clientele's
decorum and flaunting tends to be a demure,
refined atmosphere regardless of the
efforts of the musicians.

MINT LEAF
● ● ● ● ○

Suffolk Place (off Haymarket), Trafalgar
Square, London, SW1Y 4HX, England

Tel: +44 (0)20 7930 9020,
www.mintleafrestaurant.com
Hours: Mon-Fri noon-3pm & 5.30pm-
11pm, Sat 5.30pm-11pm

Type:	Lounge/restaurant bar
Alfresco:	No
Entry:	Subject to management and capacity
Highlights:	Cocktails, bar snacks
Atmosphere:	Chilled
Clientele:	Young & not so young professionals
Dress code:	Smart
Price guide:	££££
Food:	Modern Indian fusion

Mint Leaf is tucked away in the basement
of an apartment block on the corner of
Haymarket. Its location and minimal
signage make it easy to miss but once
down the stairway and into the slick
modern space you'll know you've arrived.
Those familiar with Hakkasan will notice a
similarity in the way the bar is separated
from the restaurant by dark wooden slatted
screens. Subdued lighting, leather
banquettes, dark walnut and slate
combine to give a warm, informal feel.

While the restaurant, which serves
modern Indian food, has received mixed
reviews, the bar is highly regarded and
attracts many drinks industry types. Many
of the drinks reflect the restaurant's theme
and mint, chilli and spices are often used.

Depending on when you visit you're
likely to find a suited business crowd mixed
with younger fashionistas but I've yet to
encounter this huge space truly busy.

Mint Leaf

The Red Lion

The Red Lion

THE RED LION

●●●◐○

2 Duke of York Street (btwn Jermyn St & St. James's Sq), St. James's, London, SW1Y 6JP, England

Tel: +44 (0)20 7321 0782
Hours: Mon-Sat 11:30am-11pm (closed Sun & bank holidays)

Type: Traditional pub
Alfresco: Stand on pavement
Entry: Open door
Highlights: Beautiful interior
Atmosphere: Relaxed
Clientele: Upscale office crowd
Dress code: Suits - casual
Price guide: £££
Food: Some food available lunchtimes

Just around the corner from the smart gentlemen's outfitters of Jermyn Street lies this equally upmarket and old school little pub. Built in 1821 on the site of a previous pub, its 300 square feet of floor space were originally subdivided into several small bars. However, those Victorians were a canny lot and they covered the Red Lion's walls with ornate cut and bevelled glass mirrors to make it appear much larger. They also embellished this little gin palace with etched glass and ornate carved woodwork, all wrapped around an island bar counter.

As with the shops around the corner, the regulars here tend to be a certain class and predominantly male. They enjoy a choice of between two and five ales with champagne also popular, as is the wine of the month. In summer they spill out onto the pavement.

The steep spiral staircase which leads to the basement toilets is a test of your sobriety.

ROCKWELL BAR

●●●◐○

Trafalgar Hotel, 2 Spring Gardens, Trafalgar
Square, London, SW1A 2TS, England

Tel: +44 (0)20 7870 2900,
www.thetrafalgar.hilton.com
Hours: Mon-Sat 9am-1am,
Sun 9am-10.30pm

Type:	Lounge bar
Alfresco:	No
Entry:	Fairly relaxed door policy
Highlights:	Cocktails
Atmosphere:	Relaxed
Clientele:	Hotel guests, funksters & after workers
Dress code:	Jeans to business suits
Price guide:	££££
Food:	Fish and chips to pastrami and buffalo mozzarella

Rockwell Bar

Just off Trafalgar Square lies the Hilton's
Trafalgar hotel, the home of this airy, modern
lobby bar. Polished concrete pillars rise to
the high ceilings from a wooden floor
scattered with sofas and low tables.

This bar is big on Bourbon. For most
spirit categories, there is only one choice of
brand (although all are super premium).
There are, however, over eighty American
whiskeys to choose from. Cocktail wise, the
list majors on Bourbon but other spirits are
also well represented.

Considering Rockwell operates within
the corporate limitations of a Hilton hotel lobby,
it is a stylish bar. Sadly, it is not consistently
busy and once the after work drinkers have
left can lack atmosphere and soul. In clement
weather a few special guests are invited up to
the roof terrace bar to enjoy the views.

Recent refurbishment and expansion
has incorporated a new staircase to
encourage more traffic to the restaurant
below. However, the basement remains
somewhat austere so I'd only use these
stairs as a new route to the toilets.

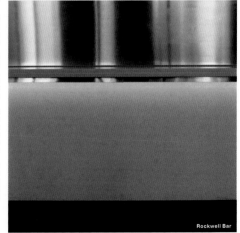

Rockwell Bar

DEMON MARTINI
BY SALVATORE CALABRESE

AVAILABLE @ SALVATORE

Glass: Martini
Garnish: Small red chilli & half sugar rim
Method: MUDDLE pomegranate flesh in base of
shaker. Add other ingredients, SHAKE with ice and
fine strain into glass.
50ml Beefeater gin
20ml Kina Lillet
¼ Fresh pomegranate (flesh only)
1 barspoon White castor sugar
2 thin slices Fresh chilli

SALVATORE
● ● ● ● ○

Ground Floor, Fifty, 50 St James' Street, London, SW1A 1JT, England

Tel: +44 (0)20 7491 4678,
www.fiftylondon.com
Hours: Daily midday-late

Type: Members' lounge / casino bar
Alfresco: No
Entry: Strictly members & guests
Highlights: Cognacs, cocktails
Atmosphere: Calm, relaxed
Clientele: Wealthy players
Dress code: Jacket preferred for gents
Price guide: ££££
Food: Prawn satay, tuna spring roll, club sandwich etc.

This Grade II listed building in the heart of St James's has been home to London's most opulent casino since 1827. In 2004, London Clubs International and the entrepreneur Robert Earl set about an ambitious refurbishment, which has incorporated several new upscale bars and restaurants.

Salvatore's, to the right of the lobby on the ground floor, is named after and run by the Inspector Clouseau lookalike and renowned former manager of the Library Bar at the Lanesborough, Salvatore Calabrese. He now holds court from the 25 ft long bar in this chocolate box lounge, which is strewn with comfy chairs and low tables. Fifty of Salvatore's favourite cocktails are listed, ranging from classics to his more recent creations. There's also an impressive Cognac and Armagnac collection with vintages dating back to 1788. (A double will set you back a cool £1,500.)

Members in search of more excitement can head down to 'Fifty Below', the impressive basement club space with its illuminated catwalk.

SWAG & TAILS
● ● ● ● ○

10-11 Fairholt Street, Knightsbridge Village, London, SW7 1EG, England

Tel: +44 (0)20 7584 6926,
www.swagandtails.com
Hours: Mon-Sat 11am-11pm,
Sun noon-10:30pm

Type: Gastro pub
Alfresco: No
Entry: Open door
Highlights: Food & ambience
Atmosphere: Calming
Clientele: Wealthy locals & businessmen
Dress code: Suits to upscale casual
Price guide: £££
Food: Seasonally changing Mediterranean menu

Minutes away from Harrods but hidden in the la-di-da and tranquil back streets of Knightsbridge is this upmarket little neighbourhood gastro pub. Set in the middle of a terrace, it's as quaint as you like with hanging baskets and window boxes aplenty. The interior is surprisingly bright and airy. Stripped pine floors, panelling and tables make a pleasant change from the dark and dreary woods common to most pubs of its era. Behind the main bar with its open fire lies a small dining area and conservatory. The blond wood and excellent food combine to create a country kitchen feel.

A team of smartly presented and friendly barstaff provide superlative service and recommendations. Both the food menus and the wine list, which boasts 11 bins by the glass, are as extensive as they are excellent. And, lest we forget this is actually a pub, there's Bombardier and Adnam's Best among the draught beers.

TOWNHOUSE
● ● ● ● ○

31 Beauchamp Place, Knightsbridge, London, SW3 1NU, England

Tel: +44 (0)20 7589 5080,
www.lab-townhouse.com
Hours: Mon-Thu 4pm-midnight, Fri noon-midnight, Sat noon-midnight, Sun 4pm-11.30pm

Type: Lounge bar
Alfresco: No
Entry: Subject to appearance & capacity
Highlights: Cocktails
Atmosphere: Posh party
Clientele: Wealthy Knightsbridge young
Dress code: Smart designer casual
Price guide: ££££
Food: Platters & tapas through to burgers

Formerly a vaguely Moroccan styled bar called Min's, this ivy-covered Georgian townhouse in Knightsbridge is now owned by the team from Soho's Lab bar. They've poshed their act up somewhat to suit the locality but naturally there's an extensive cocktail list and a DJ booth.

Townhouse is set over three floors. Dark hardwood flooring, refined décor and tall leather banquettes appear throughout. The largest space is at street level and dominated by a seven metre, lava topped bar with front panels which gradually change colour. Downstairs is an intimate area designed for private parties, while upstairs is a second bar and a very cosy lounge.

Townhouse's cocktail list is one of the most impressive in Britain, but Champagne remains the most popular choice for the Sloanes and It-girls who frequent the bar.

THE WELLINGTON CLUB
● ● ● ● ○

116a Knightsbridge, Knightsbridge,
London, SW1X 7PL, England

Tel: +44 (0)20 7823 8211
Hours: Mon-Sat 6pm-1am

Type:	Members restaurant/lounge bar/club
Alfresco:	No
Entry:	Members & guests only
Highlights:	The relaxed lounge
Atmosphere:	Lounge upstairs/club downstairs
Clientele:	Celebrities, moneyed & beautiful
Dress code:	Catwalk/casual glam
Price guide:	££££
Food:	Lamb burger, spring rolls etc

This members-only lounge bar and club is owned by Jake Panayiotou, who previously ran the legendary Browns nightclub. Like Browns when Panayiotou owned it, the Wellington attracts its fair share of celebrities, models and modelisers.

The space is set over two floors. Early in the evening the street level lounge functions as a fairly formal restaurant. The panelled walls and leather armchairs give it the feel of a gentleman's club. But as the evening progresses and the party kicks off in the club below the lounge transforms into a great place to chill and escape from the throng downstairs. The bar dishes out gallons of Champagne alongside some great cocktails.

The split-level basement has a warm, decadent feel, with cappuccino coloured walls, dark brown sofas and beanbags, plus a state of the art sound system and a 50" plasma screen. It is a clubby space, designed for seeing, being seen and dancing. The drinks selection downstairs is limited but the bubbly keeps the punters happy.

ZANDER
● ● ● ● ○

Bank Restaurant, 45 Buckingham Gate (opp.
Vandon St), Westminster, London, SW1E 6BS

Tel: +44 (0)20 7379 9797,
www.bankrestaurants.com
Hours: Mon-Tue 11am-11pm, Wed-Fri
11am-1am, Sat 5pm-1am

Type:	Lounge/restaurant bar
Alfresco:	No
Entry:	Relaxed door policy
Highlights:	Cocktails
Atmosphere:	Chilled (party at weekends)
Clientele:	Business, young trendies
Dress code:	Smart casual / suits
Price guide:	££££
Food:	Various mixed plates

Beyond Zander's fairly bland exterior is a contemporary interior which is long and narrow - very long. In fact the bar appears to go on for ever and is one of a few claiming to be the longest in Britain. Anyway it's long enough to house a good few bar stools and is the best place from which to enjoy Zander. Unless that is, you're on a romantic rendezvous, in which case you should head for one of the intimate alcoves. However, be warned that a DJ on Fridays and Saturdays can make the atmosphere more clubby than romantic.

This destination venue (who goes drinking in Westminster?) boasts a slick and well-run bar, with a friendly and personal approach to service. Cocktails from the list of classics and Zander originals are usually faultless and many have the option of a 'premium' or 'super premium' spirit base. As in the rear restaurant, the bar food is good, although pricey.

ZUMA RESTAURANT
● ● ● ● ○

5 Raphael Street, Knightsbridge, London,
SW7 1DL, England

Tel: +44 (0)20 7584 1010,
www.zumarestaurant.com
Hours: Mon-Sat noon-11pm,
Sun noon-10:30pm

Type:	Restaurant bar
Alfresco:	No
Entry:	Dress well or book a table
Highlights:	Eye candy, food, cocktails
Atmosphere:	Lively, flirtatious
Clientele:	Rich & pretty or just pretty rich
Dress code:	Designer glamour
Price guide:	££££
Food:	Sushi & other oriental nibbles

This modern pan-Asian restaurant and bar attracts more rich and pretty people in one night than were assembled in a whole series of Dallas. Zuma occupies the former site of the Chicago Rib Shack and it's not just the clientele that has changed. 108 tonnes of Italian granite was specially quarried and imported to add a cave-like feel to the clean designer interior (the largest piece forms one corner of the bar and required special lifting gear).

The front area of the large open-plan restaurant houses the island bar and surrounding lounge. Here you'll find a range of sakes and sake based cocktails along with other imaginative, contemporary and well-executed classic drinks. Sushi and other bar snacks such as the spicy beef are also superb.

This is fashionable Knightsbridge so expect some very glamorous looking It-girls, well-heeled business types and a few visiting stars of stage and screen. Zuma is one of London's places to see and be seen.

Zuma Restaurant

Trailer Happiness

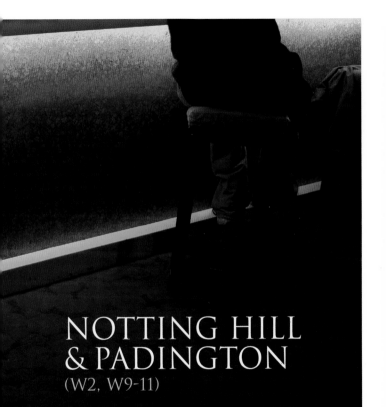

NOTTING HILL & PADINGTON
(W2, W9-11)

NOTTING HILL HAS MOVED UPMARKET SINCE THE 60S, BUT STILL RETAINS A
SLAB OF THAT BOHEMIAN CHARM WHICH ENTICED THE TRUSTAFARIANS IN
THE FIRST PLACE. SOME OF THE COCKTAIL BARS HERE ARE MUST-VISITS
FOR ANY DISCERNING DRINKER.

BEACH BLANKET BABYLON
● ● ● ○ ○

45 Ledbury Road, Notting Hill, London,
W11 2AA, England

Tel: +44 (0)20 7229 2907,
www.beachblanket.co.uk
Hours: Mon-Sun 10am-11pm

Type:	Restaurant bar
Alfresco:	Small front terrace
Entry:	Subject to management and capacity
Highlights:	Decor
Atmosphere:	Relaxed
Clientele:	Moneyed local 30-somethings
Dress code:	Designer casual
Price guide:	£££
Food:	Full Mediterranean led menu

BBB, as it's affectionately known, opened back in 1990 and is an established part of the Notting Hill bar scene. Set in an old Georgian house, it has undergone extensive renovation in recent years but retains its famously eclectic decor. Elements of Byzantine, Baroque and Gaudi blend with topiary, while out back the restaurant's interconnecting rooms continue the Baroque theme in an almost monastic setting.

The Mediterranean cuisine is as eclectic as the decor and of a reasonable standard. Sadly on our visits the cocktails have proven disappointing. BBB still attracts local, moneyed 30-somethings and the spectacular interior remains an experience. However, there are now better places nearby to imbibe cocktails.

COBDEN CLUB
● ● ● ● ○

170 Kensal Road, Notting Hill, London,
W10 5BN, England

Tel: +44 (0)20 8960 4222,
www.cobdenclub.co.uk
Hours: Mon-Sat 6pm-1:30am

Type:	Members' club
Alfresco:	No
Entry:	Members & guests only
Highlights:	Cocktails, wines, food, atmosphere
Atmosphere:	Chilled to party
Clientele:	Record & film industry types
Dress code:	Designer casual
Price guide:	££££
Food:	Full fusion menu or snacks

This exclusive den occupies three floors of the old Cobden Working Men's Club, a wonderful, Grade II listed building. The ground floor, however, is only used for functions so head up the stairs to the cosy restaurant and lounge. With the inviting look and feel of a posh pub, and oodles of comfy sofas and chairs, this is the place to relax and chat. In the party space above, a magnificent Victorian hall with a stage at one end and a thirty foot bar at the other, well-known DJs entertain a mixture of public school escapees and record industry operators.

The two bars serve some of the best cocktails in London, while the food comes in homely proportions and should be consumed with a bottle from the well conceived wine list. Entry is tricky if you're not a member. But a mere £250 per year plus £100 joining fee could assure you a place at the heart of one of London's best kept secrets.

THE COW
● ● ● ● ○

89 Westbourne Park Road (opp. Westbourne
Pk Villas), Notting Hill, London, W2 5QH

Tel: +44 (0)20 7221 5400
Hours: Mon-Sat noon-11pm,
Sun noon-10:30pm

Type:	Gastro pub
Alfresco:	Few seats at front
Entry:	Open door (subject to space)
Highlights:	Food
Atmosphere:	Relaxed
Clientele:	Local moneyed set
Dress code:	Designer casual
Price guide:	£££
Food:	Fresh seafood to sausage & mash

This is one of the most famous pubs in London – famous for being hip, rather than for some vague historical reference. In 1998 Tom Conran (son of Sir Terence) took over what was then a small boozer on its last legs and transformed it. It's still small and the design is delightfully un-Conranesque with light mustard walls, a red linoleum floor and rippled glass. While the décor is not sophisticated, the clientele is. They're drawn by the easy atmosphere and some seriously good food, particularly the seafood and oysters. The restaurant upstairs is equally relaxed and serves equally quality dishes.

This tiny pub is simply great, attracting an older and more considered audience than the Westbourne opposite. Its tiny proportions lead to much pavement drinking, particularly in the summer months.

Cobden Club

CRAZY HOMIES
●●●●○

127 Westbourne Park Road, Notting Hill, London, W2 5QL, England

Tel: +44 (0)20 7727 6771,
www.crazyhomieslondon.co.uk
Hours Mon-Sat 8am-11pm, Sun 9am-10pm

Type: Mexican restaurant & bar
Alfresco: No
Entry: Subject to capacity
Highlights: Food
Atmosphere: Better downstairs
Clientele: Attractive Notting Hillbillies
Dress code: Casual but stylish
Price guide: £££
Food: Authentic Mexican

Once a West Indian shebeen frequented by Christine Keeler and Stephen Ward of Profumo Affair fame, this is now a Mexican bar and restaurant owned by Tom Conran. The bold décor, with lipstick red banquette seats and bar stools, makes the tiny ground floor space feel rather like the inside of a sweet jar. There is a second, larger bar in the basement, which is more atmospheric than the bright space above thanks to its low ceiling.

The food is inspired by Mexican taquerias and superb tacos, tostadas, burros and enchiladas are served on plastic trays, adding to their authenticity. Drinks arrive in chunky tumblers and follow the Mexican theme. Margaritas include the wonderfully named 'Sinful Cynthia's Cadillac Margarita', which is served with a Grand Marnier float, while the good range of premium tequilas can be chased with a spicy sangrita. Two wines are offered, a Petite Syrah and a Chardonnay, both from Baja California, Mexico.

ECLIPSE
●●●○○

186 Kensington Park Road, Notting Hill, London, W11 2ES, England

Tel: +44 (0)20 7792 2063,
www.bareclipse.com
Hours: Mon-Fri 5pm-late,
Sat-Sun 4pm-late

Type: Lounge bar
Alfresco: Few pavement seats
Entry: Subject to capacity
Highlights: Atmosphere
Atmosphere: Often DJ driven party
Clientele: Notting Hill style set
Dress code: Stylishly relaxed
Price guide: £££
Food: Mediterranean/Moroccan

This Notting Hill outpost of the Eclipse bar chain lies only a stone's throw from Portobello Market. Its diminutive proportions are emphasized by the red brick walls, which, combined with the blazing log fire, make Eclipse a snug winter drinking hole. It is also a favourite with locals in summertime, as the front opens out and allows the atmosphere, along with the clientele, to spill out onto the pavement.

Thursdays and Saturdays see this laid-back lounge turn more clubby as DJs entertain a younger, up for it, party crowd. But cocktails are the mainstay here, whatever the night. There's an extensive list, shared with the other bars in the chain, and the house style leans towards fruity concoctions. In common with most Eclipse branches the most popular drink here is the Watermelon Martini.

ELECTRIC HOUSE
●●●●○

191 Portobello Road, Notting Hill, London, W11 2ED, England

Tel: +44 (0)20 7908 9696,
www.electrichouse.com

Type: Private members' lounge bar/restaurant
Alfresco: No
Entry: Members & guests only
Highlights: Exclusive retreat feel
Atmosphere: Relaxed, laid back
Clientele: Celebs & moneyed media
Dress code: Stylish, designer casual
Price guide: ££££
Food: Full meals to snacks

Between the Electric Cinema and the Electric Brasserie hides the entrance to this Notting Hill sibling of Soho House. It is also owned by Nick Jones and also a private members' club.

A staircase wrapped around a lift shaft leads to the main members' bar and restaurant. This long, loft style room with its pitched ceiling and roof lights houses a lounge bar at the front and a dining room and open kitchen at the rear. The look is seventies, with white-washed walls, chunky pale teak tables and industrial style light fittings.

The stairs continue past the glass backed projection room of the cinema and The Study, a private dining or meeting room, to The Playroom. This has its own corner bar, plasma screen and door to a small roof terrace of wooden decking.

This haven attracts celebrities and moneyed media types who enjoy well made cocktails, well selected wines and modern British comfort food.

GRAZE RESTAURANT & BAR
●●●○○

215 Sutherland Avenue, Maida Vale,
London, W9 1RU, England

Tel: +44 (0)20 7266 3131,
www.graze.co.uk
Hours: Tue-Sat 6pm-1am

Type: Lounge/restaurant bar
Alfresco: No
Entry: Via electronic sliding door
Highlights: Ambience, cocktails, service
Atmosphere: Relaxed
Clientele: Local hipsters
Dress code: Designer casual
Price guide: £££
Food: Spring rolls, chorizo, beef skewers etc.

Just down the road from Philippe Starck's
superstar the first floor of this sixties building. Formerly
the Otto Dining Room, it opened as Graze
in March this year.

While Otto had a bar in the restaurant
and a lounge with no bar, Graze has righted
this anomaly. A long bar lined with stools
now overlooks the lounge and swanky
booth seating is arranged along the
opposite wall in the time-honoured diner
style. Black leather modern chaise longues
fill the middle of the room, while an additional
seating area hides behind Missoni drapes.
In short, this is a slick looking room with
plenty of tempting spaces, although the DJs
in the glass booth appear unwilling to let you
get too comfortable.

The drinks selection is adequate.
Cocktails are proficiently made, and there
are six wines by the glass plus a couple of
beers. It is a little surprising to find this kind
of upscale lounge in Maida Vale, so let's hope
the locals discover it in greater numbers.

THE LADBROKE ARMS
●●●●○

58 Ladbroke Road (corner Wilby Mews),
Notting Hill, London, W11 3NW, England

Tel: +44 (0)20 7727 6648,
www.capitalpubcompany.com
Hours: Mon-Fri 11am-3pm & 5:30pm-
11pm, Sat 11am-11pm, Sun noon-10:30pm

Type: Gastro pub
Alfresco: Front terrace
Entry: Open door
Highlights: Cask ales, food, atmosphere
Atmosphere: Wonderfully relaxed
Clientele: Locals & upmarket 30-somethings
Dress code: Casual
Price guide: £££
Food: Eclectic gastro grub

Sat among the plants and hanging baskets
on the front terrace of this pretty pub, it's
easy to imagine you're in a quaint country
village, not opposite a police station in
downtown Notting Hill. The Ladbroke Arms
rests on a back street away from the noise
and traffic, and looks for all the world like
a little cottage pub.

The look continues inside with cream
panelled walls and a plush dark green
carpet. Tables, for both drinkers and
diners, cram every last crevice but you'll
find the Hillbilly regulars and staff a friendly
bunch so sharing with new friends only
adds to the appeal. The place stretches
back and there are many hidden alcoves
so venture beyond the small front bar in
search of a space on one of the comfy
banquette seats.

Expect as many as four well-kept real
ales and a good wine list, including eight
by the glass. However, it's the daily
changing food menu which really excels.

LONSDALE
●●●●○

44-48 Lonsdale Road, Notting Hill, London,
W11 2DE, England

Tel: +44 (0)20 7727 4080
Hours: Mon-Fri 6pm-midnight, Sat noon-
midnight, Sun noon-11pm

Type: Lounge bar
Alfresco: No
Entry: Subject to space & management
Highlights: Cocktails, atmosphere & eye candy
Atmosphere: Chilled
Clientele: Gorgeous, affluent locals & celebs
Dress code: Casual but not cheap
Price guide: ££££
Food: Tapas dishes

Originally a Truman's pub and more
recently Jac's Bar this place, situated on
a residential street in deepest Notting Hill,
was a pretty ordinary local bar. But in 2002
brothers Charles and Adam Breeden took
the place over and opened Lonsdale. It's
been widely regarded as one of London's
best bars ever since.

It's not just the cocktails that have a
wow factor. The interior, inspired by Lenny
Kravitz's Miami residence, is also worthy
of description. Hemispherical bubbles line
the walls - bronze in the downstairs bar
and chromed spun aluminium upstairs in
'Genievere', a space named in deference
to the Breedens' mother.

The sartorially elegant Henry Besant
keeps an eye on both floors and on the
beautiful and stylish Notting Hill locals who
flock here. Lonsdale is hard to fault – it's
full of beautiful people, serving balanced,
imaginative cocktails while nibbling on tasty
bar snacks, all served by skilled,
attentive staff.

CORPSE REVIVER NO. 2
BY JULIUS ELLIOTT

AVAILABLE @ LONSDALE

Glass: Marie Antoinette Coupette
Method: SHAKE all ingredients with ice and fine
strain into chilled glass.
22ml Beefeater gin
25ml Lillet blanc
22ml Freshly squeezed lemon juice
22ml Cointreau
1 dash Absinthe

BEEFEATER TRICOLORE
BY AGO PERRONE

AVAILABLE @ MONTGOMERY PLACE

Glass: Marie Antoinette Coupette
Garnish: Maraschino cherry & lime zest
Method: SHAKE all ingredients with ice and fine
strain into chilled glass.
40ml Beefeater gin
20ml Freshly squeezed lemon juice
15ml Tio Pepe sherry
10ml Pallini limoncello
1 barspoon Vanilla sugar

MONTGOMERY PLACE

● ● ● ● ○

31 Kensington Park Road, Notting Hill, London, W11 2EU, England

Tel: +44 (0)20 7792 3921,
www.montgomeryplace.co.uk
Hours: Mon-Fri 5pm-midnight, Sat 1pm-midnight, Sun 1pm-11pm

Type: Cocktail lounge	
Alfresco: No	
Entry: Subject to space	
Highlights: Classic cocktails & food	
Atmosphere: Chilled by jazz	
Clientele: Discerning cocktail lovers	
Dress code: Not shabby	
Price guide: ££££	
Food: Great tapas style dishes	

If your favourite cocktail has recently changed from a Caipirinha to a Mojito, this bar is probably wasted on you. These are indeed fine drinks, but this serious cocktail bar offers a list of previously forgotten Prohibition classics just waiting to be rediscovered. These short, very adult cocktails are served with the reverence they deserve.

Fitted out in a refined forties style, Montgomery Place is tiny. The long, narrow space leads past a small bar lined with stools to a cosy space with comfortable banquette seating and wallpaper printed with vintage string instruments. A group of thirty pretty much fills the place.

Amazingly for such a tiny venue, there is a full kitchen and a chef labours in the basement to produce a range of tasty, tapas style dishes that are all beautifully presented.

Sheer economics dictates that food and drink of this standard, served in such tasteful and intimate surroundings, only come at a price. Bring someone special and treat your taste buds.

NEGOZIO CLASSICA

● ● ● ● ○

283 Westbourne Grove (corner Portobello Rd), Notting Hill, London, W11 2QA, England

Tel: +44 (0)20 7034 0005,
www.negozioclassica.co.uk
Hours: Mon-Fri 11am-10pm, Sat 9am-10pm, Sun 11am-9pm

Type: Wine bar/liquor store	
Alfresco: Few pavement tables	
Entry: Open door	
Highlights: Wine & food	
Atmosphere: Relaxed	
Clientele: Oenophiles	
Dress code: Casual	
Price guide: £££	
Food: Italian specialities	

Negozio Classica is the flagship showroom for an Italian specialist food and wine distributor. It combines the best of an Italian delicatessen, wine bar and wine merchants, and reflects the company's skill in sourcing superb products from artisanal producers. There's a unique beer from Teo Musso, whiskies, rums, cognacs, ports, some superb grappas and a huge range of Italian wines, most available by the glass, the bottle, and, if you find you like them enough, the case.

The delicatessen offers cheeses, meats, cured hams, olive oils, balsamic vinegars and handmade Gragnano pasta. You can either buy and prepare your meal at home or enjoy a prepared meal here with a glass of wine.

Watch the world go by from one of the pavement tables or sit inside at one of the blond wood tables or the stainless steel bar. Best of all retreat to an armchair in the reading room out back.

THE PRINCE ALFRED

● ● ● ● ○

5A Formosa Street (@ Castellain Rd), Maida Vale, W9 1EE, England

Tel: +44 (0)20 7286 3287
Hours: Mon-Sat 11am-11pm, Sun noon-10:30pm

Type: Traditional / gastro pub	
Alfresco: Pavement tables / chairs	
Entry: Open door	
Highlights: Food	
Atmosphere: Buzzy	
Clientele: Notting Hillbillies	
Dress code: Casual	
Price guide: £££	
Food: Excellent meals in Formosa Dining Room	

Built in 1863, the beautiful façade of this Victorian pub is graced with the original curved and etched glass windows. Inside, a tall mahogany centrepiece is surrounded by a curved bar counter, the area around which is split into five by glazed partitions. Each zone has its own entrance but they are connected by half-height doors. Originally, the partitions reflected divisions in Victorian society and the areas are still known as the Public, the Gentlemen's, the Ladies', the Private and the Snug. Rotating, framed-glass snob screens hide you from the prying eyes of the bar staff. All this splendour is protected by a Grade II listing.

This classic old pub attracts youthful and exuberant up-market drinkers. The excellent modern British cuisine served in the attached conservatory restaurant, known as 'The Formosa Dining Room', draws a more mature crowd. There's London Pride on draught and an extensive wine list with plenty of gems and bins by the glass.

The Prince Bonaparte

THE PRINCE BONAPARTE
● ● ● ○ ○

80 Chepstow Road, Notting Hill, London, W2 5BE, England

Tel: +44 (0)20 7313 9491
Hours: Mon-Sat noon-11pm, Sun noon-10:30pm

Type:	Traditional / gastro pub
Alfresco:	No
Entry:	Open door (gets packed)
Highlights:	Atmosphere
Atmosphere:	Buzzy to loud
Clientele:	Young Hillbillies to suits
Dress code:	Casually hip
Price guide:	£££
Food:	Modern British from open kitchen

Formerly a workaday boozer called The Artesian, this large corner pub was bought by Beth Coventry and Phillip Wright who have succeeded in taking it stratospherically upmarket. Although popular with young Hillbillies the clientele is wide and varied. Suits and retired folk also enjoy the modern British food served from the open kitchen.

The large central bar is surrounded by old wooden chairs and tables. The back section, adjacent to the open kitchen and under a skylight, offers more of a restaurant feel. When busy, which is pretty much every evening, it can be raucous and the music system struggles to be heard over the bustle.

Real ale features and, while the wine list is not the longest, the reasonably priced selection covers most bases.

RUBY & SEQUOIA
● ● ○ ○ ○

6-8 All Saints Road (Westbourne Park Rd end), Westbourne Park, London, W11 1HH,

Tel: +44 (0)20 7243 6363,
www.ruby.uk.com
Hours: Mon-Thu 6pm-12:30am, Fri 6pm-2am, Sat 11am-2am, Sun 11am-12:30am

Type:	Restaurant / lounge bar
Alfresco:	No
Entry:	Door policy on Fri & Sat
Highlights:	Atmosphere, food
Atmosphere:	Relaxed to party
Clientele:	Notting Hillbillies
Dress code:	Casual but designer
Price guide:	££££
Food:	Snacks to full menu

Once Mas Café, then Manor, this previously ill-fated site at the end of All Saints Road continues to be synonymous with hospitality and the good times continue to roll, particularly in the basement which goes off late in the week.

This latest incarnation, from the folk behind Ruby, uses the ground floor as a restaurant-cum-cocktail bar. The rounded walls and ceiling are covered in white and gold, space age, flock wallpaper and enclose a sea of tables surrounded by bottle-green and brown banquettes. The food, the cocktails and indeed the service are adequate but do not a destination make.

Although you'll probably have to wait till Friday or Saturday, it's the atmosphere sometimes achieved in the intimate, chocolate brown basement bar (Sequoia) that's worth seeking out. Here the DJ and mixologists shake things up amid snakeskin banquettes and tables that encase chandeliers.

Whether eating upstairs early in the week or partying in the basement later on, you'll be surrounded by young Hillbillies, implausibly blessed with both money and looks.

SALT WHISKY BAR
● ● ● ◑ ○

82 Seymour Street (corner Edgware Rd), Marble Arch, London, W2 2JB, England

Tel: + 44 (0)20 7402 1155,
www.saltbar.com
Hours: Mon-Sat 7.30am-1am

Type:	Lounge bar/nightclub
Alfresco:	No
Entry:	Subject to management & capacity
Highlights:	Cocktails, whiskies & atmosphere
Atmosphere:	Often party fueled
Clientele:	Young, moneyed hipsters
Dress code:	Designer casual
Price guide:	££££
Food:	Snacks and plates

Put aside your preconceptions: Salt may be called a "whisky bar" but it's the funkiest I've ever seen. Your traditional whisky bar tends to attract middle aged men intent on sampling drams from every Scottish distillery, particularly the most rare and collectible. Salt provides for such individuals (fortunately for me) and also carries a good range of Bourbons, Irish and Japanese whiskies.

But the bar has much more to offer than malts: amazing cocktails, a DJ driven music policy and a contemporary, designer interior. Its beautiful, 30-something customers, generally designer-clad professionals who imbibe as much Champagne as they do cocktails, are a cut above the usual whisky bar folk.

The bar team are capable of much more than just dispensing drams and the cocktails they make with the golden spirit are as unique as Salt itself.

Trailer Happiness

Trailer Happiness

Trailer Happiness

TRAILER HAPPINESS

● ● ● ● ◐

Basement, 177 Portobello Road (corner of Elgin Crescent), Notting Hill, London, W11 2DY

Tel: +44 (0)20 7727 2700,
www.trailerh.com
Hours: Tue-Sun 5pm-midnight

Type: Lounge bar
Alfresco: No
Entry: Ring in advance and book
Highlights: Cocktails & rums
Atmosphere: Relaxed
Clientele: Well spoken Notting Hillbillies
Dress code: Casual
Price guide: £££
Food: Green Chilli Fireballs & much more

In November 2003 Jonathan Downey, the man behind Match bars, took over this tiny basement space in the heart of Notting Hill and created a very special den. To quote from his press release, Trailer H has the "e-z-boy feel of a low rent, mid-60s California valley bachelor pad… a retro-sexual haven of cosmopolitan kitsch and faded trailer park glamour – cork tiles and shag pile, love songs and vol-au-vents."

Those who appreciate Trader Vic's Tiki culture and drinks will no longer have to travel to Park Lane to find Zombies, Tiki mugs and volcano bowls. Kitsch is big here and flying ducks compete for wall space with prints by J.H. Lynch and Vladimir Tretchikoff.

The A-Team bar crew produce superb, rum laced cocktails. Imaginative bar snacks include "Alabama Black Snake Sesame Shrimp" and "Dr. Jay's Green Chilli Fireballs". All in all a theme bar with fun, style and a lot of rum – crammed into a small basement.

WALMER CASTLE

● ● ● ◐ ○

58 Ledbury Road, Notting Hill, London,
W11 2AJ, England

Tel: +44 (0)20 7229 4620
Hours: Mon-Sat 11am-11pm, Sun 11am-10:30pm

Type:	Traditional / gastro pub
Alfresco:	Tables on pavement
Entry:	Open door
Highlights:	Thai food
Atmosphere:	Can be loud
Clientele:	Hillbillies
Dress code:	Casual
Price guide:	£££
Food:	Thai snacks and meals

This narrow, Victorian pub is visually unspectacular – a small, well lived in, traditional boozer with mismatched wooden tables and chairs sitting on bare floorboards. The charming little lounge behind the bar is worth bagging early if you are looking to settle in for the night with a group.

The Walmer may not be the quaintest of pubs but it is cosy enough and attracts plenty of goodlooking young Hillbillies. Part of the attraction is the candlelit Thai restaurant upstairs. Many of the dishes are also served in the bar and spicy prawn crackers make a tasty alternative to the usual salt 'n' vinegar crisps. The beer selection is distinctly bog standard with London Pride on draught and the run-of-the-mill wine list features 11 by the glass.

The music can be loud and trashy, and two plasma screens show pop videos.

Walmer Castle

Walmer Castle

Walmer Castle

THE WATERWAY

● ● ● ○ ○

54 Formosa Street (at corner of Blomfield Rd), Maida Vale, W9 2JU, England

Tel: +44 (0)20 7266 3557,
www.thewaterway.co.uk
Hours: Mon-Sat noon-11pm, Sun noon-10:30pm

Type: Gastro pub
Alfresco: Large canal side terrace
Entry: Open door
Highlights: Food
Atmosphere: Relaxed
Clientele: Hip 30-somethings
Dress code: Casual
Price guide: £££
Food: Mediterranean influenced Modern British dishes

Approaching from Formosa Street, The Waterway looks like the dodgy 70s council estate pub it once was. Fortunately that's just the back view. The entrance lies on the north bank of the Grand Union Canal by a footbridge, meaning the pub not only looks over water, but also faces South. The façade is further enhanced by an 120 foot decked terrace and floor to ceiling glass doors.

The interior is Scandinavian modern and feels a little like a theatre or museum restaurant. The fairly serious eatery is separated from the bar by pillars. The beer selection is a tad bland with no traditional ales but the wine list includes plenty by the glass.

THE WESTBOURNE PUB

● ● ● ○ ○

101a Westbourne Park Villas (corner Westbourne Park Rd), Notting Hill, London, W2 5ED, England

Tel: +44 (0)20 7221 1332
Hours: Mon-Sat 11:30am-11pm, Sun noon-11pm

Type: Contemporary pub
Alfresco: Terrace with heaters, seats 100
Entry: Dinner bookings take preference
Highlights: Atmosphere
Atmosphere: Crowded, relaxed and friendly
Clientele: Young Notting Hill set
Dress code: Casual
Price guide: £££
Food: Modern British & upmarket pub grub

Like The Cow across the road, this is a seriously hip pub that was not so long ago just workaday. Its greatest asset, apart from its corner location in a fashionable part of town, is its south facing terrace. Even on relatively cold days this area is quickly populated with young and hip Hillbillies here to see and be seen.

Inside its shabby but cool with a buzzy atmosphere. The walls are plastered with funky artwork and photographs. Built-in green leather banquettes line the walls, fronted by old wooden chairs and tables, and the ceiling is strung with fairy lights.

Blackboards offer a good selection of beers and wines while the tiny open kitchen produces some scrumptious snacks.

The Westbourne Pub

SOHO & MAYFAIR
(W1)

W1 HAS CHANGED A LOT IN RECENT YEARS BUT REMAINS LONDON'S NIGHTLIFE EPICENTRE. HEAD EAST FROM REGENT STREET FOR FUN, FROLICS AND COOL MEMBERS' HANGOUTS; HEAD WEST FOR LUXE LOUNGES AND CLASSICAL HOTEL BARS. SOHO IS AT ITS BEST MID-WEEK, BEFORE THE OUT-OF-TOWNERS HIT THE STREETS.

AKBAR

● ● ● ● ○

The Red Fort, 77 Dean Street, Soho,
London, W1D 3SH, England

Tel: +44 (0)20 7437 2525,
www.redfort.co.uk/akbar
Hours: Mon-Fri noon-1am,
Sat 5.30pm-1am

Type:	Lounge bar
Alfresco:	No
Entry:	Arrive early towards the weekend
Highlights:	Cocktails, food
Atmosphere:	Full-on/chilled
Clientele:	Young trendy media types
Dress code:	Smart/casual
Price guide:	££££
Food:	Mughal court food (posh Indian)

Soho's famous Red Fort first opened in
1983 and became instantly renowned for
its stylish design and a quality of food and
service aeons beyond that of your average
Tandoori. A serious fire in the kitchen closed
the place down and it reopened in October
2001 after a complete refurbishment.

With this phoenix-like reincarnation
came 'Akbar', the superb lounge bar in the
basement, which takes its name from the
greatest of the Mughal emperors. The small
(70 capacity) room has simple but lush
décor and includes two intimate booths
which are actually under Dean Street.

The tasty bar snacks should be
washed down with one of the sublime
cocktails which exploit typical Indian
flavours such as date, jasmine, ginger,
rosewater, mango and sweet spices.

Akbar's clientele is predominantly
young and drawn from local media
companies. The bijou space can get
packed and the atmosphere DJ charged,
but I prefer the place earlier in the week
when it is quieter.

Akbar

ANNEX 3

● ● ● ◑ ○

6 Little Portland Street, Fitzrovia, London,
W1W 7JE, England

Tel: +44 (0)20 7631 0700
Hours: Mon-Sat noon-midnight,
Sun noon-8pm

Type:	Lounge bar/restaurant
Alfresco:	No
Entry:	Best book ahead
Highlights:	Punk interior
Atmosphere:	Chilled
Clientele:	Young trendy media types
Dress code:	Designer casual
Price guide:	££££
Food:	French bistro with an Asian twist

The latest offering from the three antique
dealers behind Les Trois Garçons &
Loungelover is no more restrained despite
being their first foray out of funky
Shoreditch. Annex's eclectic interior looks
like it was designed by an ageing punk with
a penchant for gilt, glitter and hard drugs.
It's loud, bold and kitsch with snakeskin
tables, 70s chandeliers, perspex Louis XV
chairs, gold banquettes and a mosaic floor.
The centrepiece is a rotating and
illuminated fairground ride encased in a
perspex box.

When this place first opened in
November 05 the cocktail list was even
more spectacular than the decor. Sadly by
Christmas the whole bar team had walked
out and the replacement cocktail list, while
good, lacks that indefinable wow factor.

Annex is popular with young, trendy
media types. In fact, it's so popular that I'd
advise booking ahead. The food is better
than many reviews suggest but is still style
over substance.

Astor

ASTOR BAR AND GRILL

● ● ○ ○

20 Glasshouse Street, Piccadilly, London,
W1B 5DJ, England

Tel: +44 (0)20 7734 4888,
www.astorbarandgrill.com
Hours: Mon-Sat 5pm-3am

Type:	Lounge, restaurant bar
Alfresco:	No
Entry:	£10 cover after 10pm
Highlights:	Amazing interior architecture
Atmosphere:	Mellow
Clientele:	After office crowd
Dress code:	Smart with funky exceptions
Price guide:	££££
Food:	Full menu available

This splendid art deco ballroom beneath
the Regent Palace Hotel off Piccadilly
dates back to 1919, the height of the
ocean liner era. Its high coffered ceilings
and network of columns, mouldings and
friezes were concealed for years until
1994, when Oliver Peyton restored the
room to its former glory and opened The
Atlantic. Until its demise late in 2005 this
was London's foremost lounge bar.

Thankfully, the splendid art deco
space is protected by a Grade II listing and
was not left empty for long. Astor opened
in February 2006. The interior is little
changed and the columns and panelling
are as lavish as ever, but this bar-cum-
club-cum-steakhouse is less than special.
The food fails to live up to the surroundings, the cocktail list is disappointing
compared to the Atlantic's heyday and the
wine list is hardly good value.

An entrance charge (usually £10) may
be payable after 10pm, so for a quick drink
and a look at a splendid room, go early.

Astor

Astor

THE AUDLEY

●●●○○

41 Mount Street (corner South Audley St),
Mayfair, London, W1K 2RX, England

Tel: +44 (0)20 7499 1843
Hours: Mon-Sat 11am-11pm,
Sun noon-10:30pm

Type:	Traditional pub
Alfresco:	Pavement tables
Entry:	Open door
Highlights:	Traditional cask ales & grub
Atmosphere:	Relaxed
Clientele:	Surprisingly varied
Dress code:	Casual to smart suits
Price guide:	£££
Food:	Sandwiches to hearty meals

In the early 1880s the first Duke of
Westminster set about rebuilding Mount
Street and with this reconstruction came
The Audley. Built in the neo-French
Renaissance style, the red brick and pink
terracotta frontage with its lush greenery
is in harmony with the rest of the street.

Inside, this is a traditional grand old
pub with a forest of dark carved wood
offset by red leather banquettes and a floral
carpet. The original chandeliers hang from
the ornately moulded ceiling and the long
bar counter traverses the two distinct sides
of the Audley. Drinkers congregate on the
left and diners on the right.

Four regular cask ales are supplemented by a changing guest beer while 17
wines by the glass feature on a brand-led
list. Proper pub grub runs from gourmet
sausages and mash, burgers, salads and
sandwiches to roasts on Sundays.

The Audley

The Audley

The Audley

CENTURY
● ● ● ● ○

61-63 Shaftesbury Avenue (btwn Wardour & Dean Sts), Soho, London, W1D 6LQ, England

Tel: +44 (0)20 7534 3080,
www.centuryclub.co.uk
Hours: Mon-Fri 8am-1am, Sat noon-2am

Type:	Members lounge bar/restaurant
Alfresco:	Roof terrace
Entry:	Members & guests only
Highlights:	Ambience, service & roof terrace
Atmosphere:	Relaxed, home from home
Clientele:	Soho media types
Dress code:	Suits to designer jeans
Price guide:	£££
Food:	Platters to shepherds' pie

I worried about including this bar in this guide as it's the one I frequent the most. Happily it's a private members club and so a committee prevents it from getting too crowded with new drinkers - sorry.

Century opened in spring 2001 and its four floors boast three bars, a roof terrace and a restaurant (which offers good brasserie fare). The first floor bar, which is open from breakfast, is cosy with comfy chairs arranged round simple tables; modern art on the walls entertains the creative clientele which Century attracts. The second floor lounge bar opens from 4pm and tends to a living room feel, with warm lighting and a fireplace. The ambience is friendly and a comfy armchair here makes a relaxing spot to escape the bustle of Soho.

Membership costs £400 per year plus a £100 registration fee but it's worth every penny. However, please save your money and stay away - I want that armchair.

CIRCUS
● ● ● ○ ○

Basement, 1 Upper James Street (corner Beak St), Soho, London, W1R 4BP, England

Tel: +44 (0)20 7534 4000
Hours: Mon-Wed noon-1.30am, Thu-Sat 12.30pm-3am

Type:	Lounge bar
Alfresco:	No
Entry:	Possible charge for non-members after 11pm
Highlights:	Cocktails, vibe
Atmosphere:	Full-on / relaxed
Clientele:	Soho-ites and local workers
Dress code:	Chic is best
Price guide:	£££
Food:	Chips, spring rolls etc.

This split-level minimalist bar lies underneath the successful restaurant of the same name on the corner of Beak Street and Upper James Street. Black leather seating is scattered along the lengthy lower lounge which looks out onto an illuminated Japanese style garden of gravel and bamboo.

The well-stocked bar, complete with goldfish swimming in two giant bowls, knocks out classic cocktails as well as some interesting original concoctions. The food menu is short but every bit as good as that on offer in the restaurant above.

The clientele ranges from magazine styled local media darlings to the unstylish after office crowd. Circus enjoys a late licence but I'd advise arriving early as non-members have to pay an entry charge after 11pm.

CLARIDGE'S BAR
● ● ● ● ○

Claridge's Hotel, 55 Brook Street (corner Davies St.), Mayfair, London, W1A 2JQ, England

Tel: +44 (0)20 7629 8860,
www.savoygroup.com
Hours: Mon-Sat midnight-1am,
Sun 4pm-noon

Type:	Hotel/lounge bar
Alfresco:	No
Entry:	Via hotel lobby or Davies St.
Highlights:	Cocktails, service
Atmosphere:	Quiet gentleman's club
Clientele:	Mayfair set
Dress code:	Gents requested to wear jackets
Price guide:	££££
Food:	Caviar, sushi, salads, risotto etc

Tucked away under the staircase of Claridge's lobby is this quaint lounge bar, which acquired its warm Art Deco look in 1999 when the hotel embarked on its first major designer restoration since the 1930s. A Venetian chandelier drapes glass tendrils down in front of the white marble bar counter in this small but somehow stately room lined with comfy, red leather bar stools, chairs and banquettes. A similarly appointed, connecting room has a fireplace topped by a mirrored clock. Behind this lies the aptly named Snuggery, an intimate area which seats up to twenty.

Claridge's Bar boasts the best range of Louis Roederer Champagne in Britain with Vintage Cristal 1997 by the glass (£44). Service is impeccable. The skilled bartenders will make any classic you request as well as more contemporary creations from their own list.

Elderly regulars are joined by the young Mayfair set and diners from Gordon Ramsay's restaurant just across the lobby.

COCOON
● ● ● ● ◑

65 Regent Street (entrance on Air Street),
London, W1B 4EA, England

Tel: +44 (0)20 7494 7600,
www.cocoon-restaurants.com
Hours: Mon-Fri noon-3pm & 5:30pm-midnight,
Sat 5:30pm-midnight, Sun 5:30pm-11pm

Type:	Restaurant bar
Alfresco:	No
Entry:	Subject to management & capacity
Highlights:	Food, cocktails, sake & shochu
Atmosphere:	Relaxed
Clientele:	Henrys & Henriettas
Dress code:	Designer casual
Price guide:	££££
Food:	Starters from Pan-Asian menu

This long, narrow venue with views over
Regent Street was formerly the landmark
l'Odeon restaurant. The original arched
windows and claustrophobically low ceiling
remain. However, the room now hosts a
series of six spherical and interlocking dining
areas, linked by a central walkway and divided
by net drapes. The bar and lounge nestles in
the middle of the row, and shares the rather
garish space age decor of the whole.

According to Cocoon's blurb, the
design was 'inspired by the lifecycle of the
butterfly'. Yeah, right.

Whatever you may think of the high
concept, the cocktails, whether classics or
Cocoon's own Asian-influenced creations,
are superb. The wine list features some
interesting bins and there's an exceptional
selection of shochu and sake.

Those with a weak bladder should be
warned that the loos are in the basement and
the trip involves a long walk and two sets of stairs.
However, the incontinent and just plain lazy may
like to note that there's also a solitary 'disabled'
WC upstairs.

Cocoon

Cocoon

Crazy Bear

CRAZY BEAR BAR

● ● ● ◐ ○

Basement, 26-28 Whitfield Street, Fitzrovia, London, W1T 2RG, England

Tel: +44 (0)20 7631 0088,
www.crazybeargroup.co.uk
Hours: Mon-Fri 11am-11pm, Sat 6pm-11pm

Type:	Lounge bar
Alfresco:	No
Entry:	Subject to management & capacity
Atmosphere:	Relaxed
Highlights:	Interior design
Clientele:	Local office & diners
Dress code:	Smart casual
Price guide:	£££££
Food:	Oriental

The restaurant on the ground floor of this Fitzrovia enclave looks so impressive that you may not want to descend the stairs to the bar. But with its leather floor and walls, art deco lamps, ostrich-skin chairs and padded booth tunnels, the basement delivers another visual treat.

The bar itself is sunken so, when seated at the bar, the bartenders are at your level. Behind them are five matching fireplaces salvaged from the Royal Automobile Club, which now warm their admirers with premium spirits rather than flames. Naturally, the toilets do not disappoint. The gents features an incredible mirrored floor.

The bar snacks and food served in the restaurant upstairs are Thai with pan-Asian elements. The quality of the cocktails has recently improved dramatically with the arrival of a new bar manager but Crazy Bear is worth the journey for its interior alone.

Crazy Bear

Crazy Bear

THE CUCKOO CLUB

● ● ● ● ○

Swallow Street, London, W1B 4EZ, England

Tel: +44 (0)20 7287 4300,
www.thecuckooclub.com
Hours: Wed-Thu 7:30pm-3am, Fri-Sat
8pm-3:30am

Type: Members bar & club
Alfresco: No
Entry: Subject to management & capacity
Highlights: Cocktails (upstairs) & atmosphere
Atmosphere: Full-on party
Clientele: Style set
Dress code: Designer casual
Price guide: £££££
Food: Modern European food

The word 'club' usually suggests bad drinks, bad service and grotty spaces but a great party atmosphere. Thankfully there are a few clubs that manage to combine the standards of an upscale lounge with the buzz of a rave and the Cuckoo Club is a shining example.

The Cuckoo Club opened in November 2005 on the site of the former Stork Rooms and its 5,000 square feet is spread over two floors. This makes it feel more intimate than the 300 capacity might suggest.

The upstairs bar boasts an impressive array of spirits and, judging by my visit, some great cocktails. It starts off relatively sedately, picking up momentum and volume as the night turns to morning. Downstairs, the drinks offering is more basic but the atmosphere full-on from the start. Both floors feature flamboyant decor, theatrical drapes, gilded mirrors and ceilings where 350 LED lights pulsate in time with the music.

If you want to come and play here you'll need to blag your name on the list or, better, pass the A-list committee and splash out a few hundred quid on one of the coveted memberships.

The Cuckoo Club

CVO FIREVAULT
● ● ● ● ○

36 Great Titchfield Street, near Oxford Circus, London, W1W 8BQ, England

Tel: +44 (0)20 7636 2091,
www.cvo.co.uk
Hours: Mon-Sat noon-11pm

Type: Lounge bar & restaurant
Alfresco: No
Entry: Ring first
Highlights: Food, decor
Atmosphere: Wonderfully ambient
Clientele: Media types
Dress code: Designer casual
Price guide: ££££
Food: Diverse snacks & full menu

Five minutes walk from Oxford Circus, this is one of London's best hidden and most romantic bars. The unusual name is a reference to its owner, Caroline Van Outersterp, a fireplace designer who originally opened this as a basement showroom. She had the natty idea of combining her showroom with a restaurant and bar, something she's done brilliantly.

The ground level reception and cloakroom look like another of the area's many designer furniture shops. Descend the stairs and you'll find yourself in a clinical white space, divided by maze-like walls and net drapes. Fireplaces of all shapes and sizes are everywhere, set into the walls and even the tables. The combination of secluded spaces, comfy white leather sofas, ambient lighting and the warm glow of the flames is enchanting.

Such surroundings are the perfect setting for sipping cocktails and the list here features classics and twists on classics which, when ordered, are very well-made. The food is wonderfully diverse with classic French meeting Asian and North African dishes.

Highly recommended for romantic liaisons on cold winter's nights.

THE DOG & DUCK
● ● ● ○ ○

18 Bateman Street (at Frith St), Soho, London, W1D 3AJ, England

Tel: +44 (0)20 7494 0697
Hours: Mon-Fri noon-11pm, Sat 6pm-11pm, Sun 7pm-10:30pm

Type: Traditional pub
Alfresco: No
Entry: Open door
Highlights: Decor and ale
Atmosphere: Relaxed
Clientele: Local office types, tourists
Dress code: Whatever
Price guide: £££
Food: Hot & cold traditional pub grub

The name Dog & Duck is so synonymous with traditional English pubs that it's practically generic. This particular Dog & Duck is deeply traditional, from the building's fabric to the food and drink.

The first pub here was built in 1734 on the site of the Duke of Monmouth's home. This was demolished in 1897 and replaced by the present building, which remains a glorious example of a late Victorian boozer. One of Soho's oldest and smallest pubs, its original, ornamental glazed tile and mirror interior is simply gorgeous. The Victorians were a practical lot and the tiles, like the pub's yellowish glazed brick façade, were designed to repel dirt.

Although several draught lagers and eleven wines by the glass cater to modern tastes, thankfully this tiny pub still offers four traditional cask draught ales - more than most pubs several times its size. The food menu is also disproportionately large, and packed with traditional pub fare such as sausage and mash, pies, sandwiches and even pickled eggs.

THE DORCHESTER BAR
● ● ● ● ○

53 Park Lane, Mayfair, London, W1A 2HJ, England

Tel: +44 (0)20 7629 8888,
www.thedorchester.com
Hours: Mon-Sat noon-late, Sun noon-10:30pm

Type: Hotel bar
Alfresco: No
Entry: Subject to management & space
Highlights: Cocktails & spirits selection
Atmosphere: DJ driven
Clientele: Hotel guests & party animals
Dress code: Stylish
Price guide: £££££
Food: Beautifully presented snacks & plates

The Dorchester sits majestically on Park Lane, oozing elegance, decorum and staid tradition. So its new bar may come as something of a shock to older regulars.

The Dorchester is owned by the Brunei Investment Agency and oil money has bought plenty of bling. The original restrained, classical bar has been obliterated and replaced with nightclub style ostentation, while the pianist has given way to a DJ. Some 750 scarlet glass spikes form the backdrop to a room lined with high back booth seating and plenty of bronzed glass.

Fortunately tradition survives in the drinks offering. One of the oldest cocktails of all, the Martinez, heads up a classic cocktail list based around the country's largest range of vermouths. The Dorchester even boasts its own specially made Old Tom gin, which was the original British gin before the London Dry style that dominates today.

Impeccable, traditional service standards endure and ensure this bar remains one of London's best. All that bling may also make it fashionable.

BEEFEATER JADE
AVAILABLE @ THE DORCHESTER BAR

Glass: Champagne flute
Garnish: Thin slice of melon & ground black pepper
Method: MUDDLE two small cubes of honeydew melon and a pinch of ground black pepper in base of shaker. Add other ingredients, SHAKE with ice and fine strain into glass. TOP with champagne.
25ml Beefeater gin
25ml Midori
10ml Blue curaçao
5ml Freshly squeezed lime juice

5th View

43 South Moulton

43 South Moulton

5th View

5TH VIEW

●●●●○

Waterstone's, Simpson's Building, 203-205
Piccadilly, London, W1J 9HA, England

Tel: +44 (0)20 7851 2433,
www.5thview.co.uk
Hours: Mon-Sat 10am-10pm, Sun noon-6pm

Type: Café bar
Alfresco: Terrace from May 2007
Entry: Open to all
Highlights: View, beer, cocktails
Atmosphere: Relaxed
Clientele: Bookworms & shoppers
Dress code: Casual
Price guide: £££
Food: Brunch, snacks, nibbles & dips

5th View is perched atop Europe's largest book
store (two floors up from the diffordsguide
range). The splendid art deco building was
originally home to the dapper 1930s menswear
store, Simpson's, and this space was once its
café bar. The name is apt as a wall of windows
offers panoramic views towards the Palace of
Westminster, Battersea Power Station and the
London Eye, with the twin aerials of Crystal
Palace visible on the horizon.

The stark, plain white interior centres
around the view, and the window tables are
the place to be. Failing that, the attached
reading room by the design books
department is more homely, with comfortable
banquette seating and sofas.

The drinks range is superb. Twisted
classic cocktails are listed by base spirit, while
a range of sixty-odd bottled beers includes most
of the world's most famous brews. There are
22 wines, all available by the glass, and some
very sensibly priced top end champagnes.

Brunch is served from midday with salads,
nibbles and dips from 5pm. Both food and
drinks are delivered by efficient, friendly staff.

FINO RESTAURANT
● ● ● ● ○

33 Charlotte Street (entrance on Rathbone
Street), Fitzrovia, London, W1T 1RR, England

Tel: +44 (0)20 7813 8010,
www.finorestaurant.com
Hours: Mon-Fri noon-3pm & 6pm-11pm, Sat
6pm-11pm

Type:	Spanish tapas restaurant & bar
Alfresco:	No
Entry:	Around corner in Rathbone Street
Highlights:	Cocktails, food, wine list
Atmosphere:	Convivial - no music
Clientele:	Local office crowd & travelling foodies
Dress code:	Smart casual
Price guide:	££££
Food:	Superb Spanish tapas

Put all your preconceptions of tapas bars
aside and head down to this great little
place in Fitzrovia. Don't, however, head
down to the postal address, which bears
no resemblance to the location of the front
door. You need to enter from opposite the
Rathbone Hotel, on Rathbone Street,
around the corner from Charlotte Street.

The basement space feels slick,
comfortable and convivial. Brightly
coloured leather chairs and stools sit
among the pale wood walls. The cocktail
bar, tucked round to the right, is intimately
proportioned. However, they prepare the
most amazing cocktails - many of them
topped with foaming heads created with
nitrous oxide (laughing gas). My favourite
is the Vanilla Daiquiri with Camomile Foam.
The wine list is also inspired and, as the
name would suggest, the establishment
offers a superb Sherry selection.

The food is modern tapas with a focus
on fresh seafood. Order a few dishes to
nibble or opt for one of their selections and
eat at the kitchen bar.

FLORIDITA
● ● ● ● ○

Mezzo Basement, 100 Wardour Street,
Soho, London, W1F 0TN, England

Tel: +44 (0)20 7314 4000,
www.floriditalondon.com
Hours: Mon-Wed 5.30pm-2am, Thu-Sat
5.30pm-3am

Type:	Cabaret bar
Alfresco:	No
Entry:	At a price after 8pm (£10)
Highlights:	Cocktails & live entertainment
Atmosphere:	Mellow
Clientele:	After office crowd & tourists
Dress code:	Smart
Price guide:	£££££
Food:	Cuban fusion

On this site in 1964 a little known group
called the Rolling Stones played at the
Marquee Club. Much later came Mezzo, part
of Sir Terence Conran's huge gastro-empire.
And Sir Terence still has a stake in this new
venture, which is modelled on Havana's
celebrated Floridita bar and housed in the
basement of the Mezzo building.

From the ground floor tapas bar wide
stairs descend to a huge bunker
decorated in 80s shades of red, black and
white. There's a 13 metre long bar and a
stage, from which Latin American live
music is played.

Even with live langosta (lobster)
imported weekly from Cuba, the food here
is hardly authentic, but having tried the
food in Cuba that's surely a good thing.
The cocktails are much better, with
excellent classic Daiquiris and imaginative
modern twists all made by a superb
bar team.

43 SOUTH MOLTON
● ● ● ● ○

43 South Molton Street, Mayfair, London,
W1K 5RS, England

Tel: +44 (0)20 7647 4343,
www.43southmolton.com
Hours: Mon-Sat noon-3pm & 6pm-2am

Type:	Members' lounge bar/club
Alfresco:	No
Entry:	Members & guests only
Highlights:	Cocktails
Atmosphere:	Relaxed, loungy
Clientele:	City boys & trust fund babies
Dress code:	Designer casual
Price guide:	££££
Food:	Tapas & Euro dishes

OK. So the name lacks a little imagination, but
then this is one posh Mayfair address - and,
given the eccentric country house theme of
this members' club, what more appropriate
moniker could there be? Molton Street is
known for its designer boutiques and trust-
funded babes who lunch. So it's hardly
surprising that number 43 is attracting a suitably
high net worth and fashionable young crowd,
with City boys driving their Ferraris across town
in pursuit of the aforementioned ladies of leisure.

43 uses all four floors of the site, formerly
a restaurant called 'Knew'. The street level
bistro looks more like a general store from an
episode of Little Britain than an aristocratic pad.
The first and second floors are cosier and kitted
out in a shabby chic vein with mismatched
comfy old armchairs and antique light fittings.
Don't get too comfortable, however, for the
action is generally in the basement below.
Despite its grand title 'The Ballroom', this is
actually an intimate club space.

Join the Mayfair set here and you'll benefit
from sublime cocktails and great service from
friendly staff.

FRENCH HOUSE
● ● ● ○ ○

49 Dean Street, Soho, London, W1V 5HL, England

Tel: +44 (0)20 7437 2799
Hours: Mon-Fri 11am-11pm, Sun 11am-10:30pm

Type: Traditional pub	
Alfresco: No	
Entry: Subject to limited space	
Highlights: All things French	
Atmosphere: Crowded but friendly	
Clientele: Conversationalists, all ages & walks	
Dress code: Casual to suits	
Price guide: ££	
Food: Modern British restaurant above	

When this tiny Soho boozer was built in 1937 it was named the York Minster. Just before the Second World War it was taken over by a Belgian, Victor Berlemont, who made it a haunt for singers and actors. During the war it became a meeting place for French exiles, including the future president Charles de Gaulle, which led to the nickname 'The House of the French', later shortened to the 'French House'.

Today this one room pub still attracts plenty of French folk and is reputedly the country's largest retail outlet for Ricard Pastis. Its walls display a unique collection of signed photographs of French entertainers and sportsmen. The first floor restaurant has something of a reputation, but surprisingly offers a modern British menu.

Its reputation and diminutive size means that most lunchtimes and early evenings the French House is so busy that entering one of its twin doors is a challenge, let alone getting to the bar. Winter afternoons are the best time to appreciate this hospitable little pub at its best.

YE GRAPES
● ● ● ○ ○

16 Shepherd Market, Mayfair, London, W1J 7QQ, England

Tel: +44 (0)20 7499 1563
Hours: Mon-Sat 11am-11pm, Sun noon-10:30pm

Type: Traditional pub	
Alfresco: Standing room outside	
Entry: Open door	
Highlights: Traditional cask ales	
Atmosphere: Often very busy	
Clientele: Office staff, locals, tourists	
Dress code: Casual to suits	
Price guide: ££££	
Food: Peanuts and crisps only	

Ye Grapes lies in Shepherd Market, which is named after Edward Shepherd, the architect and developer who started building here in 1735, on the site of the May Fair, the annual fair which gave Mayfair its name. By 1882, when this pub was built, Shepherd Market was a well-known haunt for prostitutes.

Today the market is distinctly upscale but retains a quaint, village-like feel with narrow streets and tiny houses and shops. This very traditional, old Victorian pub with hanging baskets, green paintwork and glazed tiles fits right in.

As was common in pubs of the day, the interior was originally divided to accommodate different classes of drinker but today only high back snugs provide some anonymity. Cartoons, a deer head, a propeller and stuffed fish in cases dot the walls and abundant carved bunches of grapes recall the pub's name.

Traditional ales are a speciality here and the five pumps on the bar are often supplemented by a couple of firkins on the side.

GROUCHO CLUB
● ● ● ○ ○

45 Dean Street (just North of Old Compton St), Soho, London, W1D 4QB, England

Tel: + 44 (0)20 7439 4685,
www.thegrouchoclub.com
Hours: Mon-Sat 11am-3am, Sun 11am-midnight

Type: Private members club	
Alfresco: No	
Entry: Members & guests	
Highlights: Vibe	
Atmosphere: Mellow	
Clientele: 25-50 arts, celebs and media	
Dress code: Casual	
Price guide: ££££	
Food: Club sandwiches etc	

The legendary Groucho Club was founded in 1985 by a group including Tony Mackintosh, the chocolate multimillionaire. The name derived from Groucho Marx's quip, "I don't care to belong to any club that would accept me as a member," and it was billed as a members-only hangout for non-clubby people. It quickly attracted many celebrity members, including actors and pop stars such as Mick Jagger.

Groucho was bought in 2001 by a group led by another chocolate heir (Joel Cadbury) and PR guru Matthew Freud, who gave the club a much needed spruce up. The Groucho's three bars, brasserie and more formal dining room still offer celebs and media types an exclusive and congenial haven in which to relax. Should they need overnight accommodation, the club has 19 well appointed bedrooms.

The Groucho offers great service, great cocktails and perhaps the best drinking companions of any London bar. The only problem is gaining membership: aspirants must be signed and seconded by accredited members then accepted by the membership committee, and, even if they pass these hurdles, may have to wait more than a year for membership.

HAKKASAN

● ● ● ● ○

8 Hanway Place, Fitzrovia, London, W1T
9HD, England

Tel: +44 (0)20 7927 7000,
www.hakkasan.com
Hours: Mon-Wed noon-12.30am, Thu-Sat
noon-2.30am, Sun noon-midnight

Entry:	Dinner bookings take preference
Type:	Lounge / restaurant bar
Alfresco:	No
Highlights:	Cocktails, spirits, food, vibe
Atmosphere:	Full-on / relaxed
Clientele:	Stylish business and Soho set
Dress code:	Chic / smart
Price guide:	££££
Food:	Modern Oriental

The hubbub of Oxford Street and the grime
of Hanway Place do little to prepare the
visitor for the elegance of Hakkasan, with
its dramatic staircase leading down to a
basement lobby bathed in a blue neon
glow. The main room's architecture is
among the most impressive of any London
restaurant. Dark wood latticework screens
divide the main space into restaurant,
lounge and bar. These and the slate wall
of the 16 metre bar are much copied by
counterfeiters who always fail to achieve
Hakkasan's wow factor.

Hakkasan is the vision of Alan Yau,
who also brought us the Wagamama
noodle bar chain. It buzzes with a business
led clientele enhanced by some very
beautiful women and successfully cool
men. They are served dim sum to die for
and some highly imaginative cocktails by
waitresses who look like they have been
squeezed into Chinese lanterns.

And the name? 'Hakka' is Chinese
dialect and 'san' is the Japanese form of
addressing someone.

HUSH

● ● ● ● ○

8 Lancashire Court (off Brook Street),
Mayfair, London, W1S 1EY, England

Tel: +44 (0)20 7659 1500,
www.hush.co.uk
Hours: Mon-Sat 11am-11pm

Type:	Lounge/restaurant bar
Alfresco:	Courtyard dining in summer
Entry:	Subject to capacity
Highlights:	The atmosphere
Atmosphere:	The kitchen of a great party
Clientele:	City types & Mayfair set
Dress code:	Suits, glamour, designer jeans
Price guide:	££££
Food:	Potato wedges to caviar

Hush is owned by Jamie Barber and
Geoffrey Moore (son of Roger) and sits
serenely in its Georgian townhouse in a
cobbled courtyard off Mayfair's Brook
Street. Clement weather sees diners from
the popular ground floor brasserie spill out
into the courtyard in continental style.

The lounge bar and a second, more
upmarket restaurant known as 'Hush Up'
lie at the top of a wood and perspex
staircase. The Hush lounge is a cosy den
of 70s softness, with velour banquettes
and satin cushions. But the place to blag
is the intimate wood-lined boudoir that
seats ten and is filled with deep cushions.

Hush is close to Bond Street and
next to the Versace store, so caters for
ladies who lunch and suited young gentry
who gather to enjoy an array of superbly
conceived cocktails mixed by a very able
bar crew. All in all, a very civilised
experience which can also be great fun.

Hakkasan

ICEBAR & BELOW ZERO
● ● ● ○

29-33 Heddon Street, London, W1B 4BL,
England

Tel: +44 (0)20 7478 8910,
www.belowzerolondon.com
Hours: Mon-Sun 12:30pm-11:30pm

Type:	Lounge, restaurant & ice bar
Alfresco:	No
Entry:	Cover charge, book ahead
Highlights:	The cold experience
Atmosphere:	Chilled!
Clientele:	The curious
Dress code:	Smart casual
Price guide:	££££
Food:	Sashimi to burgers

Below Zero and the Absolut Icebar sit adjoining each other and united by a common theme. Below Zero is a two storey lounge and restaurant which is pleasant enough and serves reasonable cocktails. But it's the Icebar, perhaps wrongly, that's of more interest. This is a miniature, artificially chilled version of the bar at the legendary Icehotel in Sweden.

The London version is basically a huge industrial freezer lined with ice blocks to resemble an igloo and maintained at -5°C. The stools, the tables, the bar counter and the spectacular ice carvings are made from ice imported from northern Sweden.

A forty minute slot in the Icebar costs £12 (£15 on Thursday, Friday and Saturday evenings) and the price includes your first Absolut cocktail, served in an outsize, hollow ice cube by a bartender wearing a ski suit. You are issued with a silver cape to keep you warm and gloves so you can hold your "glass". It's certainly worth doing once for the experience - as is spending a night at the Icehotel itself.

KABARET'S PROPHECY
● ● ● ○

16-18 Beak Street, Soho, London, W1F
9RD, England

Tel: +44 (0)20 7439 2229,
www.kabaretsprophecy.com
Hours: Mon-Fri 4pm-3am, Sat 10pm-3am

Type:	Lounge bar/members' club
Alfresco:	No
Entry:	Members & guest list
Highlights:	Cocktails & vibe
Atmosphere:	Full-on
Clientele:	Style set (20-40)
Dress code:	Designer casual
Price guide:	££££
Food:	Very tasty international snacks & plates

This tiny basement club is a 70s schoolboy's dream. The bar front is made of Swarovski crystal, the walls are lined with LED pixels which produce an arcade style flicker and, naturally, the dancefloor is full of pretty young things. The frenzied design (and attractive clientele) continues in the toilets, where the walls are plastered with cartoon characters by Jamie Hewlett, the illustrator who created Tank Girl.

Unusually for a club, there is a very serious bar team - and a cocktail list to match. I can highly recommend both the bar snack menu and the cocktails, which are far above the standard for such places. Kabaret's Prophecy is open to members only from 10:30pm, but from 4-10pm Monday to Friday anyone can enjoy these delights.

With its flashing walls and pumping sound system, this is certainly no place to take your granny. However, it could be right for you.

KEMIA BAR
● ● ● ○

Momo, 25 Heddon Street (off Regent St.),
Soho, London, W1B 4BH, England

Tel: +44 (0)20 7434 2011
Hours: Mon-Tue 7pm-1am, Wed 7pm-
2am, Thu-Sat 7pm-3am

Type:	Members bar/club
Alfresco:	No
Entry:	Mon-Wed invited guests, Thu-Sat members only
Highlights:	Atmosphere
Atmosphere:	Full-on party
Clientele:	Elegant, classy, fun-loving models
Dress code:	Expensive & stylish but casual
Price guide:	££££
Food:	Mezze-style, served 7pm-11.30pm

At the end of a tiny cul-de-sac just off Regent Street, a doorway nestles alongside the fashionable Momo restaurant whence a narrow staircase leads down to a tiny basement club. Walking into Kemia Bar for the first time is like stepping into a bedouin tent which has been erected in a cave to find a visiting North African band and its entourage celebrating their first number one hit.

Authentically decorated in an Algerian/Moroccan vein, this low vaulted, incense burning den is lined with leather, organza and luxurious silk drapes. With its celebrated music policy the Kemia Bar is a gem for the sophisticated partygoer.

Drinks and food are in keeping with the theme, so mint is delivered by the truck load to supply cocktails such as the refreshing Momo Special or the Pepe. The ethos behind Momos, as Kemia Bar is better known, is fun and the place is full of sophisticated, beautiful, stylish people having lots of it.

KETTNERS CHAMPAGNE ROOMS

● ● ● ○ ○

29 Romilly Street, Soho, London, W1D 5HP,
England

Tel: +44 (0)20 7734 6112,
www.pizzaexpress.com/kettners
Hours: Mon-Sun 11am-1am

Type: Champagne bar
Alfresco: No
Entry: Subject to space and attire
Highlights: Champagne list
Atmosphere: Relaxed
Clientele: Sloane set, actors, tourists, locals
Dress code: Smart/chic
Price guide: ££££
Food: Pizzetine & ciabatta sandwiches

Kettners was opened in 1867 by Auguste Kettner, chef to Napoleon III, and it is said that both Oscar Wilde and Edward VII ate here. (It's also said that Wilde used to take rent boys to the upstairs rooms.) It underwent various incarnations until 1979, when it was purchased by Peter Boizot, founder of the Pizza Express chain.

This place looks nothing like a Pizza Express outlet (although the pizzas are very good). Consisting of a series of simply decorated yet grand rooms with comfy leather armchairs and wooden floors, it has the air of a gentlemen's club without the pretension.

Kettners is one of London's original champagne bars and remains one of few still offering 32 Grand Marques. A refined place to meet friends or lovers and chat while a bottle chills in the bucket.

THE KINGLY CLUB

● ● ● ○ ○

4 Kingly Court, Soho, London, W1B 5PW,
England

Tel: +44 (0)20 7287 9100,
www.kinglyclub.co.uk
Hours: Mon-Sat 6pm-2am,
Sun 6pm-12.30am

Type: Lounge bar, members club
Alfresco: No
Entry: Members & guest list
Highlights: Cocktails and vibe
Atmosphere: Relaxed
Clientele: Soho style set
Dress code: Anything but a tie
Price guide: ££££
Food: Sushi

This visually stunning bar sits in a subterranean tunnel that was once home to the legendary Pinstripe Club. During the 1960s it attracted famous revellers, allegedly including John Profumo and Christine Keeler, protagonists in the decade's greatest British sex scandal. However, the site was forgotten until the opening of The Kingly Club in August 2003.

The intimate space, with a capacity of only 125, is made to feel bigger thanks to mirrors, a white burnished, almost wet ice finish on the walls and some gorgeous fish tanks. Two intimate antechambers have cream leather booth seating.

This space age club can get claustrophobic but it always has atmosphere, beautiful people and great drinks.

LAB

● ● ● ○ ○

12 Old Compton Street (Charing Cross Rd end), Soho, London, W1V 5PG, England

Tel: +44 (0)20 7437 7820,
www.lab-bar.com
Hours: Mon-Sat noon-midnight,
Sun 3pm-10.30pm

Type: Lounge bar
Alfresco: No
Entry: Open to all subject to capacity
Highlights: Cocktails, atmosphere
Atmosphere: Party-like
Clientele: Young Soho set (20-35)
Dress code: Practically anything goes
Price guide: £££
Food: Food is not always available

Lab's name is a throwback to the long defunct London Academy of Bartenders, which was established by some of its founders, but this multi-award-winning venue remains a big name on the bar circuit.

The distinctive 70s retro decor sees rounded corners far outnumbering angles. The two long narrow, dimly lit bars (one on the ground floor, one in the basement) are either intimate or claustrophobic depending on your mood and the population density.

The beer and wine lists are also bijou, but if you drink anything other than a cocktail here you're missing out. The house cocktail style tends towards long fruity drinks rather than short strong ones. If the extensive list leaves you undecided, the bartenders will helpfully oblige with a recommendation.

Lab is busy pretty much nightly and even if there is no DJ expect loud music and a pumped up atmosphere. The bar attracts a friendly young crowd, mainly drawn from local offices.

The Living Room W1

THE LIVING ROOM W1

● ● ● ● ○

3-9 Heddon Street, London, W1B 4BE,
England

Tel: +44 (0)87 0166 2225,
www.thelivingroomw1.co.uk
Hours: Mon-Sat 10am-1am, Sun 11am-
midnight

Type:	Lounge bar/restaurant
Alfresco:	No
Entry:	Subject to management & capacity
Highlights:	Cocktails & vibe
Atmosphere:	Relaxed party
Clientele:	20 & 30-somethings
Dress code:	Designer casual
Price guide:	£££
Food:	Full modern British menu

Towns across the country are dotted with
this successful brand of style bars cum
restaurants, but this is the chain's flagship
and accordingly distinguished by the W1
moniker. The setting is a former Post Office
just off Regent Street, an address made
famous on the cover of David Bowie's
Ziggy Stardust album.

No living room is complete without the
homely warmth of a flickering fire and the
partition that divides the large ground floor
incorporates three gas fires. On one side
lies the lounge with its 17 metre bar, on the
other an informal dining area with café style
windows that can be thrown open in
summer. A staircase leads up to a more
formal first floor dining room with an open
kitchen and galleried view of the bar below.
A club is also set to open in the basement.

The modern British gastro grub
attracts business types at lunchtime while
evenings see their secretaries pile in for
the well made cocktails. Although it trades
until 1am, access after 11pm is by non-
fee membership.

The Living Room W1

The Living Room W1

LOTUS ROOMS

● ● ● ○ ○

Bam-Bou, 1 Percy Street, Fitzrovia, London,
W1P 0ET, England

Tel: +44 (0)20 7323 9130,
www.bam-bou.co.uk
Hours: Mon-Sat 6pm-1am

Type:	Lounge bar / members bar
Alfresco:	No
Entry:	Members only (but try your luck)
Highlights:	Atmosphere
Atmosphere:	Mellow & relaxed
Clientele:	Media types
Dress code:	Designer, cool casual
Price guide:	£££
Food:	Prawn toast, spring rolls etc

This four-floored paean to French
Vietnamese colonial style is quite
seductive. The dark and lusty rooms, with
cracked lacquered walls, are filled with
opulent antiques and authentic furniture.

The ground and first floor restaurants
serve Asian fare to diners. On the third
floor, the bar is open to all and yet further
up the winding staircase sit the
tantalisingly titled Lotus Rooms. These are
a series of small, interlocking rooms in an
opium den vein, lined with comfy chairs
and banquettes.

Appropriately themed around the
Orient, many of the original cocktails are
superb. The bar food continues the theme:
dim sum are presented in steaming
baskets. Chilled music, friendly armchair
service and an open fire complete the
karma-inducing experience.

Strictly speaking the Lotus Rooms are
only open to members and their guests.
However, my advice is to ring ahead.
Unless there is a private booking you will
probably be most welcome.

Lotus Rooms

Match Bar

Match Bar

MATCH BAR
● ● ● ● ○

37-38 Margaret Street (nr Oxford Circus),
London, W1G 0JF, England

Tel: +44 (0)20 7499 3443,
www.matchbar.com
Hours: Mon-Sat 11am-midnight

Type: Lounge/restaurant bar
Alfresco: No
Entry: Subject to space rather than dress
Highlights: Cocktails
Atmosphere: Laid-back but bustling
Clientele: Business groups, friends, couples
Dress code: Anything goes - suits to jeans
Price guide: £££
Food: Sturdy snacks

Located just a stone's throw from Regent Street, Match consists of a small raised dining zone, a lengthy bar area which feels a little like a corridor and a cosy back room which is available for hire.

Like the other bars in the group, this place is primarily about good drinks, particularly cocktails. The list (as in the other two Match bars featured here) includes all the classics you'd hope for, as well as the many original cocktails created by Match bartenders over recent years. There is also a small but good selection of wines and beers.

The clientele is a mixture of the suited and the stylish and customers tend to get younger and more lively as the week draws to a close, when the atmosphere is usually DJ assisted. In this relatively small space, both the discerning, table-bound Martini drinker and the out & out party goer can be satisfied.

Match Bar

Match Bar

Match Bar

Maze

Mews of Mayfair

MAZE

● ● ● ● ◑

10-13 Grosvenor Square, Mayfair, London,
W1K 6JP, England

Tel: +44 (0)20 7107 0000,
www.gordonramsay.com
Hours: Mon-Sun noon-1am

Type:	Restaurant lounge bar
Alfresco:	No
Entry:	Subject to capacity
Highlights:	Food, cocktails, wine
Atmosphere:	Relaxed, informal
Clientele:	Business types
Dress code:	Smart casual
Price guide:	£££££
Food:	Tiny tasting plates

Grosvenor Square is the home of the US
embassy and opposite its ugly concrete
and steel security cordon sits yet another
Gordon Ramsay restaurant. Unlike some
of his others, however, this features a very
serious bar. In fact, two bar stations jut out
into the room. Covered by canopies of
white tile and frosted glass, these illuminate
the already clinical and brightly lit space.

Ramsay pulls a crowd and the banquette
seating in the bar area fills up quickly, leading
drinkers to congregate around the bars. This
helps create a relaxed, informal atmosphere
and the business types abandon their jackets
and ties on entry in favour of open necked shirts.

The cocktail list features new creations
and twists on the classics. All are well made
and beautifully presented. Foodies are right
to rave about executive chef Jason
Atherton, but the chaps wielding the
shakers are worthy of similar praise.

THE MET BAR
● ● ● ● ○

18-19 Old Park Lane, Mayfair, London, W1K
1LB, England

Tel: +44 (0)20 7447 4757,
www.metropolitan.co.uk
Hours: Mon-Sat 10am-3am,
Sun 10am-10.30pm

Type: Members' lounge bar
Alfresco: No
Entry: Strictly members & hotel guests
Highlights: Cocktails, music, atmosphere
Atmosphere: Chilled/late night party
Clientele: Celebs, hotel guests, music & media
Dress code: Gorgeously casual
Price guide: ££££
Food: Nibbles from Nobu

When The Met first opened at the end of
last century it was consistently rammed
with 'A' list celebs while hordes of
paparazzi froze their nuts off outside.
Unfortunately, most of the celebs moved
on to the next place to be seen and some
of the magic was lost. While lesser bars
would have relaxed their door policy, The
Met stuck strictly to its members and
guests only rule. The strategy paid off for
the celebs and that famous Met
atmosphere have returned. On a good
night it's like being at a friend's house party
only with great DJs, bartenders and the
odd TV personality.

With the exception of a new mural
depicting people dancing, the decor has
changed little. The original red, diner-style
booths and tables are still crammed into a
surprisingly small space. But The Met is
about the music, the cocktails and the
atmosphere, all of which can be fantastic.
Unless you are a member, however, you'll
need to book a room.

MEWS OF MAYFAIR
● ● ● ● ○

10-11 Lancaster Court (off New Bond
Street), Mayfair, London, W1S 1EY, England

Tel: +44 (0)20 7518 9388,
www.mewsofmayfair.com
Hours: 11am-2am (last entrance 1am)
(restaurant noon-3pm & 6pm-11:30pm)

Type: Cocktail bar, lounge & restaurant
Alfresco: Stand in narrow pedestrian street
Entry: Open door
Highlights: Food & cocktails
Atmosphere: Relaxed
Clientele: Mayfair set
Dress code: Stylish
Price guide: £££
Food: Classic English with modern slant

This aptly named bar, lounge and
restaurant is housed in two old mews
buildings in Lancaster Court, a series of
narrow pedestrian cobbled streets and
courtyards in the heart of Mayfair.

The wall and chimney stack between
the two houses has been completely
removed, creating a surprisingly large and
airy ground floor cocktail bar. Distressed
antiques line the walls while old picture
frames encase deluxe spirits behind the
bar. Deep-buttoned leather sofas and
Queen Anne chairs provide opulently
luxurious seating.

The basement lounge oozes glamour
with glass beaded walls, sculptural chairs
and a striking illuminated bar. Two
secluded alcoves form retreats for those
wanting to party in private.

As we went to press Mews had only
just opened. Still, the first floor restaurant
and the chef's dining room above are
expected to gain rave reviews for their
classic British fare. Two owners with
extensive bar experience and a good team
should ensure that cocktails and other
drinks match up.

MEZZA
● ● ● ○ ○

100 Wardour Street, Soho, London, W1F
0TN, England

Tel: +44 (0)20 7314 4002,
www.conran.com
Hours: Mon-Thu noon-2am, Fri-Sat
midnight-3am

Type: Tapas bar
Alfresco: No
Entry: Subject to capacity
Highlights: Sherry, tapas & cocktails
Atmosphere: Loud, informal and fun
Clientele: After work & out of towners
Dress code: Casual to suits
Price guide: £££
Food: Spanish tapas

This bar, on the ground floor of Conran's
old Mezzo building, has attracted much
less press coverage than the larger
Floridita restaurant below. But this slick
Conran operation is certainly worthy of
attention. The sherry list alone features
more than twenty bins and the forty strong
wine list is almost exclusively Spanish. The
Hispanic theme continues throughout the
menu, which features Spanish liqueurs,
Spanish brandy and of course tasty tapas.
The extensive cocktail list features classic
drinks as well as contemporary interpreta-
tions, all prepared to a high standard.

Sit at the chef's counter, at the
sweeping, pebble-fronted bar or at one of
the many oak trimmed tables. The
fortunate few score one of the four intimate
booths. The decor is clean and modern
and the atmosphere informal and fun. You'll
find a mixed bunch of after workers
alongside Conran fans from out of town.

MILK & HONEY
●●●●●

61 Poland Street, Soho, London, W1F 7NU,
England

Tel: +44 (0)7000 655 469,
www.mlkhny.com
Hours: Mon-Fri 7pm-3am, Sat 8pm-3am

Type:	Members lounge club
Alfresco:	No
Entry:	Members only after 11pm
Highlights:	Cocktails
Atmosphere:	Relaxed/sombre
Clientele:	Media & fashion kids
Dress code:	Smart casual
Price guide:	££££
Food:	Platters, oysters, caviar, venison etc.

Jonathan Downey, the man behind the
Match bar chain, has teamed up with
Sasha Petraske, owner of Milk & Honey in
New York, to turn what was Papa Gaio into
a larger copy of the famously secretive
Manhattan club.

The austere exterior and lobby confer
a satisfying feeling of entering a seedy den.
Beyond are three dimly lit floors, all sharing
the same 30s speakeasy decor. The two
main bars are on the ground floor and
basement with the smaller VIP 'Red Room'
on the first floor.

The comfortably moody surroundings,
secretive address and calm atmosphere,
coupled with some of the best classic cocktails in
London, make this a special place for seriously
discerning drinkers. Members are requested
to ring prior to visiting. Non-members can visit
until 11pm provided a telephone reservation
is made well in advance.

MORTON'S
●●●●○

28 Berkeley Square, Mayfair, London, W1J
6EN, England

Tel: +44 (0)20 7499 0363,
www.mortonsclub.com
Hours: Mon-Sat 8am-3am

Type:	Members/lounge bar
Alfresco:	No
Entry:	Member and guests only
Highlights:	Service
Atmosphere:	Posy but relaxed
Clientele:	Sloanes & mature trustafarians
Dress code:	Smart/designer casual
Price guide:	£££££
Food:	Nibbles & platters

There has been a club called Morton's in
a Georgian townhouse on Berkeley
Square, Mayfair, for as long as I can
remember but a change in ownership saw
an altogether plusher space emerge in
May 2004.

The new interior mixes original fixtures
with contemporary decor. In the basement
private dining room guests sit among the
2,300 bins that comprise the very
impressive wine list. The ground floor bar
features tan, stitched leather on both walls
and banquettes, while handcrafted glass
adorns the bar top. Backlit panels along
one wall change hue to moderate the
mood as the day progresses. A restaurant
lies at the top of a sweeping staircase.

Five star service prevails throughout,
while the Champagne and cocktail
offerings live up to the standards set by the
sommeliers. Morton's attracts a range of
moneyed types who are happy to part with
the £800 a year membership fee.

Nobu Berkeley St

Nobu Berkeley St

NOBU BERKELEY ST

● ● ● ◐ ○

15 Berkeley Street, Mayfair, London, W1J
8DY, England

Tel: +44 (0)20 7290 9222,
www.noburestaurants.com
Hours: Mon-Fri 5pm-2am, Sat 6pm-2am,
Sun 6pm-11pm

Type:	Lounge bar/restaurant
Alfresco:	No
Entry:	Subject to management & capacity
Highlights:	Food & cocktails
Atmosphere:	Relaxed
Clientele:	Wealthy, good looking
Dress code:	Designer casual
Price guide:	£££££

Food: Amazing sushi, sashimi, tempura

This ground floor bar and upstairs
restaurant was the third Nobu to open in
London and one has the feeling that even
if they outnumbered McDonald's they'd all
be busy. The draw is of course the
faultlessly good sushi, sashimi, tempura
and famed black cod in miso. The bar is
pretty much guaranteed custom as trendy
upscale restaurant patrons wait for a table
or stop off for an after dinner drink.
However, it has also become a destination
in its own right.

The interior is so modern that it wouldn't
seem out of place in Star Trek or Star Wars.
The almost circular room is dominated by
the bar, which is backed by whitened tree
branches sprouting out over black tiles.

Able bartenders construct tasty
cocktails. There's a serious champagne
list, ten sakes and eleven wines by the
glass, while the choice of four beers
includes Asahi Black and the wonderfully
creamy and hoppy house beer, Nobu
Special Reserve. Seats and tables tend to
be reserved for VIPs.

BEEFEATER &TONIC

Last Collection Time

Glass: Tall

Garnish: Lime wedge squeezed & dropped in

Method: Pour ingredients into ice-filled glass and lightly stir.
Squeeze lemon wedge into drink and lightly stir.
Serve with straws.

2 measures Beefeater
Top up with chilled tonic water

**Sunday
2.00pm**

Other Cocktails

Additional collections will be made throughout the
day as required until the last time shown.

On Bank Holidays we collect from this letter box
at 2.00pm

Letter box numb:

The Player   The Red Lion

The Player   The Red Lion

THE PLAYER LOUNGE BAR & KITCHEN

● ● ● ● ○

8 Broadwick Street, Soho, London, W1F
8HN, England

Tel: +44 (0)20 7494 9125,
www.theplyr.com
Hours: Mon-Thu 5.30pm-1am, Fri 5.30pm-
1am, Sat 6pm-3am

Type:	Members lounge bar
Alfresco:	No
Entry:	Door charge may apply (members only after 11pm)
Highlights:	Cocktails
Atmosphere:	Club-like
Clientele:	Young Soho set
Dress code:	Designer jeans
Price guide:	£££
Food:	Spare ribs, crab fritters, cheese fondue

A simple doorway in the heart of Soho, the
entrance to The Player would look
complete if it had a sign saying 'model
downstairs', a feel which is further
enhanced by the lingerie in the window of
Agent Provocateur next door. In fact, the
basement houses a well stocked bar
complete with black leather banquette
seating and scarlet walls.

When The Player first opened in
September 1998, it enjoyed immediate
success, partly due to the presence of bar
guru Dick Bradsell. However, he left, there
were 'licensing difficulties' and eventually
the Player closed. It was reopened by
Jonathan Downey's Match group in
October 2001, looking and feeling even
better than it did before, with Dale DeGroff
(New York's legendary bar meister)
overseeing the excellent cocktails.

The Player attracts a young crowd partly
drawn from nearby media and film companies.

THE RED LION

● ● ● ● ○

1 Waverton Street (opp. Charles St.), Mayfair, London,
W1J 5QN

Tel: +44 (0)20 7499 1307
Hours: Mon-Fri 11:30-11pm, Sat
11:30pm-3pm & 6pm-11pm, Sun noon-
3pm & 7pm-11pm

Type:	Traditional pub
Alfresco:	No
Entry:	Open door
Highlights:	Heritage & atmosphere
Atmosphere:	Warm & convivial
Clientele:	Well-heeled
Dress code:	Not too casual - suits
Price guide:	£££
Food:	Fish & chips, pies, burgers etc.

With its quaint lattice windows and back
street location, The Red Lion has the look
and feel of a country pub. Originally it was.
Back in the 18th century, it stood on an
unmade road, close to the grounds of
Chesterfield House, lordly seat of the Earls
of Chesterfield. The house was demolished
in 1937 and the old stable buildings that
used to surround the pub were replaced
with the grand houses we see today.

The interior has altered over the years
as the clientele changed from stable lads to
captains of industry. However, it retains an
olde-worlde charm with open fires, a low
ceiling, bare floorboards and dark panelled
walls adorned with old prints and topped by
shelves lined with Toby jugs, tea pots and
other chinaware. Winged settles (high
backed benches) add to its traditional appeal.

This little pub is busy enough at
lunchtimes and early evening to justify as
many as five traditional cask ales on
draught. There's also a fair wine offering
and reasonably priced pub grub.

REFUEL BAR

● ● ● ● ○

The Soho Hotel, 4 Richmond Mews, Richmond Buildings
(off Dean St), Soho, London, W1D 3DH, England

Tel: +44 (0)20 7559 3000,
www.sohohotel.com
Hours: Mon-Sat noon-3pm & 6pm-11pm,
Sun noon-3pm & 6pm-10.30pm

Type:	Lounge/hotel/restaurant bar
Alfresco:	No
Entry:	Subject to capacity
Highlights:	Cocktails & champagne
Atmosphere:	Relaxed
Clientele:	Hotel guests and media office escapees
Dress code:	Smart/casual
Price guide:	£££££
Food:	Platters serve 4 (e.g. Italian or Moroccan)

The Soho Hotel opened in summer 2004
at the end of a cul-de-sac off Dean Street
and it's hard to believe that this slick
boutique environment was constructed in
the shell of a former multi-storey car park.
The Refuel bar lies next to the hotel's
restaurant, beyond the lobby and its
impressive giant bronze cat.

The fairly bland room is dominated and
brightened by a specially commissioned
mural which illustrates the site's previous
incarnation. Below it runs a long pewter bar
lined with high stools, while low slung sofas
and coffee tables occupy the narrow space
between the bar and the restaurant.

Soho's most stylish media set appear
to have settled in here, appreciating the
efficient service offered by the friendly staff.
A comprehensive champagne and wine
list and an inspired range of excellent
cocktails enhance the draw.

REX CINEMA & BAR
●●●●○

21 Rupert Street, Soho, London, W1V 7FE, England
OR 13 Coventry Street, W1V 7FE

Tel: +44 (0)20 7287 0102,
www.rexcinemaandbar.com
Hours: Tue-Sat 6pm-3am

Type:	Lounge bar/nightclub/cinema
Alfresco:	No
Entry:	Members have priority
Highlights:	Cocktails, films
Atmosphere:	Chilled to full-on party
Clientele:	Young social climbers
Dress code:	Bling
Price guide:	££££
Food:	Sushi, gourmet pizza, club sandwiches etc

A bouncer, a clipboard toting accomplice and a velvet rope protect the entrance to this subterranean art nouveau styled lounge. Deep velvets and crystal chandeliers contrast with raw exposed brickwork to create a feel rather similar to a film set.

Beyond the bar and a lobby-like space is a small but plushly appointed 75-seat cinema which screens current, classic and pre-release films (the Rex is named after a pre-war cinema group). Membership costs £250 per annum but provides free access to both bar and cinema.

The female-led bar team at Rex offer a great list of classically inspired cocktails which are brilliantly executed and delivered to your table. The atmosphere is more club-like towards the end of the week and at weekends, when DJs often play.

RIVOLI BAR
●●●●○

Ritz Hotel, 150 Piccadilly, London, W1J 9BR, England

Tel: +44 (0)20 7493 8181,
www.theritzhotel.co.uk
Hours: 11:30am-11pm (1am for hotel residents)

Type:	Hotel / lounge bar
Alfresco:	No
Entry:	Subject to dress
Highlights:	Art Deco interior, cocktails
Atmosphere:	Somewhat staid
Clientele:	Trustafarians & crusty Mayfair money
Dress code:	Gents must wear jacket & tie, no jeans
Price guide:	£££££
Food:	Posh sandwiches, sushi, salads etc

When Cesar Ritz opened this graceful old hotel on 24th May 1906 it featured spectacular innovations such as a bathroom for each guestroom and double glazing. It was the first steel framed building of any significance in London and was praised for its French chateau style architecture and Louis XVI furnishings. Thanks to recent refurbishment it still oozes style and opulence, which continue in the Rivoli Bar just off the grand 'Long Gallery'.

Entering the Rivoli is like stepping into a bygone era. The interior is classic 1920s Art Deco. An onyx marble bar is surrounded by walls of polished camphor wood and illuminated Lalique glass panels. Etched glass windows peek onto Piccadilly. Four panes of verre églomisé (gilded and silvered mirror glass) reflect gilt leaf ceiling domes and polished bamboo.

This ornate room accommodates a mere 44 guests but it does so in some style. Champagne and well made cocktails are delivered by table service.

SANDERSON HOTEL BARS
●●●●○

Long Bar & Purple Bar, 50 Berners Street, Fitzrovia, London, W1P 3AD, England

Tel: +44 (0)20 7300 1400,
www.sandersonhotel.com
Hours: Mon-Sat 11am-12.30am, Sun 11am-10.30pm

Type:	Lounge/hotel bar
Alfresco:	Courtyard
Entry:	Hotel guests only in Purple bar
Highlights:	Eye candy/pulling potential
Atmosphere:	Chilled to party
Clientele:	City boys, jet set, models
Dress code:	To the hilt
Price guide:	£££££
Food:	Finger food - foie gras, smoked salmon

The jewel of the Starck-designed Sanderson hotel, the Purple bar is like travelling celebrity class to Wonderland. It's snug and dimly lit, with miniature tables and chairs, decoratively cut mirror work and opulent deep purple furnishings in front of a solid stone bar. But you'll need to book a room as the Purple bar is designed for VVIPs and hotel residents only.

The Long Bar, Sanderson's slightly less exclusive second bar, is, well, long. The island bar sits in the centre of the white room, allowing the finance/fashion clientele, who ooze cash from every orifice, to check each other out from opposite sides.

Outside, a wooden decked courtyard with bamboo, candles, slate and running water is welcome relief. Grab yourself a seat and ask one of the waitresses who slink about in black dresses for the oversized cocktail list. Whatever you choose is likely to be eminently drinkable.

BEEFEATER & ELDERFLOWER

Glass: Tall
Garnish: Mint sprig
2 measures Beefeater
1 measure Elderflower cordial
Top up with chilled sparkling water

Method: Pour ingredients into ice-filled glass and lightly stir.

72

Shochu Lounge

SHOCHU LOUNGE
● ● ● ● ◐

Roka, 37 Charlotte Street, Fitzrovia, London,
W1T 1RR, England

Tel: +44 (0)20 7580 6464
Hours: Mon-Sat 5.30pm-midnight, Sun
5.30pm-11pm

Type:	Lounge bar
Alfresco:	No
Entry:	Subject to management & capacity
Highlights:	Cocktails, spirits & food
Atmosphere:	Chilled
Clientele:	Mature office escapees
Dress code:	Smart/casual
Price guide:	£££
Food:	Japanese farmhouse cuisine

Nestling below Roka, the West End sister
restaurant to the stratospherically
fashionable Zuma, this subterranean
lounge takes its name from the traditional
Japanese spirit. A kind of low-proof,
flavoursome vodka, Shochu is very much
the theme here and antique Japanese
brewing and distilling vessels occupy a
whole wall.

Various types of Shochu are available,
either as a cocktail base or infused with
flavours such as cherry blossom or green
tea in one of the many glass jars that line
the wall. Infusions are served in wonderful
hand blown tumblers with a single huge
ice cube chiselled from a large block of ice
as you watch.

Beyond the natural timber island bar
is a lounge area. I recommend the
Japanese farmhouse nibbles from the
kitchen above.

Shochu Lounge

SKETCH
● ● ● ◐ ○

9 Conduit Street, Mayfair, London, W1S
2XG, England

Tel: +44 (0)8707 774 488,
www.sketch.uk.com
Hours: Mon-Sat noon-2am

Type:	Restaurant bar/supper club
Alfresco:	No
Entry:	Members and diners only
Highlights:	Peeing in a pod
Atmosphere:	Clinical to debauched
Clientele:	Business types and the glamorous
Dress code:	To the hilt
Price guide:	££££
Food:	Foie gras, smoked salmon etc.

The interior of Sketch sets clinical 70s
futurism against a grand backdrop. The
high ceilings and detailing are original to
the Georgian, Grade II listed building which
houses this Michelin-starred restaurant,
lounge and club.

Along with The Lecture Room, which
is notoriously London's most expensive
restaurant, Sketch also boasts a 150-seat
brasserie-style restaurant with moving
wallpaper called the Gallery, the East Bar
and an affordable restaurant, Glade, in
what was once the West Bar.

The East Bar is known as the capsule
due to its ovoid design and is encircled by
a double staircase which leads to the
much talked about toilets, each housed in
its own egg shaped white pod.

Sketch attracts a glamorous, well-
heeled crowd, admitted because they
have paid for annual membership or have
previously reserved a table at one of the
restaurants. Thanks to wonderfully polite
staff the whole experience is far more
approachable than it sounds - that's if your
credit card is up to it.

SOHO HOUSE
● ● ● ● ○

40 Greek Street (corner Old Compton St),
Soho, London, W1D 4EB, England

Tel: +44 (0)20 7851 1178,
www.sohohouse.com
Hours: Mon-Sat noon-3am, Sun noon-
10:30pm

Type:	Members' club/restaurant/ lounge bar
Alfresco:	Small roof deck
Entry:	Members & guests only
Highlights:	Exclusive retreat feel
Atmosphere:	Relaxed, laid-back
Clientele:	Folk from film, media & arts
Dress code:	Stylish, designer casual
Price guide:	££££
Food:	Plates to full meals

Soho House was founded in 1995 by Nick
Jones, the husband of the TV newsreader
Kirsty Young. It is a private members' club
of some repute, popular with folk from the
film and media industries - many of
them celebrities.

There are two distinct sides to Soho
House. One, accessed from an entrance
at 21 Old Compton Street, houses a series
of rooms and a loft terrace which can be
hired by non-members for private functions
or meetings. The other, quite separate,
side is accessed from the members'
entrance around the corner on Greek
Street. This also consists of a series of
rooms laid out over three floors with a first
floor restaurant, second floor circle bar and
a drawing room. My favourite area is the
third floor Kitchen & Bar, an informal, open-
plan restaurant and bar. A small roof deck
offers views across the rooftops of Soho
and is great for al fresco breakfasts,
lunches or dinners.

TAMAN GANG
● ● ● ◐ ○

140a Park Lane (@ Oxford St), London,
W1K 7AA, England

Tel: +44 (0)20 7518 3160,
www.tamangang.com
Hours: Daily midday-1am

Type:	Lounge/restaurant bar
Alfresco:	No
Entry:	Subject to management & capacity
Highlights:	Cocktails & service
Atmosphere:	Restrained
Clientele:	Diners and a varied crowd
Dress code:	Smart casual/designer
Price guide:	££££
Food:	Pan-Asian

Owned by the founders of London's
fashionable Chinawhite club, Taman gang
takes its named from the Balinese for 'Park
Lane'. Hidden in a basement under the
Marriott Hotel near the corner of Park Lane
and Oxford Street, its unassuming entrance
belies the impressive space below.

The interior resembles a hidden
chamber from Raiders Of The Lost Ark.
Craftsmen were flown in from Bali to carve
the limestone walls. The lighting is dim and
the ceiling low, adding intimacy to the large
room. The men's toilets feature erotic
carvings and the women's have stalagmite
and stalactite wash and dry units. These
are something of a talking point among the
glamorous folk Taman gang attracts.

This is primarily a restaurant but the
small bar area is worth a visit in itself.
Service is slick and both food and drinks
are great. Cocktails are inventive, high
quality and made with love.

TRADER VIC'S
● ● ● ● ○

Hilton Hotel (basement), 22 Park Lane, Mayfair, London, W1Y 4BE, England

Tel: +44 (0)20 7208 4113, **www.**tradervics.com
Hours: Mon-Thu 11.30am-3.30pm & 5pm-1am, Fri 11.30am-3.30pm & 5pm-3am, Sat 5pm-3am, Sun 5pm-10.30pm

Type:	Lounge/cabaret/restaurant bar
Alfresco:	No
Entry:	Subject to management & capacity
Highlights:	Cocktails
Atmosphere:	Relaxed
Clientele:	Suited older crowd
Dress code:	Smart (but not strictly)
Price guide:	£££££
Food:	Tidbits & 'bar bites' (try the Piri Piri Prawns)

In 1934, Victor Jules Bergeron, or Trader Vic as he became known, opened his first restaurant 'Hinky Dink's' in Oakland, San Francisco. Here he served Polynesian food with a mix of Chinese, French and American dishes cooked in Chinese wood-fired ovens. As well as his then exotic menu, Vic became famous for the rum based cocktails he created, particularly the Mai Tai.

He acquired the 'Trader' nickname due to offering free food and drinks to customers who brought him aged rums, which were then hard to obtain. After a trip to Tahiti in 1937 he changed the restaurant's name to Trader Vic's and the Tiki theme was born.

Vic died in 1984, but his brand lives on with branches around the world. I've visited a few and found this one to be by far the best. Here you'll find Vic's take on Polynesian food, great rum cocktails and South Pacific themed decor including shark's teeth, puffer fish and hand carved Tiki poles.

VOLSTEAD
● ● ● ● ○

9 Swallow Street (btwn Regent Street & Piccadilly), Mayfair, London, W1R 7HD, England

Tel: +44 (0)20 7287 1919,
www.volstead.com
Hours: Tue-Sat 7pm-3am

Type:	Lounge bar / micro club
Alfresco:	No
Entry:	Arrive early towards the weekend
Highlights:	Cocktails
Atmosphere:	Chilled to mini party
Clientele:	Mayfair in-crowd
Dress code:	Designer lounge
Price guide:	££££
Food:	Posh mini burgers, chips & caviar

Volstead is a 1920s inspired lounge-cum-club ironically named after Andrew Volstead, who created the act which launched Prohibition in the US. Although this is an intimately sized space – the capacity is only 150 - the owners, who also run Cocoon, have managed to squeeze in a small dancefloor complete with a decanter encrusted DJ booth. They have also managed to entice the flamboyant Mikey and Andreas away from Kemia Bar to draw Mayfair's moneyed and gorgeous set to their new place.

Banquettes line walls still clad with original strip mirrors from a previous incarnation as Sybilla's Club, an elite 1960s venue backed by the Beatle George Harrison and friends. The lighting is suitably dim and the DJ steers the mood from early evening cocktail jazz through lounge to out & out club as the atmosphere picks up.

The spirits offering is dominated by American whiskies and gin, as is the cocktail list, which features audacious contemporary creations rather than the predictable classics you might expect in a retro lounge. Alternatively wash the wagyu beef burgers down with vintage Veuve Clicquot, Dom Perignon or Krug, which are all available by the glass.

WINDOWS
● ● ● ○ ○

The London Hilton, 22 Park Lane, Mayfair, London, W1K 1BE, England

Tel: +44 (0)20 7493 8000,
Hours: Mon-Thu noon-3am, Fri-Sat noon-3am, Sun noon-10:30pm

Type:	Lounge bar
Alfresco:	No
Entry:	Subject to management & capacity
Highlights:	View
Atmosphere:	Tad stuffy
Clientele:	Hotel guests & glamour seekers
Dress code:	Make an effort
Price guide:	£££££
Food:	Modern French cuisine next door

This restaurant and bar space on the 28th floor of the Hilton on Park Lane has long been famous for its views but recently also known for its rather dated appearance. However, thanks to a £1.5 million refurbishment, things have changed. The renamed Galvin at Windows restaurant now boasts the acclaimed, classically trained Chris Galvin as chef-patron and the bar next door has also benefited from the refit.

Windows now sports a decidedly contemporary look. Apparently "inspired by 1930s glamour" it feels more corporate than louche. The room is dominated by an illuminated halo which hangs menacingly over drinkers corralled into the fenced-off central area. Sadly, the light this emits detracts from the loungy atmosphere.

We were disappointed by all the cocktails we sampled on our visit, especially considering their premium price. However, it is the expanse of floor to ceiling glass on both sides of the room which give this bar its name and make it worth visiting.

ZETA

●●●◐○

35 Hertford Street (under Hilton Hotel),
Mayfair, London, W1Y 7TG, England

Tel: +44 (0)20 7208 4067,
www.zeta-bar.com
Hours: Mon-Tue 5pm-1am, Wed-Fri 5pm-
3am, Sat 5pm-3am, Sun 8pm-1am

Type:	Lounge bar
Alfresco:	No
Entry:	Members take precedence
Highlights:	Atmosphere
Atmosphere:	Party
Clientele:	City crowd & the style set
Dress code:	Casually couture
Price guide:	££££
Food:	Oriental influence

Zeta is one of London's funkiest hotel bars,
so you'll be surprised to hear that the name
was inspired not by the sixth letter of
the Greek alphabet, but by the brand name
of a fire bell Robbie Bargh (the consultant
behind this bar) spotted in another
bar's toilets.

The interior has a subtly Oriental
theme with delicate looking illuminated
walls that appear to be made from brown
packing paper. Apart from the odd out of
place guest from the Hilton upstairs and
businessmen celebrating winning or losing
an award in another Park Lane hotel, Zeta
is packed with City boys and model types
enjoying sublime drinks from the
impressive cocktail list.

Friday and Saturday nights here are
huge. Subdued lighting, comfy chairs,
attentive staff and DJs spinning chilled
tunes drive the party.

Trader Vics

Zeta

SOUTH BANK
(SE1, SE11, SE16)

FAMED FOR ITS CULTURAL ATTRACTIONS, THE SOUTH BANK IS ALSO HOME
TO HORDES OF OFFICES AND FRIDAY EVENINGS SEE POST-WORKERS OUT
EN MASSE. BUT BOTH HERE AND FURTHER EAST ARE SOME PLEASANT
BARS AND HISTORIC PUBS.

ANCHOR & HOPE
● ● ● ○

36 The Cut, Waterloo, London, SE1 8LP,
England

Tel: +44 (0)20 7928 9898
Hours: Mon 5pm-11pm, Tue-Sat 11am-
11pm (lunch noon-2:30pm, dinner 6pm-
10:30pm)

Type: Gastro pub
Alfresco: None but has café-style windows
Entry: Open door
Highlights: Food, wine, beer
Atmosphere: Relaxed
Clientele: Foodies & office escapees
Dress code: Suits to scruffy jeans
Price guide: £££
Food: Excellent snacks and mains

Appearances can be deceiving and the
exterior of the Anchor & Hope looks
unpromising to say the least. The interior,
with its burgundy walls, swirling ceiling fans
and the usual mismatched second-hand
tables and chairs, is merely nice enough.

But the Anchor & Hope takes the best
elements of pub and restaurant, and
combines them in a relaxed, informal,
friendly setting. The food varies from
outstanding to damn good and leads
gastrophiles to trek across London to join
hordes of local office workers in the
scramble for one of the unbookable tables.

Waiting for a table in the bar area is a
pleasure with three traditional ales on
draught (including St Austell Tribute) and
a good selection of wines chalked up on
the board behind the bar, including
eighteen by the glass. There's also a none
too shabby range of cocktails and sherries
should the mood take you. While you wait
I'd suggest snacking on a couple of the
tasty tapas plates.

THE ANGEL
● ● ● ○

101 Bermondsey Wall East (@ Cathay St),
Rotherhithe, London, SE16 4NB, England

Tel: +44 (0)20 7237 3608,
www.famousangel.co.uk
Hours: Mon-Sat noon-11pm, Sun noon-
10:30pm

Type: Traditional pub
Alfresco: Riverside gallery & side terrace
Entry: Open door
Highlights: View
Atmosphere: Very relaxed
Clientele: Local residents, odd tourist
Dress code: Casual
Price guide: ££
Food: Finger snacks to full blown pub grub

Lost downriver in Rotherhithe suburbia,
opposite the ruins of a fourteenth century
manor house built for Edward III, lies one of
London's most historic pubs. The original
inn was built in the 15th century by monks
at the nearby Bermondsey Priory for use as
a guesthouse called the Salutation. After the
Reformation, it was renamed the Angel in
honour of the local lord of the manor and is
said to have been patronised by Samuel
Pepys and Captain James Cook.

The present building dates back to the
1850s and was thankfully saved by a loving
restoration in 2005. The old sash windows
of both the ground floor bar and the upstairs
lounge offer spectacular views up and down
the river. A side door leads out onto a narrow
gallery over the Thames where water laps
the timber piles below.

Like many other historic London pubs
this is owned by Samuel Smith's so sadly
only that brewery's brands are available.
However, the drinks are cheap and it's a very
comfortable spot from which to appreciate
Tower Bridge.

BALTIC
● ● ● ○

74 Blackfriars Road (@ The Cut), Waterloo,
London, SE1 8HA, England

Tel: +44 (0)20 7928 1111,
www.balticrestaurant.co.uk
Hours: Mon-Fri noon-11pm, Sat 6pm-
11pm, Sun noon-10.30pm

Type: Eastern European restaurant & bar
Alfresco: Few tables out front
Entry: Subject to capacity
Highlights: Home flavoured vodkas & cocktails
Atmosphere: Friendly local
Clientele: Locals & those in the know
Dress code: Office attire to hip
Price guide: £££
Food: Blinis & other Polish snacks

Lying behind Baltic's narrow frontage is a
deceptively large modern Polish bar and
a vast, barn-like restaurant. Baltic is noted
for its extensive list of Polish vodkas and
beers and the staff flavour the in-house
vodkas in huge glass demijohns behind
the bar. The Karmelówka (caramel) and
Wisniówka (cherry) are particularly worth
a try, whether neat or as part of one of the
many outstanding cocktails on the list.

Poland & Eastern Europe are bar
snack heaven and the Slavs even manage
to turn beetroot broth into a delicacy, so
be sure to try the Ukrainian barszcz.

Baltic draws a friendly crowd of locals
and after work drinkers who are joined by
travelling foodies and fun seekers in
the know.

BERMONDSEY KITCHEN

● ● ● ○ ○

194 Bermondsey Street, Bermondsey,
London, SE1 3TQ, England

Tel: +44 (0)20 7407 5719,
www.bermondseykitchen.co.uk
Hours: Mon-Fri noon-3pm & 6:30pm-
10:30pm, Sat 9:30am-3.30pm & 6:30pm-
10:30pm, Sun 9:30am-3:30pm

Type: Eastern European restaurant & bar
Alfresco: Few tables out front
Entry: Subject to capacity
Highlights: Home flavoured vodkas & cocktails
Atmosphere: Friendly local
Clientele: Locals & those in the know
Dress code: Office attire to hip
Price guide: £££
Food: Blinis & other Polish snacks

As its name suggests, the Bermondsey
Kitchen is primarily a restaurant. However,
it is wonderfully relaxed and you're welcome
just to pop in for a drink.

Originally an engineering workshop, the
interior follows the classic gastro pub formula
of bar counter leading to open kitchen, bare
floorboards and mismatched old wooden
tables and chairs. More distinctive styling
comes from 70s lampshades and a white
horizontal panel which runs the length of one
wall, resembling a gallery space awaiting
artwork. The frontage has panes that slide
open in the summer, and gives the room a
bright airy feel, offering views of St. Mary
Magdalen opposite.

The food is both excellent and multi-
cultural with dishes from Europe, South
America and Asia. Wash these down with
one of the well priced wines (7 by the glass)
or choose from the cocktail list.

While weekdays attract folk from local
offices, weekends draw an older crowd and
even the odd child.

BREW WHARF

● ● ● ● ○

Brew Wharf Yard, Stoney Street, London,
SE1 9AD, England

Tel: +44 (0)20 7378 6601,
www.brewwharf.com
Hours: Mon-Fri 11.30am-11pm,
Sat 11am-11pm

Type: Contemporary pub & brasserie
Alfresco: Courtyard with tables
Entry: Open door
Highlights: Beer
Atmosphere: Sobered by lighting
Clientele: Office escapees & occasional tourist
Dress code: Office attire to casual
Price guide: £££
Food: Full Alsatian bistro menu

Set within three vast, high railway arches just
behind Borough Market, Brew Wharf combines
brasserie, beer hall and microbrewery.

You enter via the venue's own walled
yard, complete with outside tables, and
through a café style open frontage. The
first arch houses a bar counter bristling
with gleaming beer pumps, the middle
arch an open kitchen and a glass fronted
beer cellar, while the last offers a view of
the brewing vessels behind. All three
arches are furnished with simple wooden
tables and contrast a white mosaic floor
with towering bare brickwork.

Two real ales are brewed on site, one
with Fuggles hops and the other with
Goldings Kentish hops. The other draught
beers come from the celebrated Meantime
brewery in Greenwich, including the
excellent Vienna-styled Union lager.

The wine list and the brasserie menu
are heavily influenced by France's Alsace
region. Ingredients are sourced exclusively
from the famous market across the street.

THE BRIDGE HOUSE

● ● ● ○ ○

218 Tower Bridge Road, London, SE1 2UP,
England

Tel: +44 (0)20 7407 5818,
www.adnams.co.uk
Hours: Mon-Sat 11am-11pm, Sun noon-
10:30pm

Type: Gastro pub
Alfresco: No
Entry: Open door
Highlights: Beer, food & wine
Atmosphere: Relaxed
Clientele: Office workers & tourists
Dress code: Suits to casual
Price guide: £££
Food: Modern British posh gastro grub

The Bridge House is one of the first
buildings you encounter on the south side
after crossing Tower Bridge. It's also the
first London pub to be owned and
operated by Adnams, the Suffolk brewer
which makes Broadside, the flavoursome
traditional British ale with the strap line "a
blast from the past". Not only is Broadside
served at the bar, but the gastro menu
offers haddock baked in batter flavoured
with the ale and served with mushy peas.

The old building has real character,
particularly appreciated when you
approach from the back entrance in
Horselydown Lane. Its soulless, modern
and bland interior is comfortable but
disappointing.

These days Adnams is as noted for its
wines as its beers and the reasonably
priced, democratic list offers 16 by the
glass. However, the main attraction remains
the food. Whether you're here to dine or
drink ale, expect great table service.

THE GARRISON

● ● ● ○ ○

99-101 Bermondsey Street, Bermondsey, London, SE1 3XB, England

Tel: +44 (0)207 089 9355,
www.thegarrison.co.uk
Hours: Mon-Fri 8am-11pm, Sat 9am-11pm, Sun 9am-10:30pm

Type: Gastro pub
Alfresco: No
Entry: Open door
Highlights: Food
Atmosphere: Relaxed
Clientele: New media types
Dress code: Relaxed
Price guide: ££££
Food: Superb modern Brit snacks to mains

Bermondsey Street is hardly short of quality gastro pubs, but the Garrison is perhaps its most praised - so much so that I'd advise ringing ahead to be sure of securing a table.

The green-tiled exterior has a quaint, almost country pub look and the theme continues inside with sage coloured, country kitchen panelling. But that's where the coordination ends for this is an interior of vastly contrasting styles: plush wallpaper, silk lamps, American diner-style booths and space age bucket seats collaborate implausibly.

The homely feel, coupled with an excellent modern British menu and great service, has proved a major hit with Bermondsey's newly found crowd of hip creatives. They are made further at home by a cinema room in the basement.

The Garrison may be a fantastic restaurant but it retains all the essential elements of a great pub and regulars still prop up the bar. The wine list has some real gems and draught offerings include Adnams Best and Leffe Braun.

THE GEORGE INN

● ● ○ ○

George Inn Yard, 77 Borough High Street, Borough, SE1 1NH, England

Tel: +44 (0)20 7407 2056,
www.nationaltrust.org.uk
Hours: Mon-Sat 11am-11pm, Sun noon-10:30pm

Type: Traditional pub
Alfresco: Large courtyard with tables
Entry: Open door
Highlights: Heritage, traditional ale
Atmosphere: Varies
Clientele: Tourists, office workers
Dress code: Casual
Price guide: £££
Food: Pub food

London's only surviving galleried coaching inn is tucked away in a cobbled courtyard just off Borough High Street. The George was rebuilt in 1676, after a fire swept through Southwark. Then in the late 19th century the Great Northern Railway demolished two of its façades to make way for warehousing, leaving just the south face. Now owned by the National Trust, it is leased to private operators.

Behind the pretty lattice windows it is a little touristy but olde world. Interconnecting bars feature low ceilings, oak beams, old settles, alcoves and chimney corners. The upstairs, galleried part with its dark panelling originally housed bedchambers and is now a restaurant and function rooms.

They say that Shakespeare once performed in the cobbled courtyard. Today this is overlooked by an ugly modern office block but it remains a popular summer time drinking spot.

Beware coachloads of tourists and the far from special food and drinks offering.

THE MARKET PORTER

● ● ● ● ○

9 Stoney Street, Borough, London, SE1 9AA, England

Tel: +44 (0)20 7407 2495
Hours: Mon-Sat 6:30am-8:30am & 11:30am-11pm, Sun noon-10:30pm

Type: Traditional pub
Alfresco: Pavement (no chairs)
Entry: Open door
Highlights: Range of cask ales
Atmosphere: Warm & friendly
Clientele: Market/office workers
Dress code: Suits to jeans
Price guide: £££
Food: Snacks & full meals (not Saturday)

Aptly named after its clientele, The Market Porter is one of a few London pubs which operate market hours, opening early in the morning to allow market workers to enjoy a drink after a hard morning's graft.

It opened in 1620 but is looking smarter than ever after a refit in 2005, although some say this was to the detriment of its character. It now boasts freshly painted burgundy walls contrasting with exposed brickwork and bare wooden floor.

The market opposite has also been subject to a spruce-up in recent years. It has become a destination for food lovers who flock here on Saturdays to buy supplies from the excellent farmer's market and that is the only day when food is not served in the pub.

The Market Porter has something of a reputation for traditional cask ales and the choice of eight brews changes regularly.

BEEFEATER LIME & TONI
2 SHOTS BEEFEATER
CHILLED TONIC WATER
1 LIME WEDGE

MAYFLOWER

● ● ● ○ ○

117 Rotherhithe Street, Rotherhithe, London, SE16 4NF, England

Tel: +44 (0)20 7237 4088
Hours: Mon-Sat 11am-11pm, Sun noon-10:30pm

Type:	Traditional pub
Alfresco:	Jetty over river
Entry:	Open door
Highlights:	Ales, steaks & jetty
Atmosphere:	Warm & friendly
Clientele:	Locals & tourists
Dress code:	Casual
Price guide:	£££
Food:	Pub grub, steaks a speciality

Originally named the Shippe, this picturesque Thameside pub was built in 1550. Its modern name celebrates the voyage of the Pilgrim Fathers, who set off for the New World seventy years later on board the Mayflower. They departed from moorings behind the pub and the captain who brought the ship home is buried in the graveyard of St Mary's nearby. Some time in the early 18th century, the Shippe was rebuilt with its original cellars, supposedly using timbers from the Mayflower, whose name it acquired when restored in 1957.

This beautifully restored and kept hostelry boasts its own jetty built on piles in the river, from which thirty or so drinkers can enjoy views of Tower Bridge and the site of Execution Dock, where convicted pirates were taken to drown. Inside, the small, wood panelled bar is lined with narrow settles "that fit all buttocks".

Three Greene King ales are offered alongside a fair wine list. Steaks are something of a speciality.

OXO TOWER

● ● ● ● ○

8th Floor, Oxo Tower Wharf, Barge House Street, London, SE1 9PH, England

Tel: +44 (0)20 7803 3888,
www.oxotower.co.uk
Hours: Mon-Sat 11am-11pm,
Sun noon-10.30pm

Type:	Lounge/restaurant bar
Alfresco:	Only for diners
Entry:	By elevator from the 1st floor
Highlights:	Cocktails and the view
Atmosphere:	Crowded but friendly
Clientele:	Tourists, City boys & girls
Dress code:	Suits to designer jeans
Price guide:	£££
Food:	Prawn toast, fish cakes, wedges etc

In the late 1920s the makers of OXO stock cubes and gravy granules bought this now famous South Bank landmark. Their architect, Albert W Moore, proposed to spell out OXO in electric lights on the tower but was refused permission so he incorporated the name into the windows, hence branding the building forever.

The bar lies on the eighth floor and is accessed by an express elevator from the first floor. Windows on two sides offer stunning views of London. With its louvred ceiling incorporating blue neon lights, the interior design is modern touching on industrial.

City boys, sightseers, hen parties and the style set crowd this small space so the comfy-as-hell blue orchid chairs are in short supply, as is space around the curvaceous padded island bar. There's a great selection of classic and contemporary cocktails and an excellent range of beers, wines and spirits.

SOUTH LONDON PACIFIC

● ● ● ○ ○

340 Kennington Road, Oval, London, SE11 4LD, England

Tel: +44 (0)20 7820 9189,
www.southlondonpacific.com
Hours: Tue-Wed 5pm-midnight, Thu 5pm-1am, Fri 5pm-2am, Sat noon-2am, Sun noon-midnight

Type:	Tiki bar
Alfresco:	No
Entry:	Open door
Highlights:	Kitsch
Atmosphere:	Locals' pub to Tiki party
Clientele:	Locals, Tiki enthusiasts
Dress code:	Jeans & T-shirt
Price guide:	£££
Food:	Elvis snacks

The theme of this kitsch emporium, like the name, is South Pacific Polynesian island and to appreciate it you'll have to forget the fact that it's situated in insalubrious Kennington, South London.

The inside is a celebration of Tiki kitsch. Bamboo supports the grass roof of the bar, elongated Tiki faces cover the walls, the space is crammed with bamboo furniture and hula girls, and DJ Aloha provides the Polynesian tunes. Rum based tropical cocktails are the drink of choice and the list includes all the Tiki classics.

On a good night this place rocks but sadly on other nights the location lets it down and it feels like a rather tacky theme bar. Diehard Tiki fans should also be warned that the interior shows signs of budgetary constraint and lacks many of the more exotic accoutrements of the genre. All the same, I recommend dusting off your Hawaiian shirt and heading here for a Mai Tai. Aloha!

H

VILLAGE EAST
● ● ● ○

171-173 Bermondsey Street, Southwark,
London, SE1 3UW, England

Tel: +44 (0)20 7357 6082
www.villageeast.co.uk
Hours: Mon-Sat noon-11pm, Sun noon-
10:30pm

Type:	Gastro bar
Alfresco:	None
Entry:	Open door
Highlights:	Food & wine
Atmosphere:	Relaxed
Clientele:	Office escapees
Dress code:	Suits to casual (not scruffy)
Price guide:	££££
Food:	Excellent snacks and mains

Confusingly, the newly gentrified, 'villagey'
neighbourhood referenced in this bar's name
is South-East London's Bermondsey, not
somewhere in the East End. I suppose
'Village South-East' just doesn't have the
same ring.

The interior of Village East straddles the
ground floor of two buildings which have
been knocked into one. The left side is
modern while the right is, typically for the area,
a refurbished Victorian warehouse. Each side
has a bar at the front and a dining room
behind. Smokers are relegated to the new
building but the old building is the place to
be: its dining room is discreet and cosy, while
its bar is ample and lounge with squashy
leather seating, low tables, exposed
brickwork, and an oak floor and bar counter.

As well as an extremely appealing
interior, Village East also boasts a superb,
modern and eclectic food menu, plus an
equally impressive wine list, with 15 wines
by the glass, and some well conceived and
made cocktails. It attracts young
professionals from the local offices and lofts.

THE WHITE HART
● ● ● ○

29 Cornwall Road (corner Whittlesey St),
Waterloo, London, SE1 8TJ, England

Tel: +44 (0)20 7401 7151
Hours: Mon-Sat noon-11pm, Sun noon-
10:30pm

Type:	Traditional / gastro pub
Alfresco:	Four pavement tables
Entry:	If there's room
Highlights:	Beers, food
Atmosphere:	Busy / bustling
Clientele:	Office escapees
Dress code:	Suits to tatty jeans & T-shirts
Price guide:	£££
Food:	Gourmet burgers, steaks and sandwiches

At first glance The White Hart is a fairly
unassuming back street boozer but the
Mitchell & Butler pub company have
introduced a touch of 70s kitsch as part of
a gastro makeover. The old pub retains its
dark wood panelling and a square island
bar that takes up more of the space than
a modern designer would allow, while
gastro furnishings include old kitchen
chairs, wooden tables and slouchy sofas.
The low lighting is brightened by 70s light
fittings and sparkly dangly bits.

An impressive parade of beer fonts
includes two ales on hand pump (Spitfire
and Pride) and posh foreign brews such
as Hoegaarden, Leffe, Fruli and Kuppers
Kolsch. A chalkboard lists a further
selection of bottled brews which includes
some of the world's finest.

This place is packed with after-work
20-somethings most nights but the
burgers are legendary if you can find a
space to eat one in.

WINE WHARF
● ● ● ○

Stoney Street, Borough Market, Borough,
London, SE1 9AD, England

Tel: +44 (0)20 7940 8335,
www.winewharf.com
Hours: Mon-Fri 11.30am-11pm,
Sat 11am-11pm

Type:	Wine bar
Alfresco:	No
Entry:	Subject to capacity
Highlights:	Wines
Atmosphere:	Informal/relaxed
Clientele:	Vinopolis visitors, the young and the old
Dress code:	Suits to jeans
Price guide:	£££
Food:	Mediterranean snacks to rhubarb crumble

Close to Borough Market and at the
southern end of the huge wine museum,
Vinopolis, this wine bar is one of the best
in London. The interior of this old
warehouse contrasts bare bricks, wooden
beams and painted iron with concrete,
modern fittings and contemporary
furnishings. A mezzanine level which
overlooks the bar area is more lounge with
plenty of comfy sofas.

Pleasant though the interior is, Wine
Wharf finds its way into these pages mainly
due to its wine range and the educated
staff who not only offer recommendations
but also aren't shy of giving honest tasting
notes such as "car tyres and petrol". To
complement the wines there's an extensive
range of champagne, port, sherry and
cognac, while a small open kitchen
prepares a snack friendly Mediterranean
influenced menu.

WANDSWORTH & BATTERSEA
(SW18, SW11)

THESE RESIDENTIAL LOCALES BOAST THE SUB-DISTRICT 'NAPPY VALLEY' AND PLAY HOST TO WELL-HEELED YOUNG FAMILIES AND NOT-YET-BREEDING YOUNG PROFESSIONALS. THE GASTRO PUBS AND EATERIES ARE PLEASANT ENOUGH FOR LOCALS BUT HARDLY VAUT LE VOYAGE FROM THE CENTRE.

The Alma

THE ALMA
● ● ● ● ○

499 Old York Road, Wandsworth, London, SW18 1TF, England

Tel: +44 (0)20 8870 2537,
www.youngs.co.uk
Hours: Mon-Fri 8am-11pm, Sat 11am-11pm, Sun noon-10:30pm

Type: Gastro pub
Alfresco: No
Entry: Open door
Highlights: Food & interior
Atmosphere: Buzzy local
Clientele: Upscale locals
Dress code: Casual
Price guide: £££
Food: Modern / traditional British

This Victorian corner pub sits majestically opposite Wandsworth Town station, decked out in green glazed tiles and hanging baskets, and crowned with a dome. It was built in 1866, twelve years after the battle from which it takes its name.

Many Victorian features, including a splendid mahogany staircase and carved fireplace, remain intact, although the delicately painted mirrors were a later addition. These form the backdrop to a large, open plan room with a central island bar, plenty of old tables and the odd leather armchair.

The rear dining room, with its ornate frieze discovered during restoration works in 1987, is one of the most attractive of all London's pubs and The Alma has something of a reputation for its food. This is a Young's pub so much of the beer offering is supplied by the Ram Brewery just up the road - at least until October, when brewing operations move to Bedford.

B@1
● ● ● ● ○

85 Battersea Rise (nr Northcote Rd), Battersea, London, SW11 1HW, England

Tel: +44 (0)20 7978 6595,
www.beatone.co.uk
Hours: Mon-Sat 5pm-11pm, Sun 5pm-10:30pm

Type: Cocktail bar
Alfresco: No
Entry: Subject to management & space
Highlights: Cocktails, atmosphere
Atmosphere: Cocktail fuelled party
Clientele: 30-something locals
Dress code: Casual
Price guide: £££
Food: Not a place to eat

This tiny bar has something of a reputation for cocktails and unpretentious fun. Way back in 1998 a trio of bartenders left TGI Friday's, pooled small loans and redecorated a rundown Indian restaurant. B@1 has been busy ever since and so successful have our three heroes been that this little place has proved the start of a chain.

Simply and sparsely decorated, B@1 is usually filled to bursting point with sweaty, frisky locals. The friendly bartenders put Tom Cruise in Cocktail to shame as glasses and bottles fly around the tiny space. Amazingly, given all the commotion, they not only manage to hear orders but also to keep up with demand. The thick cocktail menu runs from classics through to disco drinks so, whatever your taste, there's a mix for you.

This is a place to come for a blast with mates, not a first date venue.

DUSK BAR, KITCHEN & LOUNGE
● ● ● ○ ○

339 Battersea Park Road, London, SW11 4LS, England

Tel: +44 (0)20 7622 2112,
www.duskbar.co.uk
Hours: Mon-Thu 6pm-12:30am, Fri-Sat 6pm-1:30am

Type: Lounge bar
Alfresco: Garden area
Entry: Members have priority
Highlights: Cocktails & atmosphere
Atmosphere: Party
Clientele: Young funky things of Battersea
Dress code: Cool casual
Price guide: £££
Food: Platters, oysters, potato wedges, meatballs

Dusk's website proudly boasts "Battersea's No.1 style bar". Not much of a boast, I hear you cry. Well, this once down-at-heel boozer is better than that.

Outside may look unpromising but inside is warmly lit and homely, decked out in shades of coffee and chocolate with dark wood, leather stools, sofas and banquettes. There's even garden seating for those rare warm evenings.

Early week Dusk is a cool lounge bar with mellow music, great cocktails and table service. Late week sees private parties in the Red Room and DJ driven frolics out front, and only those on a guest list or holding a 'member's privilege card' are assured entry.

Dusk is hardly positioned in the centre of things, even for residents of Battersea. But what it lacks in position it makes up for with its warm interior, party atmosphere, well-made drinks and motivated staff.

East Hill Free House

Iniquity

East Hill Free House

EAST HILL FREE HOUSE

● ● ● ◖ ○

21 Alma Road (corner Fullerton Rd),
Wandsworth, London, SW18 1AA, England

Tel: +44 (0)20 8874 1833,
www.geronimo-inns.co.uk
Hours: Mon-Sat 11am-11:30pm, Sun
noon-10:30pm

Type: Gastro / contemporary pub	
Alfresco: Small front terrace	
Entry: Open door	
Highlights: Food	
Atmosphere: Buzzy local	
Clientele: Upscale locals	
Dress code: Casual	
Price guide: £££	
Food: Eggs Benedict to grilled monkfish etc.	

Formerly known as 'the pub with no name',
this back street corner boozer lies in the
middle of a part of Wandsworth known
formally as The Tonsleys and informally as
Nappy Valley.

East Hill Free House is part of the
Geronimo Inns gastro empire, founded
by Rupert Clevely and his wife Joanna,
and shares the homely, book shelf look
of the rest of their estate. Here, however,
the ornate plaster of the high ceiling gives
the room a warm, parlour feel. Ye
traditional old wooden tables and church
hall chairs dot the bare floorboards, while
the walls are hung with some fetching
contemporary art.

Food is an important part of this pub's
offering and, combined with several ales,
a good wine list and that neighbourhood
feel, makes it popular with upmarket locals.

THE FOX & HOUNDS
● ● ● ● ○

66 Latchmere Road (corner Amies St), Battersea, London, SW11 2JU, England

Tel: +44 (0)20 7924 5483
Hours: Mon 5pm-11pm, Tue-Fri noon-3pm & 5pm-11pm, Sat noon-11pm, Sun noon-10:30pm

Type:	Gastro pub
Alfresco:	Appealing rear courtyard
Entry:	Open door
Highlights:	Food
Atmosphere:	Relaxed local
Clientele:	Locals & travelling foodies
Dress code:	Casual
Price guide:	£££
Food:	Modern British / Mediterranean

At first blush this place seems like a workaday corner boozer. Despite a fresh lick of paint and a large display of cut flowers, the furniture looks as if it came from a junk shop and the pub's best attributes, the food and the garden, are hidden.

Richard and George Manners bought The Fox & Hounds early in 2001. The names may ring a bell, since the brothers originally worked at The Eagle in Farringdon before going on to buy their first pub, The Atlas in Fulham. They now have an established foodie reputation and The Fox & Hounds is justly noted for the superb nosh emanating from their kitchen. While the lounge area has been stylishly extended, head for the secluded yard with its pot plants and ivy covered walls whenever the weather permits.

Although it's been gastrofied, this old boozer is not quite gentrified, and some regular old geezers mingle with the new hip clientele. Both enjoy the well kept real ales.

THE GREYHOUND
● ● ● ● ○

136 Battersea High Street, Battersea, London, SW11 3JR, England

Tel: +44 (0)20 7978 7021,
www.thegreyhoundatbattersea.co.uk
Hours: Tue-Sat noon-11pm, Sun noon-10:30pm

Type:	Gastro pub
Alfresco:	Small front terrace & back yard
Entry:	Open door
Highlights:	Wine & food
Atmosphere:	Relaxed
Clientele:	Locals, oenophiles
Dress code:	Casual
Price guide:	£££
Food:	Excellent full menu

When I describe The Greyhound as a gastro pub I use the term loosely as the furnishings, food and wine here are far removed from anything one would normally expect to find in a pub environment.

This refurbished, tile fronted, Victorian boozer is owned by Australian Mark van der Goot, who was previously the sommelier at Mayfair's Greenhouse, as evidenced by the extraordinary wine list with over 500 bins and twenty wines by the glass. Mark's restaurant experience also tells in his choice of chef, Tom Martinovic, a fellow Australian who served time under Heston Blumenthal at The Fat Duck. With three starters, three mains and three desserts, the menu may be simple to read but what turns up on your plate is a sumptuous work of art, although those after gastro pub portions may be disappointed by the size of the helpings.

Although there are hints of exposed brickwork, The Greyhound's interior with its plush leather seating is altogether more polished than yer average pub. Gentrification has certainly come to this part of Battersea.

INIQUITY
● ● ● ● ○

8-10 Northcote Road (corner Abyssinia Close), Battersea, London, SW11 1PG

Tel: +44 (0)20 7924 6699,
www.iniquitybar.com
Hours: Mon-Thu 4pm-11pm, Fri-Sat noon-midnight, Sun noon-10:30pm

Type:	Lounge bar
Alfresco:	Narrow pavement terrace
Entry:	Subject to management & capacity
Highlights:	Cocktails & atmosphere
Atmosphere:	Chilled early, party later
Clientele:	Fun loving 30-somethings
Dress code:	Casual but to impress
Price guide:	£££
Food:	Comfort food, world tapas, burgers

Arrive late on a Saturday night and this den of Iniquity lives up to its name as Clapham's 'up for it' 30-somethings indulge in all kinds of shenanigans and the DJ drives the party. Earlier in the week, however, Iniquity offers a more refined lounge bar experience, complete with table service.

The swanky interior is predominantly black and red with a glowing crimson bar counter, burgundy velvet curtains and black leather banquette seating. The L-shaped room wraps around the bar, creating cosy, hidden corners. A Rat Pack theme is evident: both the menu and the walls are graced with photographs of and quotes from Sinatra and his chums. Three double doors open out in summer and bring café society to Northcote Road.

My Dark Daiquiri was one of many classics on the menu and proved fantastic, while there are plenty of contemporary creations for the adventurous. Food revolves around 'world tapas' although there are burgers for those in search of comfort food.

The Masons Arms

The Masons Arms

THE MASONS ARMS

● ● ● ○ ○

169 Battersea Park Road (opp. Battersea
Park BR), Battersea, London, SW8 4BT

Tel: +44 (0)20 7622 2007
Hours: Mon-Sat noon-11pm,
Sun noon-10:30pm

Type: Gastro pub
Alfresco: Bench tables on pavement
Entry: Open door
Highlights: Food
Atmosphere: Relaxed local
Clientele: Young professionals & footballers
Dress code: Casual
Price guide: £££
Food: Modern British fare – lunch & dinner

The Masons Arms lies just down the road
from Battersea Dogs Home and directly
opposite Battersea Park station. And, yes,
it's another big old boozer that's been given
the stereotypical gastro treatment. It's open
plan with light walls, wooden furniture and
a long bar with, yes, you guessed it, an
open kitchen at one end. The one
distinguishing feature is someone's record
collection randomly glued to the walls.
Early in the week the vast interior can
appear sparse and soulless but at the
weekend local young professionals flood
in, joined by footballers from the nearby
AstroTurf.

A change of ownership seems to
have knocked both popularity and
reputation but the modern British food
served here, while not a subject of
reverence, is more than satisfactory and
reasonably priced. The beer, wine and
spirit offering is unremarkable.

MICROBAR

●●●○○

14 Lavender Hill (nr corner of Queenstown Rd), Battersea, SW11 5RW, England

Microbar

Tel: +44 (0)20 7228 5300
Hours: Mon-Fri 6pm-11pm, Sat-Sun 4pm-11pm

Type:	Beer/lounge bar
Alfresco:	No
Entry:	Most welcome
Highlights:	Beer selection
Atmosphere:	Friendly, relaxed
Clientele:	Beer lovers (not CAMRA members)
Dress code:	Casual
Price guide:	£££
Food:	Nuts, crisps etc.

Brothers Steve and Jeff Pickthall established Microbar in 2000, as part of their mission 'to rescue good beer from the clutches of weirdy-beardies'. They suggest drinkers avoid all beers claiming to be the following: 'lite', 'cold filtered', 'ice', 'smooth', 'cream' (or 'creamy'), 'clean' or 'crisp'. They also advise steering well clear of 'beers advertised with words ending in flow, beers advertised on television, beers with sports tournaments named after them and beers with the small print "brewed under licence in the UK".'

New owner Alex Poland-Smith follows the same manifesto. While laudable, this means Microbar is devoid of the brands which appeal to the average lagerhead. Coupled with the distance from the tube, this means it's usually pretty quiet. However, those wise enough to frequent this little place enjoy some of the best and most interesting brews the world has to offer, including Anchor Liberty Ale on draught.

Microbar

RECOMMENDED

PARTICULARLY RECOMMENDED FOR:

ALFRESCO

BREW WHARF - BREW WHARF YARD, STONEY STREET, BOROUGH, SE1 9AD - **203**

BROWN'S RESTAURANT & BAR - HERTSMERE ROAD, WEST INDIA QUAY, E14 8JJ - **85**

CENTURY - SHAFTESBURY AVENUE, SOHO, W1D 6LQ - **170**

CORNEY & BARROW - 19 BROADGATE CIRCLE, BROADGATE, CITY, EC2M 2QS - **39**

COVE BAR (THE) - 1 PIAZZA, COVENT GARDEN MARKET, WC2E 8HB - **77**

CUTTY SARK (THE) - 5 BALLAST QUAY, GREENWICH, SE10 9PD - **104**

EALING PARK TAVERN (THE) - 222 SOUTH EALING ROAD, EALING, W5 4RL - **130**

FREEMASONS ARMS - 32 DOWNSHIRE HILL, HAMPSTEAD, NW3 1NT - **108**

GEORGE INN (THE) - GEORGE INN YARD, 77 BOROUGH HIGH STREET, SE1 1NH - **204**

GREENWICH UNION (THE) - 56 ROYAL HILL, GREENWICH, SE10 8RT - **104**

GUN (THE) - 27 COLDHARBOUR, BLACKWALL, ISLE OF DOGS, E14 9NS - **86**

HILL (THE) - 94 HAVERSTOCK HILL, BELSIZE PARK, NW3 2BD - **108**

JUNCTION TAVERN (THE) - 101 FORTESS ROAD, TUFNELL PARK, NW5 1AG - **111**

LADBROKE ARMS (THE) - 58 LADBROKE ROAD, NOTTING HILL, W11 3NW - **154**

LIGHT (THE) - 233 SHOREDITCH HIGH STREET, SHOREDITCH, E1 6PJ - **67**

MAYFLOWER - 206 ROTHERHITHE STREET, ROTHERHITHE, SE16 4NF - **204**

PROSPECT OF WHITBY - 57 WAPPING WALL, WAPPING, E1W 3SH - **49**

SALT HOUSE (THE) - 63 ABBEY ROAD, ST JOHN'S WOOD, NW8 0AE - **113**

SCARSDALE - 23A EDWARDES SQUARE, KENSINGTON, W8 6HE - **132**

SPANIARDS INN - SPANIARDS ROAD, HAMPSTEAD HEATH, NW3 7JJ - **113**

WATERWAY (THE) - 54 FORMOSA STREET, MAIDA VALE, W9 2JU - **162**

WHITE HORSE (THE) - 1-3 PARSONS GREEN, PARSONS GREEN, SW6 4UL - **99**

BEER (INTERNATIONAL)

5TH VIEW - WATERSTONE'S, 203-205 PICCADILLY, W1J 9HA - **176**

BREW WHARF - BREW WHARF YARD, STONEY STREET, BOROUGH, SE1 9AD - **203**

DOVETAIL (THE) - 9 JERUSALEM PASSAGE, CLERKENWELL, EC1V 4JP - **60**

LOWLANDER BEER CAFÉ - 36 DRURY LANE, COVENT GARDEN, WC2B 5RR - **79**

MICROBAR - 14 LAVENDER HILL, BATTERSEA, SW11 5RW - **215**

PORTERHOUSE (THE) - 21-22 MAIDEN LANE, COVENT GARDEN, WC2 7NA - **80**

WHITE HORSE (THE) - 1-3 PARSONS GREEN, PARSONS GREEN, SW6 4UL - **99**

ZERODEGREES - 28-31 MONTPELIER VALE, BLACKHEATH, SE3 0TJ - **104**

BEER (REAL ALE)

COVE BAR (THE) - 1 PIAZZA, COVENT GARDEN MARKET, WC2E 8HB - **77**

EALING PARK TAVERN (THE) - 222 SOUTH EALING ROAD, EALING, W5 4RL - **130**

GRENADIER PUB (THE) - WILTON ROW, KNIGHTSBRIDGE, SW1X 7NR - **139**

MARKET PORTER (THE) - 9 STONEY STREET, BOROUGH, SE1 9AA - **204**

RED LION (THE) - 1 WAVERTON STREET, MAYFAIR, W1J 5QN - **193**

ROSEMARY BRANCH (THE) - 2 SHEPPERTON ROAD, ISLINGTON, N1 3DT - **125**

SPANIARDS INN - SPANIARDS ROAD, HAMPSTEAD HEATH, NW3 7JJ - **113**

WHITE HORSE (THE) - 1-3 PARSONS GREEN, PARSONS GREEN, SW6 4UL - **99**

YE GRAPES - 16 SHEPHERD MARKET, W1J 7QQ - **178**

BOWLING / SKITTLES

ALL STAR LANES - VICTORIA HOUSE, BLOOMSBURY PLACE, HOLBORN, WC1 4DA - **23**

FREEMASONS ARMS - 32 DOWNSHIRE HILL, HAMPSTEAD, NW3 1NT - **108**

CHAMPAGNE

AMUSE BOUCHE - 1 PARSONS
GREEN LANE, PARSONS GREEN,
SW6 4JA - **92**
CORNEY & BARROW - 10
PATERNOSTER SQUARE, CITY OF
LONDON, EC4M 7DX - **39**
CORNEY & BARROW - 19
BROADGATE CIRCLE,
BROADGATE, CITY OF LONDON,
EC2M 2QS - **39**

KETTNERS
CHAMPAGNE ROOMS - 29
ROMILLY STREET, SOHO, W1D
5HP - **181**
VATS WINE BAR - 51 LAMBS
CONDUIT STREET, HOLBORN,
WC1N 3NB - **27**
VERTIGO 42 - TOWER 42, OLD
BROAD STREET, BANK,
EC2N 1HQ - **44**

CINEMA
(FILM SCREENING)
EIGHT - 1 CHANGE ALLEY, CITY
OF LONDON, EC3V 3ND - **40**
ELECTRIC HOUSE - 191
PORTOBELLO ROAD, NOTTING
HILL, W11 2ED - **153**
GARRISON (THE) - 99-101
BERMONDSEY STREET,
BERMONDSEY, SE1 3XB - **204**
REX CINEMA & BAR - 21
RUPERT STREET, SOHO,
W1V 7FE - **194**
SAND - 156 CLAPHAM PARK
ROAD, CLAPHAM, SW4 7DE - **55**

CLASSIC
(OLD-SCHOOL) BARS
AMERICAN BAR (THE) - THE
STAFFORD HOTEL, ST JAMES'S
PLACE, SW1A 1NJ - **136**
BLUE BAR - THE BERKELEY
HOTEL, WILTON PLACE,
KNIGHTSBRIDGE, SW1X 7RL - **137**
CLARIDGE'S BAR -
CLARIDGES'S HOTEL, 55 BROOK
STREET, MAYFAIR, W1A 2JQ - **170**
LIBRARY BAR -
LANESBOROUGH HOTEL, HYDE
PARK CORNER, SW1X 7TA - **139**
MILK & HONEY - 61 POLAND
STREET, SOHO, W1F 7NU - **189**
MONTGOMERY PLACE - 31
KENSINGTON PARK ROAD,
NOTTING HILL, W11 2EU - **157**
RIVOLI BAR - RITZ HOTEL, 150
PICCADILLY, W1J 9BR - **194**
SALVATORE - GROUND FLOOR,
FIFTY, 50 ST JAMES'S STREET,
SW1A 1JT - **145**

COCKTAILS

43 SOUTH MOLTON - 43 SOUTH
MOLTON STREET, MAYFAIR, W1K
5RS - **177**
ALL STAR LANES - VICTORIA
HOUSE, BLOOMSBURY PLACE,
HOLBORN, WC1 4DA - **23**
AURORA BAR - GREAT EASTERN
HOTEL, LIVERPOOL STREET,
EC2M 7QN - **38**
B@1 - 85 BATTERSEA RISE,
BATTERSEA, SW11 1HW - **210**
COCOON - 65 REGENT STREET,
W1B 4EA - **171**
DORCHESTER BAR (THE) -
53 PARK LANE, MAYFAIR,
W1A 2HJ - **174**
**DUSK BAR KITCHEN &
LOUNGE** - 339 BATTERSEA PARK
ROAD, SW11 4LS - **210**
ECLIPSE - 111/113
WALTON STREET, CHELSEA, SW3
2PH - **94**
ECLIPSE - 186 KENSINGTON
PARK ROAD, NOTTING HILL, W11
2ES - **153**
GREEN & RED - 51 BETHNAL
GREEN ROAD, SHOREDITCH,
E1 6LA - **65**
HAWKSMOOR - 157
COMMERCIAL STREET,
SPITALFIELDS, E1 6BJ - **86**
KOSMOPOL - 138 FULHAM
ROAD, CHELSEA, SW10 9PY - **95**

LONSDALE - 44-48 LONSDALE
ROAD, NOTTING HILL,
W11 2DE - **154**
LOST SOCIETY - 697
WANDSWORTH ROAD, CLAPHAM,
SW8 3JF - **51**
MATCH BAR - 37-38 MARGARET
STREET, W1G 0JF - **184**
MATCH EC1 - 45-47 CLERKENWELL
ROAD, CLERKENWELL,
EC1M 5RS - **68**
MILK & HONEY - 61 POLAND
STREET, SOHO, W1F 7NU - **189**
MINT LEAF - SUFFOLK PLACE,
TRAFALGAR SQUARE,
SW1Y 4HX - **140**
MONTGOMERY PLACE - 31
KENSINGTON PARK ROAD,
NOTTING HILL, W11 2EU - **157**
PLAYER LOUNGE - 8
BROADWICK STREET, SOHO, W1F
8HN - **193**
SALVATORE - GROUND FLOOR,
FIFTY, 50 ST JAMES'S STREET,
SW1A 1JT - **145**
SHOCHU LOUNGE - ROKA, 37
CHARLOTTE STREET, FITZROVIA,
W1T 1RR - **196**
SOSHO - 2A TABERNACLE STREET,
SHOREDITCH, EC2A 4LU - **70**
TRADER VIC'S - THE HILTON
HOTEL, 22 PARK LANE, MAYFAIR,
W1Y 4BE - **198**

GASTRO

ABINGDON (THE) - 54
ABINGDON ROAD, KENSINGTON,
W8 6AP - **128**
ADMIRAL CODRINGTON (THE) -
17 MOSSOP STREET, BROMPTON,
SW3 2LY - **92**
ANCHOR & HOPE - 36 THE CUT,
WATERLOO, SE1 8LP - **202**
ANGLESEA ARMS (THE) - 15
SELWOOD TERRACE, SOUTH
KENSINGTON, SW7 3QG - **136**
ANGLESEA ARMS (THE) - 35
WINGATE ROAD, CHISWICK,
W6 0UR - **128**
BALTIC - 74 BLACKFRIARS ROAD,
WATERLOO, SE1 8HA - **202**
BARNSBURY (THE) - 209-211
LIVERPOOL ROAD, ISLINGTON, N1
1LX - **118**
BEDFORD & STRAND - 1
BEDFORD STREET, COVENT
GARDEN, WC2E 9HH - **74**
BERMONDSEY KITCHEN -
194 BERMONDSEY
STREET, BERMONDSEY,
SE1 3TQ - **203**
BLACK LION - 274 KILBURN
HIGH ROAD, KILBURN,
NW6 2BY - **108**
BLEEDING HEART TAVERN -
19 GREVILLE STREET,
HATTON GARDEN,
EC1N 8SQ - **58**
BOUNTIFUL COW (THE) - 51
EAGLE STREET, HOLBORN, WC1R
4AP - **24**
BULL (THE) - 13 NORTH HILL,
HIGHGATE, N6 4AB - **119**
BUTCHER'S HOOK (THE) - 477
FULHAM ROAD, FULHAM,
SW6 1HL - **93**
CHARLES LAMB - 16 ELIA
STREET, ISLINGTON, N1 8DE,
ENGLAND - **120**
COACH & HORSES (THE) - 26-28
RAY STREET, CLERKENWELL,
EC1R 3DJ - **60**
COW (THE) - 89 WESTBOURNE
PARK ROAD, NOTTING HILL,
W2 5QH - **150**
CRAZY HOMIES - 127
WESTBOURNE PARK ROAD,
NOTTING HILL, W2 5QL - **153**

GASTRO CONT.

DRAPER'S ARMS (THE) - 44 BARNSBURY STREET, ISLINGTON, N1 1ER - **120**

EAGLE (THE) - 159 FARRINGDON ROAD, FARRINGDON, EC1R 3AL - **62**

EALING PARK TAVERN (THE) - 222 SOUTH EALING ROAD, EALING, W5 4RL - **130**

EAST HILL FREE HOUSE - 21 ALMA ROAD, WANDSWORTH, SW18 1AA - **212**

EBURY (THE) - 11 PIMLICO ROAD, PIMLICO, SW1W 8NA - **138**

ENGINEER (THE) - 65 GLOUCESTER AVENUE, PRIMROSE HILL, NW1 8JH - **31**

FENTIMAN ARMS (THE) - 64 FENTIMAN ROAD, VAUXHALL, SW8 1LA - **50**

FOX & HOUNDS (THE) - 66 LATCHMERE ROAD, BATTERSEA, SW11 2JU - **213**

GARRISON (THE) - 99-101 BERMONDSEY STREET, BERMONDSEY, SE1 3X - **204**

GILGAMESH - THE STABLES, CHALK FARM ROAD, CAMDEN, NW1 8AH - **32**

GREAT EASTERN - 54-56 GREAT EASTERN STREET, SHOREDITCH, EC2A 3QR - **62**

GREEN & RED - 51 BETHNAL GREEN ROAD, SHOREDITCH, E1 6LA - **65**

GREYHOUND (THE) - 136 BATTERSEA HIGH STREET, BATTERSEA, SW11 3JR - **213**

GUN (THE) - 27 COLDHARBOUR, BLACKWALL, ISLE OF DOGS, E14 9NS - **86**

HAVELOCK TAVERN - 57 MASBRO ROAD, BROOK GREEN, W14 0LS - **131**

HOLLY BUSH (THE) - 22 HOLLY MOUNT, HAMPSTEAD, NW3 6SG - **110**

HOUSE (THE) - 63-69 CANONBURY ROAD, ISLINGTON, N1 2DG - **122**

JUNCTION TAVERN (THE) - 101 FORTESS ROAD, TUFNELL PARK, NW5 1AG - **111**

LADBROKE ARMS (THE) - 58 LADBROKE ROAD, NOTTING HILL, W11 3NW - **154**

GASTRO CONT.

LANSDOWNE - 90 GLOUCESTER AVENUE, PRIMROSE HILL, NW1 8HX - **33**

LORD PALMERSTON - 33 DARTMOUTH PARK HILL, DARTMOUTH PARK, NW5 1HU - **112**

LOTS ROAD DINING ROOM - 114 LOTS ROAD, CHELSEA, SW10 0RJ - **96**

LOWLANDER BEER CAFÉ - 36 DRURY LANE, COVENT GARDEN, WC2B 5RR - **79**

MARQUESS TAVERN (THE) - 32 CANONBURY STREET, ISLINGTON, N1 2TB - **122**

MORGAN ARMS - 43 MORGAN STREET, BOW, E3 5AA - **89**

NORTH STAR (THE) - 188-190 NEW NORTH ROAD, ISLINGTON, N1 7BJ - **124**

NORTHGATE (THE) - 113 SOUTHGATE ROAD, ISLINGTON, N1 3JS - **124**

PEASANT (THE) - 240 ST. JOHN STREET, CLERKENWELL, EC1V 4PH - **68**

PRINCE ALFRED (THE) - 5A FORMOSA STREET, MAIDA VALE, W9 1EE - **157**

PRINCESS (THE) - 76 PAUL STREET, SHOREDITCH, EC2A 4NE - **69**

QUEEN'S HEAD & ARTICHOKE - 30-32 ALBANY STREET, MARYLEBONE, NW1 4EA - **35**

RAPSCALLION & SEQUEL (THE) - 75 & 78 VENN STREET, CLAPHAM, SW4 0BD - **55**

SEVEN STARS (THE) - 53A CAREY STREET, WC2A 2JB - **81**

ST. JOHN BAR - 26 ST. JOHN STREET, SMITHFIELD, EC1M 4AY - **70**

SWAG & TAILS - 10-11 FAIRHOLT STREET, KNIGHTSBRIDGE VILLAGE, SW7 1EG - **145**

VILLAGE EAST - 171-173 BERMONDSEY STREET, SOUTHWARK, SE1 3UW - **207**

WELLS (THE) - 30 WELL WALK, HAMPSTEAD, LONDON, NW3 1BX - **115**

WILLIAM IV - 7 SHEPHERDESS WALK, HOXTON, N1 7QE - **71**

MEMBERS ONLY

43 SOUTH MOLTON - 43 SOUTH MOLTON STREET, MAYFAIR, W1K 5RS - **177**

APARTMENT 195 - 195 KING'S ROAD, CHELSEA, SW3 5ED - **92**

CENTURY - 61-63 SHAFTESBURY AVENUE, SOHO, W1D 6LQ - **170**

COBDEN CLUB - 170 KENSAL ROAD, NOTTING HILL, W10 5BN - **150**

CUCKOO CLUB (THE) - SWALLOW STREET, OFF REGENT STREET, W1B 4EZ - **173**

EIGHT - 1 CHANGE ALLEY, CITY OF LONDON, EC3V 3ND - **40**

G.E. CLUB - GREAT EASTERN HOTEL, LIVERPOOL STREET, EC2M 7QN - **41**

GROUCHO CLUB - 45 DEAN STREET, SOHO, W1D 4QB - **178**

KINGLY CLUB (THE) - 4 KINGLY COURT, SOHO, W1B 5PW - **181**

MET BAR (THE) - 18-19 OLD PARK LANE, MAYFAIR, W1K 1LB - **187**

MILK & HONEY - 61 POLAND STREET, SOHO, W1F 7NU - **189**

MORTON'S - 28 BERKELEY SQUARE, MAYFAIR, W1J 6EN - **189**

SALVATORE - GROUND FLOOR, FIFTY, 50 ST JAMES' STREET, SW1A 1JT - **145**

SOHO HOUSE - 40 GREEK STREET, SOHO, W1D 4EB - **197**

WELLINGTON CLUB (THE) - 116A KNIGHTSBRIDGE, SW1X 7PL - **146**

HISTORIC INTEREST

ANGEL (THE) - 101 BERMONDSEY WALL EAST, ROTHERHITHE, SE16 4NB - **202**

BLACK FRIAR (THE) - 174 QUEEN VICTORIA STREET, BLACKFRIARS, EC4V 4EG - **38**

CHESHIRE CHEESE (YE OLDE) - 145 FLEET STREET, CITY OF LONDON, EC4A 2BU - **41**

GEORGE INN (THE) - GEORGE INN YARD, 77 BOROUGH HIGH STREET, SE1 1NH - **204**

GRENADIER PUB (THE) - WILTON ROW, KNIGHTSBRIDGE, SW1X 7NR - **139**

HOLLY BUSH (THE) - 22 HOLLY MOUNT, HAMPSTEAD, NW3 6SG - **110**

MAYFLOWER - 117 ROTHERHITHE STREET, ROTHERHITHE, SE16 4NF - **206**

MITRE TAVERN (YE OLDE) - 1 ELY COURT, FARRINGDON, EC1N 6SJ - **68**

PRINCE ALFRED (THE) - 5A FORMOSA STREET, MAIDA VALE, W9 1EE - **158**

PROSPECT OF WHITBY - 57 WAPPING WALL, WAPPING, E1W 3SH - **89**

SPANIARDS INN - SPANIARDS ROAD, HAMPSTEAD HEATH, NW3 7JJ - **113**

TOWN OF RAMSGATE - 62 WAPPING HIGH STREET, WAPPING, E1W 2PN - **89**

WINDSOR CASTLE (THE) - 114 CAMPDEN HILL ROAD, KENSINGTON, W8 7AR - **139**

YE GRAPES - 16 SHEPHERD MARKET, MAYFAIR, W1J 7QQ - **178**

SPIRITS (SELECTION)

ALBANNACH & DOON (WHISKY) - 66 TRAFALGAR SQUARE, WC2N 5DS - **23**

BAR POLSKI (POLISH VODKA) - 11 LITTLE TURNSTILE, HOLBORN, WC1V 7DX - **23**

CAFÉ PACIFICO (TEQUILA) - 5 LANGLEY STREET, COVENT GARDEN, WC2H 9JA - **76**

COCOON (SHOCHU & SAKE) - 65 REGENT STREET, W1B 4EA - **171**

COTTONS (RUM) - 55 CHALK FARM ROAD, CAMDEN, NW1 8AN - **30**

DORCHESTER BAR (VERMOUTH) - 53 PARK LANE, MAYFAIR, W1A 2HJ - **174**

GREEN & RED (TEQUILA) - 51 BETHNAL GREEN ROAD, SHOREDITCH, E1 6LA - **65**

SALT WHISKY BAR (WHISKY) - 82 SEYMOUR STREET, MARBLE ARCH, W2 2JB - **159**

SALVATORE (COGNAC) - GROUND FLOOR, FIFTY, 50 ST JAMES'S STREET, SW1A 1JT - **145**

SHOCHU LOUNGE (SHOCHU) - ROKA, 37 CHARLOTTE STREET, FITZROVIA, W1T 1RR - **196**

VIEW

VERTIGO 42 - TOWER 42, OLD BROAD STREET, BANK, EC2N 1HQ - **44**

WINDOWS - THE LONDON HILTON, 22 PARK LANE, MAYFAIR, W1K 1BE - **198**

WATERSIDE

ANGEL (THE) - 101 BERMONDSEY WALL EAST, ROTHERHITHE, SE16 4NB - **202**

CUTTY SARK (THE) - 5 BALLAST QUAY, GREENWICH, SE10 9PD - **104**

MAYFLOWER - 117 ROTHERHITHE STREET, ROTHERHITHE, SE16 4NF - **206**

PROSPECT OF WHITBY - 57 WAPPING WALL, WAPPING, E1W 3SH - **89**

TOWN OF RAMSGATE - 62 WAPPING HIGH STREET, E1W 2PN - **89**

WATERWAY (THE) - 54 FORMOSA STREET, MAIDA VALE, W9 2JU - **162**

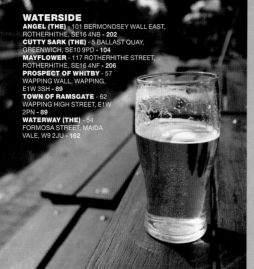

WINE

BEDFORD & STRAND - 1 BEDFORD STREET, COVENT GARDEN, WC2E 9HH - **74**

CELLAR GASCON - 59 WEST SMITHFIELD, SMITHFIELD, EC1A 9DS - **60**

CORNEY & BARROW - 10 PATERNOSTER SQUARE, CITY OF LONDON, EC4M 7DX - **39**

CORNEY & BARROW - 19 BROADGATE CIRCLE, BROADGATE, CITY OF LONDON, EC2M 2QS - **39**

EL VINO - 47 FLEET STREET, EC4Y 1BJ - **42**

GORDON'S WINE BAR - 47 VILLIERS STREET, CHARING CROSS, WC2N 6NE - **78**

GREYHOUND (THE) - 136 BATTERSEA HIGH STREET, BATTERSEA, SW11 3JR - **213**

NEGOZIO CLASSICA - 283 WESTBOURNE GROVE, NOTTING HILL, W11 2QA - **157**

PEARL RESTAURANT & BAR - 252 HIGH HOLBORN, WC1V 7EN - **24**

VILLAGE EAST - 171-173 BERMONDSEY STREET, SOUTHWARK, SE1 3UW - **207**

WINE WHARF - STONEY STREET, BOROUGH MARKET, BOROUGH, SE1 9AD - **207**

L aresser

Hope you can read the scrawl

Desmond

Fax transmission from: Sauceguides

Sauceguides Limited
Milngavie Business Centre, 17 Station Road, Milngavie, G62 8PG.
Enquiries telephone: +44 (0)870 242 5035
Email: simon@diffordsguide.com

Date: 4-July-2006
FAO: Desmond Payne

How did you get to be a Master Distiller? In the traditional way — by training under a Master Distiller, Philip Milner at Seagers Gin in Deptford London.

What's your local? And what's your usual?
My local is a Youngs pub in Wandsworth. Excellent bitter. — & I don't know what I'll do when the brewery closes!

You travel a lot for work. What's the greatest place you've visited, and why were you there? One of the places that impressed me was in Fukuoka in Southern Japan. After a long week of seminars I was taken by my host to a small stall on the quaiside. Inside was an

What's your favourite cocktail? Why does it work with your gin?
The Gimlet, for its sheer simplicity — & I like it shaken ice cold. Beefeater gin has immaculate D.J. - clad bartender mixing Beefeater Mar[...] plenty of flavour to balance the lime.

Do you have a home bar? What's it like?
Certainly not! but there is a cupboard in the kitchen. Two in the sideboard and several boxes under the stairs ...

What's your favourite place for a drink in London, and why?
The bar at Dukes Hotel for the perfect Beefeater Martini in relaxed surroundings, or either Lab bar or Crazy Bear for top of the range modern cocktails